Food Lovers' Guide
to Colorado

HELP US KEEP THIS
GUIDE UP TO DATE

Every effort has been made by the author and editors to make this guide as accurate and useful as possible. However, many things can change after a guide is published—establishments close, phone numbers change, facilities come under new management, etc.

We would love to hear from you concerning your experiences with this guide and how you feel it could be improved and kept up to date. While we may not be able to respond to all comments and suggestions, we'll take them to heart and we'll also make certain to share them with the author. Please send your comments and suggestions to the following address:

The Globe Pequot Press
Reader Response/Editorial Department
P.O. Box 480
Guilford, CT 06437

Or you may e-mail us at:

editorial@GlobePequot.com

Thanks for your input, and happy travels!

INSIDERS' GUIDE®

FOOD LOVERS' SERIES

Food Lovers' Guide to Colorado

SECOND EDITION

Best Local Specialties, Markets, Recipes,
Restaurants, Events, and More

Eliza Cross Castaneda

INSIDERS' GUIDE®

GUILFORD, CONNECTICUT
AN IMPRINT OF THE GLOBE PEQUOT PRESS

The prices and rates listed in this guidebook were confirmed at press time. We recommend, however, that you call establishments to obtain current information before traveling.

To buy books in quantity for corporate use
or incentives, call **(800) 962–0973, ext. 4551,**
or e-mail **premiums@GlobePequot.com.**

INSIDERS' GUIDE®

Text design: Nancy Freeborn
Maps created by Rusty Nelson © Morris Book Publishing, LLC.
Illustrations: page ix by Carleen Moira Powell; beer mug by M. A. Dubé. All other illustrations © Jill Butler.
Front cover photo © Getty Images
Back cover photo © Eliza Cross Castaneda

ISSN 1540-9341
ISBN 0-7627-3450-7

Manufactured in the United States of America
Second Edition/First Printing

To my mother, Betty, whose love
illuminates us all.

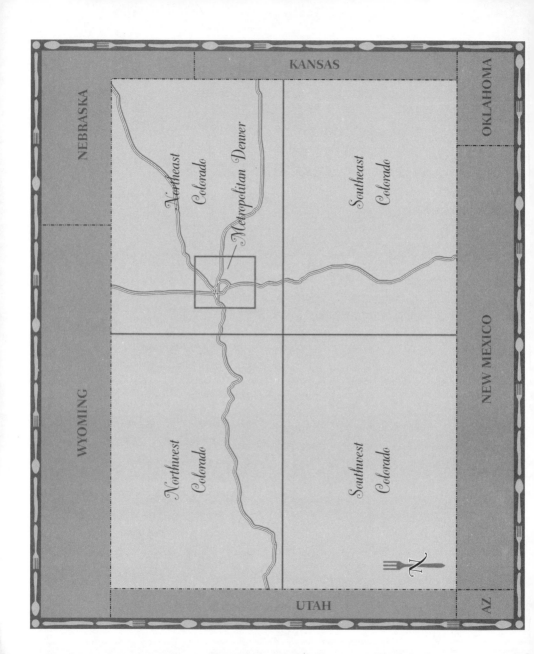

Contents

Preface

I became a Colorado food lover at an early age. We moved to Boulder when I was a toddler in the early 1960s, and I remember family picnics on the vast lawn of Chautauqua Park, noisy spaghetti dinners at the Blue Parrot in nearby Louisville, and trips out to Munson Farms' Stand for fresh peaches. My mother is a splendid cook, and I grew up spoiled on her specialties like homemade granola, freshly baked bread, hearty soups, and old-fashioned strawberry-rhubarb jam. Mom wrote a food column for the local paper, and I loved perusing the notebook she kept of her articles.

Colorado's utility company, called Public Service at that time, offered kids' cooking classes, which provided my first training in the techniques of cooking and baking. (Perhaps they were trying to get us youngsters in the habit of using electricity and natural gas at an early age.) My parents endured years of my cooking experiments as I made everything from Rice Krispies bars to chocolate fondue. Like many young women in the 1970s, I took home economics classes in school and aced my final exam at Boulder High School by preparing Crêpes Suzette.

As a young adult, I continued to study cooking and began a collection of cookbooks that now threatens to collapse my bookshelves. Single and carefree, I traveled to France and shopped in the markets of Nice and St. Tropez. I visited Corsica and Sardinia and tasted just-caught fish roasted over an open fire; the tiny, savory green olives of the region; and the potent local wine. I dined in the restaurants of Amsterdam, Paris, and London, taking notes on napkins in the hopes of re-creating the recipes.

Back home, I pursued a career in the magazine publishing business, where I began to learn about the importance of good, relevant editorial copy, and what makes people read a magazine. On evenings and weekends, my best friend and I catered small parties, learning as we went along. Soon I was teaching cooking classes for Colorado Free University, demonstrating everything from making basic soup stocks to creating authentic risotto.

In 1990 I began writing food articles for local and regional magazines, including *Colorado Homes & Lifestyles* and *Mountain Living*. Since then my assignments have taken me all over the state in search of local specialties, fresh produce, little-known restaurants, and interesting recipes.

This book is a culmination of all those experiences and passions, and although I have been deeply involved in our state's food scene for a long time, I continue to be amazed at the wide range of choices there are for Colorado food lovers.

Acknowledgments

To the Colorado farmers, shop owners, entrepreneurs, instructors, chefs, restaurateurs, vintners, and brewmeisters who were so generous with their time and thoughts.

Special thanks to editor Gia Manalio, whose calm presence and attention to countless details made the project a joy.

To Kristin Browning, Linda Hayes, Holly Arnold Kinney, John Lehndorff, Marty Meitus, and Ellen Sweets, who weighed in on the question, "Does Colorado have its own trademark cuisine?" (see Introduction). I am grateful for your collective experience and wise insights.

To Anne, Darla, Gail, Irene, Myrna, and Rachel—the circle of talented writers who provide so much support and encouragement.

To Amy, Beth, Corine, Debbie, Janice, and Laura for all the laughter, love, life, and great meals we have shared.

The journey is brighter when there are caring people who encourage your pursuit of purpose. Claire, Madeline, Pauli, Pat, and Ted are some of my guiding lights.

To Ann Marie Swenson, the gifted teacher who continues to inspire me—these thirty years later.

Finally, my love and gratitude to my family: Dad, Mom, Pop, Jose, Gracie, Michael, Catherine, Emilie, Bonnie; and always, Jorma.

Many thanks to the following individuals and establishments for graciously providing recipes. Many recipes were adapted for home cooks, and these individuals and companies are not responsible for any inadvertent errors or omissions.

Ancho Chili Roasted Duck Breast with Orange Cider Chipotle Glaze and Grilled Tomatillos: Eric Viedt and Pati Davidson, The Margarita at PineCreek

Basic Quinoa: Paul New, White Mountain Farm

Betty's Eminently Edible Golden Fruitcake: Betty Crosslen

Blue Cheese and Port Wine Fondue: Pascal Coudouy and Maryann Yuthas, Park Hyatt Beaver Creek Resort and Spa

Catherine's Foolproof Pie Crust: Catherine Cavoto

Colorado Peach Pecan Sour Cream Coffee Cake: Phyllis Stanley, Colorado Nutritional Bread Baking Supplies

Crusted Lemon Crackers with Pistachio Boursin Cheese Rolls: Jorge de la Torre and Lindsay Morgan Tracy, Johnson & Wales University

The Fort's Buffalo Gonzales Steak: Samuel P. Arnold and Holly Arnold Kinney, The Fort

Grilled Colorado Lamb Chops with Mint Salsa: Paul Ferzacca, La Tour

Highland Haven's Baked Orange Pecan French Toast: Gail Riley and Tom Statzell, Highland Haven Creekside Inn

Insalata di Cipolle e Rucola (Red Onion & Arugula Salad): Elizabeth Montana, Dream Italia

Judi's Granola: Judi Schultze, The Inn on Mapleton Hill

Mile High Watermelon Pyramids: Harry Schwartz and Leslie A. Coleman, National Watermelon Promotion Board

Peaches and Cream: Christine Jasper, the Palisade Chamber of Commerce and Linda Quarles

The Penrose Room's Butternut Squash and Green Pea Risotto: Siegfried Werner Eisenberger and Kathryn Wohlschlaeger, The Broadmoor

Queen City Pound Cake: Catherine Cavoto

Quick Caramel Sauce: Harry Schwartz and Leslie A. Coleman, National Watermelon Promotion Board

Quinoa Griddle Cakes: Paul New, White Mountain Farm

Roasted Garlic Soup: Liv Lyons, TheGarlicStore.com

Rocky Mountain Diner's Buffalo Meatloaf: Rocky Mountain Diner

San Luis Potato and Smoked Salmon Salad: Linda Weyers, Colorado Potato Administrative Committee

Seared Diver Scallop with Foie Gras Flan, Mâche and Apple Salad: Matt Morgan and Bruce Yin, Sweet Basil

Seasons' Green Chile Cheddar Smashed Sweet Potatoes: Karen Barger, Seasons Rotisserie & Grill

Ship Tavern Rocky Mountain Trout with Herb Butter Sauce: Michael Beck and Deborah Dix, The Brown Palace Hotel

Thelma's Washboard Cookies: The Manitou Springs Historical Society and Thelma Eastham

Introduction

It's a great time to be a food lover in Colorado. Since we published the first *Food Lovers' Guide to Colorado* in 2002, our state has exploded with new offerings and more choices for those who love to eat and drink.

Most significantly, we are seeing a welcome swing of the culinary pendulum away from the "agribusiness" practices of the recent past back toward eating and buying food grown as naturally as possible, and a growing trend toward purchasing foods directly from the producer. More farmers' markets are sprouting up in every region of the state, and for the first time in several decades, there is renewed hope for the small farmer.

I can remember years ago when the small organic produce section of the grocery store had spotty fruits and vegetables, high prices, and limited selection. No more. As the demand for organic products grows and organic farming gains mainstream acceptance, top-quality naturally grown produce is more readily available at the grocery store. As demand increases, my hope is that we will see less of a price difference between organic and non organic produce and that people of all income levels can enjoy healthy, natural produce.

The same kind of development is changing the meat industry. Free-range chickens, heritage turkeys, grass-fed beef, and naturally-raised buffalo are providing flavorful and more humane choices that we can all feel better about eating. With increasingly good information, we can make more informed decisions about seafood, too. Consumers are shunning seafood varieties with high methylmercury levels, and actively seeking types of fish and shellfish that have been fished or farmed in environmentally friendly ways.

Colorado's wine industry is growing like crazy, and many of our wineries are winning awards and producing wines that compete with the best. We continue to enjoy our microbrewed beers, too; Colorado is the third-largest market in the United States for handcrafted beers. Artisan cheese makers like Bingham Hill and MouCo in Fort Collins are producing an exciting selection of handcrafted, small-batch cheeses. In turn there are a number of new cheese shops that have opened in the state, and we are seeing a renaissance of the "cheese course" following dinner at many area restaurants.

The restaurant side of the equation just gets better and better. Another Colorado chef—Frasca's Lachlan Mackinnon-Patterson (see Northeast Colorado chapter)—was honored as one of *Food & Wine* magazine's top new chefs for 2005, and culinary luminaries like Mizuna's Frank Bonanno (see Metropolitan Denver and Suburbs chapter) and The Kitchen's Kimbal Musk and Hugo Matheson (see Northeast Colorado chapter) are transforming Colorado's culinary landscape, offering exciting, creatively prepared cuisine utilizing our region's best natural and organic ingredients.

Given all this, I'd like to make a bold assertion: There is no other state in the country that offers the diversity, variety, or quality of cuisine that Colorado does. The Front Range—including metropolitan Denver, Boulder, Colorado Springs, and Fort Collins—supports hundreds of international markets and ethnic eateries with alternatives for every palate. There are fantastic specialty shops and markets, new cooking schools, and even a host of "make your own meals" shops cropping up in our major cities. The sophisticated ski towns of Aspen, Beaver Creek, Vail, and Telluride attract top restaurateurs and award-winning chefs from around the world. The Western Slope is home to Colorado's wine country and countless acres of unspoiled fruit orchards. The southern part of the state, with its unique blend of cuisine that borrows from New Mexican and Latin American influences, is home to the second-largest group of potato growers in the country. The eastern prairie—Colorado's heartland—is where our farmers and ranchers grow and raise the quality produce and meats we love. Our crops and cuisine are reflected in Colorado's colorful food festivals, county fairs, farm stands, farmers' markets, and chili cook-offs.

The combination of Colorado's unique history, terrain, and people raises an interesting question. A reader of *The Denver Post* wrote columnist Ellen Sweets in her wonderful "Search Me" column: "Does Colorado have its own trademark cuisine? New England has its steamed lobsters and clam chowder, and the South has its grits and hush puppies, Wisconsin has its cheese, and Kansas City has its barbeque; what about Colorado?" An intriguing query, don't you think? To explore the answer, I spoke to some local experts—starting with Ellen.

"My father swooned over brook trout before I was even sure where Colorado was," Ellen says. "He assured us that there was nothing like fresh Colorado trout, so that's one of the foods I associated with the state long before I moved here three years ago. I also enjoy Colorado's vast array of ethnic foods, a host of choices often available within blocks of one another. I adore Italian, Chinese, Thai, and Vietnamese food." She adds, "But I still love grilled trout and scrambled eggs with country fried potatoes and sliced tomatoes."

For Holly Arnold Kinney, co-owner of The Fort restaurant (see Northeast Colorado), the answer is pretty straightforward. "Buffalo, buffalo, buffalo!" she says. "The Fort restaurant serves over 70,000 buffalo entrees per year. Colorado is also known for its fresh trout . . . and mushrooms. Beautiful chanterelles, morels, and cépes pop up all over the mountains in July and August, and many chefs have foragers who pick the good ones for them."

"Ask most people what crops the state of Colorado is famous for, and they're likely to name Palisade peaches, Rocky Ford cantaloupes—and amber waves of grain," says Marty Meitus, food editor of the *Rocky Mountain News* and author of the book *Recipe Please* (see Appendix C). "But these days they might just as easily mention purple potatoes, quinoa, and organic produce. What we always have in Colorado is diversity, whether it's Olathe corn, San Luis Valley potatoes, beef, lamb, buffalo, turkey, or organic meats."

"This question comes up all the time, because people are always looking for a cuisine that is indigenous to Colorado," says Linda Hayes, the food editor for *SKI* magazine. "We are known for our lamb, as well as wild game like elk, venison, and buffalo—in part, because these animals still roam outside here. These meats make hearty stews and comfort foods in the winter, while in the summertime our fresh produce plays a much larger role; the popularity of farmers' markets has also created a bigger connection between farms and people."

"One of the things that makes our state unique is that it attracts people from all over the country," says John Lehndorff, dining critic at the *Rocky Mountain News* and author of the book *Denver Dines—a Restaurant Guide and More* (see Appendix C). "People bring what they like with them, which has created a diversified cuisine here. We also tend to enjoy more outdoor dining. From March to October, people in Colorado cook, live, eat, and play outside. We do a lot of grilling, smoking, and open-fire 'cowboy' cooking, and of course, we say that food cooked outside always tastes better."

While there is no simple definition for Colorado's cuisine, one thing is certain: Colorado is a state rich in culinary delights, and it's only going to get better for food lovers. I hope this book leads you down new roads in our state, to your own delicious discoveries and to the making of many well-seasoned memories.

How to Use This Book

This guide has been organized into five chapters, beginning with metro Denver and then branching out into four fairly evenly divided sectors of our state: Northwest, Southwest, Northeast, and Southeast Colorado. Each chapter includes a map of the region, which can help you plan day trips to do your own exploring. Within each chapter, you'll find the following categories:

Made Here

Here you'll find local producers of everything from chocolates to cheeses, and growers of everything from popcorn to pinto beans. Most of the companies in this section offer their products directly to consumers; a handful of larger manufacturers are featured because they offer interesting tours and samples. Among them you'll meet our state's award-winning cheese makers, a pair of Belgian chocolatiers who call Colorado their home, and a busy granola maker.

Specialty Stores & Markets

This part of each chapter includes a wide cross-section of bakeries, candy shops, ethnic markets, coffee and tea shops, cheese shops, delis, butchers, and purveyors of gourmet foods and cooking accessories. You'll also find some secret sources that were known only by the locals . . . until now.

Farmers' Markets

Farmers' markets offer fresh produce, the opportunity to meet and buy directly from the grower, and a festive atmosphere. Because of the growing number of markets that are cropping up—pun intended—each year, it's a good idea to double-check times and locations. Telephone numbers and Web sites for checking those details are included at the beginning of the listings in each chapter.

Farm Stands

There are nearly 30,000 farms in Colorado, many with roadside stands offering fresh-off-the-vine produce. Often these farmers sell other goodies like honey from their own hives, homemade pickles and preserves, roasted chiles, and fresh eggs. The listings include a sampling of farm stands that keep fairly regular hours, but it's always a good idea to call ahead.

Food Happenings

Throughout the year, a surprising number of food and drink festivals, fairs, cook-offs, and other culinary events are held in our state. You'll find the details in this section, from the decadent Chocolate Lovers' Fling in Boulder to the spicy Salsa Festival in Creede.

Learn to Cook/Learn about Wine

Whether you want to pursue a professional career as a chef or just learn how to bake a brioche, there are many Colorado schools and private instructors that regularly offer cooking classes, hands-on workshops, and demonstrations. You'll also find information about wine tastings and classes for both casual sippers and serious oenophiles.

Landmark Eateries

In each region I've recommended a handful of one-of-a-kind restaurants that are sure bets for a memorable meal. I've included information about what makes each one unique as well as a

---

RESTAURANT PRICE KEY

$ = inexpensive; most entrees under $12

$$ = moderate; most entrees in the $12 to $20 price range

$$$ = expensive; most entrees over $20

pricing guideline. This book isn't a restaurant guide, so the list represents a very small selection of gastronomic gems, many of which are not commonly mentioned in the surveys and "best of" articles. What is the common denominator that these remarkable restaurants share? Great food, plus a generous dash of heart and soul. We have plenty of restaurants from which to choose; according to the Colorado Restaurant Association there are over 10,500 eateries in our state, serving roughly 2 million meals a day. (For a list of books that offer more in-depth information about Colorado dining, see Appendix C.)

Brewpubs & Microbreweries

We do love our beer. Colorado is ranked third in the country in volume of brewpubs and craft breweries. In this section, you'll learn where to go for the state's best handcrafted beers—unusual brews like Dostal Alley's Powder Keg Raspberry Porter or Steamworks' Backside Stout. Space didn't permit us to include every microbrewery, but those that made the cut have their own tasting rooms or pubs.

Wine Trail

Colorado's wine industry is growing rapidly, and the state's Grand Valley area is recognized as a viticultural area, a federal designation similar to the French *appellation contrôllée*. To help you plan your own trip to Colorado's wine country, this section includes established wineries that have tasting rooms and welcome visitors.

Recipes, Etc.

The book is peppered with a collection of recipes that utilize ingredients readily found in Colorado. Some recipes came from restaurant chefs who were persuaded to share their secrets, others were provided by growers and shop owners, and a few are old family favorites. I've also included a few choices for Colorado's Best, such as "Best Cinnamon Roll" and "Best Mexican Hamburger." Such declarations are bound to be controversial, so please don't hesitate to send your comments and suggestions for the next edition of *Food Lovers' Guide to Colorado* to:

> The Globe Pequot Press
> Reader Response/Editorial Department
> P.O. Box 480
> Guilford, CT 06437
> editorial@GlobePequot.com

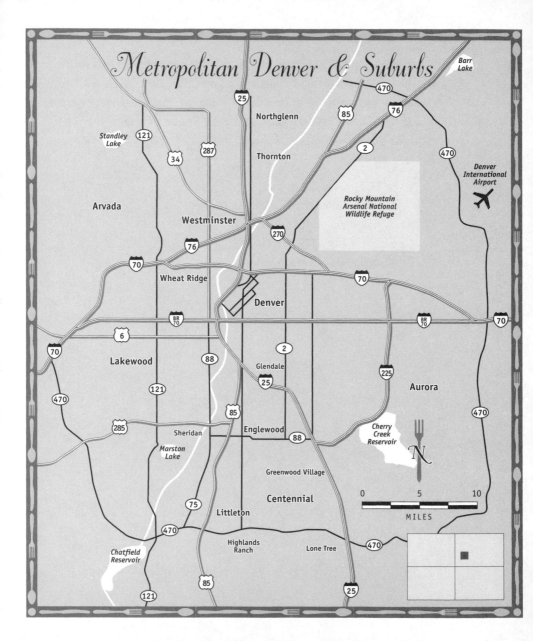

Metropolitan Denver & Suburbs

Denver, Colorado's capital, has experienced unprecedented growth and development in recent decades. The six-county metro area has a population exceeding 2.5 million people, yet Denver still offers many benefits of smaller-town living. Within the metropolitan area, there are numerous historic and redeveloped neighborhoods, many with their own business districts, individual personality, and sense of community. A diverse population supports ethnic markets and restaurants from dozens of cultures, particularly the Hispanic and Asian communities. At the same time, growth has brought the city numerous cultural offerings, first-class eateries, and enough festivals and events to fill the calendar all year.

The city is rarely called a "cow town" anymore, but we still love our beef; steak houses are one of the strongest sectors of the city's restaurant market, and the National Western Stock Show, held in Denver every January, is a major event for the cattle industry. Many bemoan the fact that the growth of the surrounding suburbs has brought a wave of chain restaurants to the metropolitan area, but the upside is that more independent restaurants are opening, too, bringing innovative cuisine to a city hungry for good food.

Microbreweries have proliferated in the city, particularly in the LoDo (Lower Downtown) area near Coors Field. With four major league sports franchises in town, the pubs stay busy year-round.

Farmers' markets are extremely popular in the Denver metro area, with nearly two dozen markets taking place all over the city during the summer and early autumn months. Three professionally accredited cooking schools attract serious chefs-in-training, and a number of other instructors host informal classes. Wine seminars and tastings are gaining in popularity, and even long-time citizens may be surprised to discover two little-known working vineyards and wineries within the city limits.

Made Here

5280 Salsa, (303) 770–5280 or (877) 879–5280; www.vhighway.biz. Using a family recipe, this popular salsa with the mile-high moniker is made with whole peeled tomatoes, onions, crushed red pepper, roasted jalapeños, cilantro, and spices. The salsa is available in mild and medium versions in local stores and online.

Big Mike's Original Barbecue Sauce, 3003 Arapahoe Street, Denver 80205; (303) 450–7091; www.bigmikes.com. Big Mike, Michael McCrea that is, manufactures and sells his own homemade recipe barbecue sauces. The tangy sauce—available in Original, Spicy, and Hottt!—is Big Mike's original creation. The sauce has won numerous barbecue competitions and is available online or at several local farmers' markets.

Boba Tea Direct, 13683 Detroit Street, Thornton, 80602; (303) 881-6146; www.bobateadirect.com. Bubble tea—the blended drink filled with chewy tapioca balls that looks like something out of a Dr. Seuss book—is wildly popular in Taiwan and catching on fast with younger consumers in many major U.S. cities. Whether it permanently piques the taste buds of Coloradoans is anyone's guess. If you're curious, though, you can purchase the *boba,* also known as tapioca pearls, QQ balls, or "zhen zhu" from Boba Tea Direct, a major supplier in Thornton. The *boba* are derived from the starch of the cassava root and when they're cooked properly, they have a chewy, Gummy Bear-like texture and a slightly sweet taste. *Boba* are commonly added to drinks like cold or hot milk tea, ice-blended drinks, smoothies, juice, and coffee. Order your own *bobas* online or via telephone.

Chico's Chili & Spices, P.O. Box 32174, Aurora 80012; (303) 366-6411; www.chicoschilispices.com. Chico's Chili & Spices offers an award-winning sauce mix, which is a special blend of spices with the authentic flavor of Mexican chili. Both red and green chili mixes, which can be cooked with pork or beef, as well as an authentic enchilada chili sauce mix, are available. Chico's mixes are available in local stores and may also be ordered by mail or online.

BIRTHPLACE OF THE CHEESEBURGER

The first cheeseburger was invented in Denver at the now-defunct Humpty Dumpty Drive-In in 1935. Owner Louis Ballast claimed he came up with the idea while experimenting with hamburger toppings.

East-West Specialty Sauces, 2045 South Valentia Street, Denver 80231; (303) 695–6369; www.eastwestsauces.com. For nearly thirty years, Denver's Jade Palace Restaurant delighted Denver diners with authentic Asian cuisine. Although the restaurant is gone, the flavors remain with East-West Specialty Sauces' delicious products. The company has "created Asian flavors for the Western palate," with offerings like Sweet Ginger Teriyaki Sauce, Tangy Mandarin Barbecue Sauce, and Sesame Soy Dressing. While the flavors are rich, the sauces are all low-fat or fat-free and cholesterol-free, and they contain no MSG. Gift sets are available, and you can order online (check out the recipes section of the Web site while you're there) or by telephone.

Hammond's Candy Company, 5735 North Washington Street, Denver 80216; (303) 333–5588; www.hammondscandies.com. Since 1920, Hammond's Candy Company has been delighting young and old alike with its homemade hard candies. Today Hammond's is the largest producer in the country of entirely handmade hard candy. Old-fashioned favorites include peppermint pillows, ribbon candy, twisted lollipops, and candy sticks ("barber poles"). Our family loves the company's famous

Mitchell Sweets—marshmallows wrapped in caramel. The company hosts free tours, Monday through Friday, every twenty minutes from 9:00 A.M. to 3:00 P.M., and Saturday from 10:00 A.M. to 3:00 P.M. (Groups of ten or more, and those with special needs should call first and schedule a tour time.) Hammond's products are also available by mail order and online.

La Popular Mexican Food, 2033 Lawrence Street, Denver, 80205; (303) 296–1687. For really, really fresh corn and flour tortillas, you've got to come to La Popular. The company grinds its own corn and supplies many of Denver's best Mexican restaurants. The shop is best known for its delicious homemade tamales; Christmas Eve is the busiest day of the year. Want to make your own tamales? A refrigerator case holds five- and ten-pound bags of prepared *masa*, and owner Susana Herrera will gladly give you a recipe. The shop has a large case of tempting sweets as well: gingerbread pigs called *marranitos,* fruit-filled fried empanadas, crumbly cookies, and Mexican pastries.

Mrs. Mauro's Potica, 9015 West Tanforan Drive, Littleton 80123; (303) 948–8589; www.shopfest.com/mrsmaurospotica. *Potica* (Po-tee-sa) is a thinly rolled sweet bread dough with a moist walnut filling that tastes like the rich homemade pastries from the good old days. Indeed it was the late 1890s when sixteen-year-old Albina Kormornik arrived in Colorado from her native city of Bratislava, today part of the Slovak Republic. Among her treasure trove of family recipes was the popular *potica*, also called *kolachi, povitica,* or nutbread. Albina soon started a tradition of baking *potica* during the holidays as a gift of love for her family and friends. Albina passed on the secret recipe to her daughter

Taking It Slow

If you're truly passionate about good food, there is no better organization to join than Slow Food. The group, which originally began in Italy in 1986, promotes the kind of eating that is the antithesis of fast food: dining as a source of pleasure, knowing and understanding where your food comes from, and preserving the traditions of regional food and wine. Being at a Slow Food event is like attending a family reunion where all your relatives know about your multiple divorces but they love you anyway. No one thinks it's weird to talk about, say, heritage turkeys or where the wild asparagus is growing or how surprisingly good the Cabernet Franc tastes with the Havarti. The events are fun and educational, you'll meet producers and growers galore, make friends, and enjoy some amazing meals along the way. Members also receive the organization's international magazine, *Slow: Herald of Taste and Culture,* and the national newsletter, *The Snail.* In Colorado there are six local chapters; see Appendix C for more details. To join, visit www.slowfoodusa.org. For more information about the Denver convivium, visit www.slowfooddenver.com.

Emily Rozbroil Mauro, who began selling the rich bread commercially in 1962. Today Mrs. Mauro's company sells thousands of loaves each year, especially during the holiday season. You can find the famed *potica* at Tony's Meats (see later in chapter), or order by telephone or online.

Stephany's Chocolates, 6770 West 52nd Avenue, Arvada 80002; (303) 421–7229 or (800) 888–1522; www.stephanyschocolates.com. Stephany's Chocolates invented Denver's namesake candy, the Denver Mint. These luscious squares of thinly layered pale green mint-flavored white chocolate sandwiched around a layer of milk or dark chocolate are brisk sellers to locals and tourists alike. The plant offers tours daily on weekdays; call to make a reservation.

Two Hot Chili Peppers, 1131 Fulton Street, Aurora 80010; (303) 367-5952; www.twohotchilipeppers.com. "Only in America," says Two Hot Chili Peppers founder Anita Criticos, "can a Greek lady make a living selling Mexican food!" Her award-winning Caliente Salsa beat out every competitor in America to win First Place honors at the Fiery Food Challenge for two years running. Along with a half-dozen different salsas, the company makes delicious soup, stew, chili, and dip mixes that are sold at select area stores and are available online or via mail order.

Specialty Stores & Markets

Carbone's Italian Sausage Market & Deli, 1221 West 38th Avenue, Denver; (303) 455-2893. When you go to Carbone's, there is no doubt that you are in a real Italian market. From the Catholic icons on the walls to the ravioli cutters on the shelves, this is as authentic as it gets. Fresh, homemade Italian sausage is the big draw, but the shop also offers a large selection of meats and cheeses, plus oversized sandwiches, tortellini, manicotti, sauce, meatballs, imported pastas, olive oils, and other Italian specialties.

The Cheese Company & More, 5575 East Third Avenue, Denver; (303) 394–9911. After twenty-five years in the Belcaro shopping center, The Cheese Company moved to its new snazzy store at Third and Holly—a fitting location for the upscale foodstuffs the shop carries. Along with dozens of tempting cheeses from around the world, the store stocks homemade Bavarian sausage and bratwurst, soups, pâtés, and gourmet foods like olive oils, syrups, mixes, crackers, olives, vinegars, plus unusual items like quince paste and raclette irons. The shop gets filled up at lunchtime when people flock in for the freshly prepared sandwiches with fillings like homemade chicken salad or smoked turkey paired with Brie and honey mustard.

The Chocolate Foundry, 2625 East 3rd Avenue, Denver; (303) 388–7800; www.chocolatefoundry.com. Need a ski mountain built of fudge, blanketed with edible snow? No problem. How about a white chocolate metatarsal bone for your favorite podiatrist? Piece of cake. The Chocolate Foundry claims it can make just about any image in chocolate, and it has been crafting creative chocolates for happy customers for more than twelve years. Stop in the Cherry Creek shop and your lips will tremble; the shelves are loaded with truffles, hand-dipped chocolates, fudge, caramel apples, chocolate sauces, and much more. And for the pampered pooch, the shop offers Fido's Cookies—dog biscuits dipped in a white vanilla coating and decorated with sugar sprinkles. (Ask for a "Barker's Dozen.")

Compleat Gourmet and Gifts, 7592 South University Avenue, Centennial; (303) 290–9222; www.compleatgourmet.com. This is the place to come for the holidays; the shop stocks an abundance of Valentine's Day chocolates, unusual Easter candy, Halloween treats, Christmas stocking stuffers, and all manner of festive tableware and accessories. A specialty food section offers salsas, jams, sugars, and necessities like Mexican vanilla, and the gadget area is packed with wonderful gizmos for cooks. You'll also find a huge selection of pepper grinders and cookie cutters, plus bakeware, coffeemakers, knives, spice racks, and much, much more.

Cook's Fresh Market, 8000 East Belleview Avenue, Greenwood Village; (303) 741–4148; www.cooksfreshmarket.com. You may never have to resort to boiling bags again, once you visit this upscale shop serving the Denver Tech Center area. A popular spot for busy executives to pick up dinner to go, the shop has glass cases filled with all sorts of mouth-watering entrees and salads. The menu changes daily and the shop bakes its own breads daily. Temptations abound, from a fully stocked butcher case to hundreds of gourmet food items, a deli, an assortment of fresh fish, and a cooler full of local and imported cheeses. The shop offers cooking classes taught by professionals; call or check the Web site for a schedule.

Cook'sMart, 3000 East 3rd Avenue, Denver; (303) 388–5933; www.cooksmart.com. A cornerstone in the tony Cherry Creek North shopping area, this store is jam-packed with gourmet foods, great gadgets, professional cookware, and fun table settings. The shop stocks specialty vinegars and oils, candies, popcorn and nuts, olives, mustards, marinades, jams and preserves, dessert sauces, barbecue

Queen City Pound Cake

Catherine Cavoto has worked as a restaurant cook, caterer, personal chef, wedding cake baker, and chocolatier. She teaches cooking classes at the Seasoned Chef Cooking School (see later in chapter) and she also happens to be my sister. When she made this incredible pound cake for Dad's birthday and we raved about its flavor, she said, "that's because it's made with mace—the pound cake spice." She's always saying things like this, but it's nice to be kin, and therefore privy to the secret ingredients of her always-fabulous recipes. Catherine says this cake won't be as good if you don't get some freshly ground blade mace. She gets hers at Savory Spice Shop (see later in chapter).

Cake

3 cups unbleached flour

1 ¾ cups sugar

1 teaspoon baking powder

½ teaspoon baking soda

1 teaspoon salt

1½ teaspoons ground blade mace

1 cup plus 2 tablespoons buttermilk

1 cup softened salted butter

2 teaspoons vanilla

4 eggs

Soaking Syrup

½ cup salted butter

¼ cup water

¾ cup sugar

½ teaspoon blade mace

2 teaspoons vanilla (or rum) extract

sauce, and a good selection of baking mixes. Its happy atmosphere is a credit to its friendly staff and also, perhaps, to the mouthwatering aromas that sometimes waft through the place—it regularly

1. Preheat oven to 350° F. Generously grease and flour a 12-cup Bundt pan.
2. Put all cake ingredients in a large bowl and combine at low speed until moistened. Beat at medium speed for about 3 minutes, scraping bowl and making sure mixture is well combined. Pour into prepared pan; smooth with a spatula.
3. Bake for 55 to 70 minutes until cake springs back when lightly touched, and a toothpick inserted in the center comes out clean. Set on a rack to cool while preparing the syrup.
4. Brown the ½ cup of butter lightly in a small saucepan over low heat. When it reaches a light brown color, add the water (carefully!) and stir in the sugar, blade mace, and the vanilla. Stir until dissolved and well combined.
5. Poke the cake all over (still in the pan) with a skewer, toothpick, or even a fork. Pour two thirds of the glaze carefully over the cake, as evenly as you can. Allow the cake to cool for about 10 minutes, or until the syrup is absorbed. Invert onto a serving platter, and use a pastry brush to "paint" the remainder of the syrup over the top and any dry places. Allow to cool completely, and serve with whipped cream, fresh fruit, or just as it is!

Makes 12 to 16 servings.

hosts in-house cooking demonstrations. Call for a schedule and, while you're at it, ask for a copy of its free newsletter, which often includes recipes and special discounts.

A charming neighborhood ice-cream shop with a red and white striped awning, Bonnie Brae Ice Cream serves dozens of flavors of handmade ice cream. The flavors change with the whims of the staff, and while vanilla is a perennial favorite, combinations like Grand Marnier Chocolate Chip and Amaretto Peach attract the crowds that wind out the door during the summer. The smell of homemade waffle cones is hard to resist, especially since the shop offers them dipped in chocolate

Bonnie Brae Ice Cream

799 South University Boulevard
Denver 80209
(303) 777–0808

and candy sprinkles. A glass case marked with children's nose prints is full of additional topping temptations: chocolate jimmies, Gummi bears, nuts, marshmallows, fruits, and chopped candy bars. In the summertime you can sit outside and watch the cars whiz by on University Boulevard. Right across the street is one of Denver's favorite pizza places, **Bonnie Brae Tavern,** 740 South University, Boulevard, Denver; (303) 777–2262. There is a well-worn path between the two establishments.

Danish Scandinavian Bakery, 7475-4 East Arapahoe Road, Englewood; (303) 771-3314. You have to be diligent to find this little bakery in the busy 'burbs, where there's a chain coffee shop at every turn. But walk through the door of Danish Scandinavian Bakery, inhale the aroma of fresh-from-the-oven pastries, and you'll feel like you've stumbled into a tiny cafe in a European village. Tucked away in a strip mall on Arapahoe Road, this cozy shop has glass cases filled with fresh-baked Scandinavian pastries, Danish, tortes, tarts, cakes, cookies, and other temptations. There's always good, hot coffee and a nice selection of gourmet food specialty items, too.

Diana's Greek Market & Deli, 1035 Lincoln, Denver; (303) 629-1624. This busy little shop sells not only scores of Greek specialties, but many Middle Eastern ingredients as well. You'll find olives and olive oil, frozen phyllo dough and pastries, feta and other specialty cheeses, coffee, yogurt, and exotic spices. Stop in the deli for a fresh gyros sandwich on pita bread while you're there.

East Side Kosher Deli, 499 South Elm Street, Glendale; (303) 322-9862. The next time a cold strikes and you need a dose of home-made chicken soup, you're in luck. The East Side Kosher Deli sells rich, fragrant, nourishing chicken soup by the quart, complete with a little container of noodles to add during cooking. This immaculate shop offers a grocery, butcher shop, delicatessen, restaurant, and catering operation, and every one of the more than 1,000 items it sells is certified kosher. Try a slice of noodle kugel, a rotisserie chicken, or one of the more than two dozen salads that grace the huge, glass deli case. One of the most popular items on the restaurant menu is—surprise—fajitas. Open daily except on Saturday and Jewish holidays.

English Tea Cup, 1930 South Havana Street, Aurora; (303) 751-3032. The English Tea Cup looks like a tiny, charming antique shop that was lifted by aliens from a back alley in London and dropped in a nondescript strip

BEST LADIES LUNCH

Why has Andre's attracted the cultivated women of Denver for so many years? Let's just say that this charming little European cafe tucked away in the east part of Cherry Creek is the antithesis of Hooters. The atmosphere is pleasant, the food is always remarkable, and the lunch crowd is decidedly upper crust. A fully-clothed waitperson politely describes Andre's two luncheon entrees of the day, and all a lady has to do is pick one—or the other. It's a safe bet that both choices will be excellent. No buffalo wings here, but the daily menu might include homemade roast beef with polenta, quiche, goulash, chicken curry with pasta, meat popovers, open-faced sandwiches, spaetzle dumplings, or any number of homemade European specialties. Save a little room because dessert is included and your waitress will bring around an all-too-tempting tray of fresh pastries and hot coffee. More temptations await when you pay your check in the little shop at the front of the restaurant. No cropped t-shirts, no calendars—but a large glass case filled with pastries beckons, and the shelves are lined with Swiss chocolates and specialty foods. Andre's serves lunch starting at 10:45 A.M. Closed Sunday and Monday.

Andre's Restaurant & Confiserie Suisse
370 South Garfield Street
Denver 80209
(303) 322–8871
$

mall in Aurora. The shop is full of lovely antique teapots and cups. In addition to a wide assortment of teas, you'll also find traditional English foods: jars of lemon curd, Chocolate Flake bars, and a medicine called "Nurse Harvey's Gripe Mixture," which might be just the thing to help you navigate Havana Street at rush hour.

India Bazaar, 12200 East Cornell Avenue, Unit U, Aurora; (303) 368–1758. Oh, Calcutta! More than 600 authentic Indian items are packed in this fascinating, well-stocked shop in Aurora. You'll find unusual produce like Indian eggplant and bitter melon, Indian spices, basmati rice, beans, sweets, snacks, drinks, and specialties like *nam*, a flatbread similar to pita. This is a terrific place to buy a colorful sari to wear or drape over the table. The shop also sells gift items, cosmetics, and authentic music.

Le Bakery Sensual, 300 East 6th Avenue, Denver; (303) 777–5151; www.lebakerysensual.com. If you're in charge of bringing the dessert for the bachelorette party, you've got to visit Le Bakery Sensual. You won't believe your eyes when you feast them on the erotic cakes, candies, and other treats prepared at this offbeat bakery. The cakes' decorations, which are crafted with larger-than-life features and a humorous touch, are made from edible almond marzipan. The bakery also makes nonerotic cakes for young and old alike. (The "over the hill" styles are especially outrageous.) For a special wedding touch, custom wedding cake–toppers can be created as caricatures of the happy couple.

Lily's, 3455 West 32nd Avenue, Denver; (303) 561-3025. Open the door of this shop in the Highlands neighborhood and the sweet scent of lilies greets you, along with a tantalizing selection of temptations for the kitchen, garden, and home. Jars of freshly ground spices line the shelves behind the cash register, where brother and sister Ethan and Michelle Bontrager supply the Highlands locals with specialty foods like jams, teas, and pasta. The shelves are also packed with cookware, teapots, bakeware, linens, and much more.

Marczyk Fine Foods, 770 East 17th Avenue, Denver; (303) 894-9499; www.marczyk.com. Peter Marczyk and his wife Barbara Macfarlane run this fabulous market with passion and commitment.

BIG APPLE BAGELS

Bagel *aficionados* know that nothing beats a real New York bagel. Manhattan-based H&H Bagels claims to have the "World's Best," and indeed, the kosher, hand-rolled bagels have a marvelous chewy texture and authentic flavor. Fortunately, the New York Deli News regularly flies in fresh H&H Bagels for grateful Denverites and transplanted Easterners. Call the shop to find out when the next shipment is due.

New York Deli News
7105 East Hampden Avenue
Denver 80224
(303) 759-4741
$

Locals stop by for staples like coffee and eggs and leave with hard-to-find specialties like figs and escargot shells. The butcher shop offers hand-cut steaks, chops, and charcuterie. The seafood market features beautiful, fresh fish laid on crushed ice with nary a whiff of fishy smell in the air. House-made crab cakes are a popular offering, as are whole fish. The "cheese cave" holds dozens of choices, and the cheese monger fashions fresh mozzarella in appealing little balls. The produce section has basics plus unusual items like French haricots verts and fennel. The small bakery area offers fresh pastries and desserts. Prepared foods lean toward comfort—dishes like turkey tetrazzini and lasagna. Sign up for Barbara's e-mail newsletter and you'll be privy to all of the shop's events, tastings, and specials.

Marczyk Fine Wines, 770 East 17th Avenue, Denver; (303) 894–9499; www.marczyk.com. Wander into this cozy wine shop adjacent to Marczyk Fine Foods and you'll find the wines thoughtfully arranged by food pairings: beef, game, lamb, poultry, seafood—plus a selection of wines that are just plain good to drink. The staff enjoys helping customers find the right wine to pair with dinner and always has some surprises, like a great French Bordeaux for under $20.

Middle East Market, 2254 South Colorado Boulevard, Denver; (303) 756–4580. Hundreds of unusual ingredients line the walls of this exotic shop. The sights and smells of spices, dates, figs, cookies, Turkish Delight (a sweet made from ground nuts, honey, and dried fruit), juices, rice, lentils, pita bread, and seasonal produce will assault your senses. The shop also sells incense, coffee pots and cups, and books.

Pacific Mercantile, 1925 Lawrence Street, Denver; (303) 295–0293. There are many Oriental markets in Denver, but none is as immaculate and well stocked as Pacific Mercantile. The store has an excellent reputation for fresh seafood and produce. Wandering the aisles is almost overwhelming; there is a dizzying array of sauces, condiments, spices, and snacks. It would help very much to be fluent in Chinese, as many of the aisles sell mysterious dried ingredients in plastic bags that are completely unfamiliar to the average Western cook. The coolers are filled with prepared foods, sushi, unusual ginseng drinks, and jars of kimchi, the eye-wateringly hot Korean cabbage condiment. One side of the store sells cooking gadgets, including some hard-to-find sushi-making tools, as well as gifts, toys, and books.

Parisi, 4401 Tennyson Street, Denver; (303) 561–0234; www.parisi denver.com. Parisi has always offered some of Denver's finest Italian foods, but since it moved into its gorgeous new location at 44th and Tennyson, it's positively irresistible. Just walk in the front door and face the glass case of gelatos and you'll know you're done for. That's before you've even seen the pastas, olive oil, fresh-made mozzarella, frozen stocks and sauces, tortellini, ravioli, biscotti, and candies. In the cafe, quality reigns with offerings like pizza, calzones, pasta, and *crostones*—grill pressed sandwiches. Try the Michelangelo, a master-piece of pancetta, Brie, sliced pears, and balsamic vinegar. Don't forget to finish your meal with a scoop of gelato.

Savory Spice Shop, 1537 Platte Street, Denver; (303) 477–3322; www.savoryspiceshop.com. For a dose of culinary aromatherapy, visit Mike Johnston and Janet Chambers's cozy spice shop in the eclectic

Best Rocky Mountain Oysters

Colorado landlubbers know that our region's oysters, just like the mollusks gathered from the ocean, are an acquired taste. In the classic Western preparation of this cowboy delicacy, bull testicles are battered or dusted with seasoned flour, deep-fried, and served hot with pepper sauce. Some folks say the oysters taste like a cross between calamari and chicken tenders.

The Buckhorn Exchange

1000 Osage Street
Denver 80204
(303) 534-9505
www.buckhorn.com
$$

If you've got out-of-town visitors who want to try the famous fritters, take 'em to Denver's oldest restaurant, The Buckhorn Exchange. Founded in 1893 and the proud holder of Liquor License Number 1, this establishment's walls and corners are decorated with more taxidermy than you will probably ever see under one roof. The Buckhorn serves a generous appetizer portion of Rocky Mountain Oysters accompanied by a tasty horseradish dipping sauce. The menu also includes prime steaks, buffalo, quail, elk, and other Rocky Mountain specialties (try the Buffalo Reuben at lunchtime).

Platte Street neighborhood, where the scent of freshly ground herbs and spices will clear your head and might even inspire you to cook. All of the spices are freshly ground, and the staff will happily sell you a quantity as small as one-half ounce. Along with just about every spice on the planet, the shop stocks bags of sea salt, pepper blends, herbs, and top-quality essences including vanilla and almond, plus unusual ones like cherry and coconut. The shop makes all of its own spice

Best Burrito

All of the burritos at Chez Jose are huge, fresh and tasty, but the ultimate is the Burrito de Inferno or "Burrito from Hell." This monster is packed with grilled chicken and steak, creamy guacamole, black beans, rice, lettuce, tomatoes, onions, jalapeños, cheese, and sour cream. It begs to be accompanied with a generous side of salsa from Chez Jose's homemade salsa bar, where you can choose from a mild, fresh salsa cruda or spicy red and green salsas.

Chez Jose

3027 East 2nd Avenue
Denver 80206
(303) 322–9160
and
5910 South University Boulevard
Greenwood Village 80121
(303) 798–8753
www.chez-jose.com
$

blends and offers wonderful gift sets—perfect for the food-loving cook who has everything.

Spinelli's Market, 4621 East 23rd Avenue, Denver; (303) 329–8143. The people in Park Hill are so lucky it's almost not fair. They have the kind of charming neighborhood grocery store that we all reminisce about and long for, and on top of that, it's stocked with more top-quality temptations than a lot of supermarkets. When you need a carton of milk or a sack of flour all the staples are here, but the store also has a butcher, a plentiful produce area (fresh fava beans, sugar snap peas, and wild mushrooms were among the offerings the last time I visited), imported pastas, cheeses, pâtés, and a whole lot more. Owners Jerry and Mary Ellen Spinelli also own the Adagio Bakery right across the street, and with all that culinary abundance in 1 block I can't see why anyone would ever need to leave the 'hood.

St. Kilian's Cheese Shop, 3211 Lowell Boulevard, Denver; (303) 477–0374. You could be blindfolded and led into St. Kilian's, and I bet you'd figure out your location pretty quickly. The aroma of imported and domestic cheeses is pungent in this charming little shop in the eclectic Highlands neighborhood. The store also packs in a nice assortment of specialty foods and a few loaves of crispy bread, but cheese is the star. Owners Hugh O'Neill and Ionah deFreitas delight in offering their clientele unusual and hard-to-find varieties, and there's always something new to taste.

Tony's Meats and Specialty Foods, 4991 East Dry Creek Road, Littleton; (303) 770–7024; www.tonysmarket.com. As you're driving to Tony's Meats, you might want to heed this practical suggestion: Swing by the bank on your way and pick up a bag of money. That way, you'll be set when you encounter the myriad temptations at Tony's: pastries, produce, cookbooks, gadgets, a fully stocked deli counter, a butcher, imported and local cheeses, frozen hors d'oeuvres, candies, and everything good. This is the place to order box lunches for your next business meeting, too; who else offers sandwich combinations like smoked turkey, peppers, sun-dried tomatoes, provolone, and pesto on homemade *panella* loaf?

In addition to the original store, Tony's has two other locations in Littleton. Cooking classes are offered at the shop located at 7421 West

HOT FOR DOGS

Denver's old Mile High Stadium was the record-holder for the most hot dogs sold at a single location. The stadium sold 2.3 million hot dogs and bratwurst in 1993, with 1.8 million during the year's baseball season alone. The second-place honor goes to Chicago O'Hare Airport, which sells more than 1.5 million hot dogs a year.

Bowles Avenue (720–377–3680). Taught by local chefs and instructors, the classes offer hands-on training in a variety of basic, ethnic, and seasonal cuisine; call for a schedule. Tony's third location is at 151 West Mineral Avenue (303–795–7887), and a new fourth store is at 847 Happy Canyon Road in Castle Rock (303–814–3888).

The Truffle Artisan Cheese and Exotic Foods, 2906 East 6th Avenue, Denver; (303) 322–7363; www. denvertruffle.com. The next time a recipe calls for, say, hazelnut flour or kumquats, you'll know where to go. The Truffle stocks a wonderful assortment of gourmet foods and hard-to-find specialty items. The shop is best known for its selection of cheeses, offering everything from the mildest to the stinkiest and everything in between. Owners David and Kate Kaufman are fond of offering samples of new cheeses and politely insist that you try a taste of whatever you're considering before you buy. Dozens of other treats make it tough to leave without adding a few more things to your shopping bag: creamy pâtés and foie gras, fine caviar, olives and olive oils, vinegars, homemade jams and chutneys, and of course, truffles. On the second Monday of every month, the shop sponsors a wine and cheese tasting; call for reservations.

Denverites flock enthusiastically to farmers' markets, and as a result there are more locations cropping up each year. Often held in a parking lot, these open-air markets offer farm-fresh produce and booths with a huge variety of other items. A great place for people watching, farmers' markets offer a wide variety of organic and conventionally grown fruits and vegetables. Top-sellers include just-picked sweet corn, vine-ripened tomatoes, Rocky Ford melons, freshly roasted chile peppers, herbs, and Western Slope peaches. The cut-flower booths, with gorgeous sunflowers, delphiniums, and other seasonal blooms, are always busy. In addition to a wide assortment of fresh produce and fresh-cut and potted flowers and plants, you may also find products like home-made pasta, breads, wild rice, cider, honey, maple syrup, baked goods, tortillas, pesto, jams and jellies, candy, and fresh and dried herbs and spices. Live musicians commonly provide entertainment, which adds to the fun. For the most up-to-date farmers' market locations and times, call your county extension office, the farmers' market hotline at (303–877–FARM) or visit www.ag.state.co.us. Some markets are also listed at www.coloradofarmersmarket.com.

Alameda Village Farmers' Market, West Alameda and Wadsworth, Lakewood; (303) 887–FARM; www.denver farmersmarket.com. Thursday sfrom 11:00 A.M. to 3:00 P.M., from June through October.

Aurora Farmers' Market, 9800 East Colfax Avenue, Aurora; (303) 361–6169; www.aurorabusiness.com. Saturdays from 7:00 A.M. until everything is sold out. Starts in mid-July and runs through the first frost.

Aurora South Farmers' Market, 15324 East Hampden Circle, Aurora; (303) 361–6169, Wednesdays from 7:00 A.M., June through October.

Buckingham Square Farmers' Market, Havana and Mississippi by the west entrance, Aurora; www.denverfarmersmarket.com. Tuesdays from 11:00 A.M. to 3:00 P.M., from June through October.

Cherry Creek Fresh Market, 1st Avenue and University (the Bed, Bath & Beyond parking lot), Denver. Saturdays starting at 7:30 A.M., from early May through October. Wednesdays starting at 9:00 A.M., from early June through late September.

City Park Esplanade Fresh Market, City Park Esplanade between 17th and Colfax (by East High School), Denver. Sundays starting at 9:00 A.M., from early June to late October.

Eldorado Natural Spring Water Farmers' Market, Historic Elitch Gardens at West 38th Avenue and Tennyson, Denver; (303) 232–2935. Saturdays from 7:30 A.M. to 12:30 P.M., June through October.

Highlands Ranch Farmers' Market, 9568 University Boulevard, Highlands Ranch; (303) 471–8828; www.hrcaonline.org. Wednesdays from 8:30 A.M. to 1:30 P.M. and Saturdays from 8:30 A.M. to 1:30 P.M., June through October.

Larimer Street Farmers' Market, 2300 Larimer Street, Denver; (303) 808–0804; www.larimerstreetmarket.com. Saturdays from 8:00 A.M. to 1:00 P.M., May through October.

Littleton Farmers' Market, Broadway and Ridge Road (Broadridge Plaza Shopping Center), Littleton, www.denverfarmersmarket.com. Wednesdays starting at 11:00 A.M. to 3:00 P.M., mid-June through late October.

Lowry Farmers' Market, Stanley British Primary School, 350 North Quebec Street, Denver; (303) 621–8081; www.laughingdogfarms.net. Sundays from 8:30 A.M. to 1:00 P.M., from late May through October.

The Market at Belmar, Alaska Drive between Teller and Saulsbury streets, Lakewood; (303) 936–7424; www.belmarcolorado.com. Sundays from 10:00 A.M. to 2:00 P.M., late May through early October.

Olde Town Arvada Farmers' Market, Arvada Olde Town Square, Arvada; (303) 420–6100. Saturdays from 9:00 A.M., starting in mid-June and running through September.

Old South Pearl Street Farmers' Market, 1500 block of South Pearl Street, Denver; (303) 778–7754. Sundays from 9:00 A.M. to 1:00 P.M., June through late October.

STALKING COLORADO'S WILD ASPARAGUS

In early May, tender stalks of wild asparagus appear along the banks of some of Colorado's streams and ditches, including some areas of the Highline Canal. The asparagus is a delectable, very edible springtime treat that's ripe for the picking, but it's important not to pull up the delicate stalks. Instead: Take a sharp kitchen knife and insert it in the ground near the stalk, then cut the stalk about two inches underground. (Leaving a visible stump above the ground can allow the plant to become diseased, which can then propagate through to the roots, so the stalks are best cut below the soil line.) Be sure to wash the asparagus thoroughly before eating it, and of course, if you are unsure about the identity of any wild plant it's better to leave it undisturbed.

Southwest Plaza Farmers' Market, West Bowles Avenue and South Wadsworth Boulevard, Littleton; www.denverfarmersmarket.com. Saturdays from 8:00 A.M., starting in mid-June and running through the end of October.

Stapleton Farmers' Market, 29th Avenue and Quebec Street, Denver; (303) 442–1837. Sundays from 8:30 A.M. to 12:30 P.M., early June through late September.

Tamarac Square Farmers' Market, Tamarac Square Shopping Center, Denver; (303) 887–FARM; www.denverfarmersmarket.com. Mondays from 11:00 A.M. to 3:00 P.M., June through October.

Tri-County Farmers' Market, Smokey Hill Baptist Church at 19315 E. Smokey Hill Road, Centennial; (303) 621–8081; www.laughingdog farms.net. Thursdays from 10:00 A.M. to 2:00 P.M., June through October.

Union Station Farmers' Market, 17th Avenue and Wynkoop Street, Denver; www.denverfarmersmarket.com. Sundays from 8:00 A.M. to 1:00 P.M., starting in late June and running through October.

Westminster Farmers' Market, Westminster City Park at 105 Sheridan Boulevard, Westminster; www.coloradofarmersmarket.com. Sundays from 10:00 A.M. to 4:00 P.M., May through October.

Farm Stands

BellFlower Farms, 4704 West Bowles Avenue, Littleton; (303) 738–9788; www.bellflowerfarms.com. BellFlower Farms' nursery opens in early April with a wide assortment of bedding plants, and beginning in July, you can buy more than eighty-five varieties of fruits and vegetables. Children and grown-ups will delight in the llamas, miniature donkeys, and goats on the property. This is a great place to come on an October weekend; the farm offers tractor rides, a maze, Oktoberfest food, and the unusual sport of pumpkin bowling. Plus, you're sure to find the perfect pumpkin in the farm's enormous inventory of over a hundred thousand pounds of pumpkins. BellFlower Farms closes at the end of October, but it has a year-round kiosk at the east side of the Park Meadows mall (near

Best Sausage Roll

Vinnola's sausage roll is a treasure to behold, a spicy homemade Italian link swaddled in cheese, sprinkled with hot peppers, and encased in fresh bread dough. It is baked to a golden brown and served hot with a bowl of spaghetti sauce for dipping. Magnifico! Vinnola's, with its own deli and bakery, is one of the nicest Italian markets in the Denver area. The shop carries a huge

Vinnola's Italian Market
7750 West 38th Avenue
Wheat Ridge 80033
(303) 421–3955

assortment of imported pasta, olive oil, peppers, and Italian ingredients.

Crate & Barrel) selling its own jams and jellies, salad dressings, pickles, hot sauce, and fresh-cut flowers.

Forté Farms, 4021 South Federal Boulevard, Sheridan; (303) 789–3845; www.fortefarms.com. Open from mid-June through the end of October every day from 9:00 A.M. to 6:00 P.M. This busy farm stand is the retail outlet for Forté Orchards of Palisade, the largest growers of plums and apricots in the state. The orchards also produce fifteen varieties of peaches, as well as pears and apples. In addition to fresh fruit, the stand features dozens of varieties of fresh vegetables in season.

Heinie's Market, 11801 West 44th Avenue, Wheat Ridge; (303) 425–9955. Yes, it's pronounced just like you think it is. Beginning

May 1, Heinie's opens with a nice assortment of bedding and vegetable plants, hanging baskets, and colorful patio pots. From early summer through November, it sells a wide variety of fresh produce as well as cider, juices, eggs, dairy products, baked goods, local honey, pinto beans, specialty jams and jellies, canning supplies, and crocks. Heinie's bottled Orange Mustard Glaze, brushed on ham and chicken, is a family favorite.

Malara Gardens, 7190 Kipling Street, Arvada; (303) 424–1452. Malara Gardens opens in April with bedding plants, including flowers, herbs, and vegetables, and beautiful hanging baskets. In the summertime, the market sells a huge assortment of fresh produce and other local favorites like cider, honey, roasted chiles, and baked goods. The freshly baked Italian bread is always a crowd-pleaser. Open daily April through Halloween.

Mazzotti's Garden Center & Farm Market, 6821 East 104th, Northglenn; (303) 453–1573. A great source of Colorado-grown produce, Mazzotti's sells vegetables grown at the family's Hudson, Colorado, farm. Starting in mid-July, the market offers dozens of varieties of vegetables and Western Slope fruit. In the autumn, Indian corn, gourds, and thousands of pumpkins are harvested in all different colors and sizes; the pumpkin patch is a popular tour for school groups during October. Open early April through Halloween.

Williams Farm, 11100 West 38th Avenue, Wheat Ridge; (303) 422–5134. This twelve-acre country farm is an oasis in the city. If

Denver Omelet

The Mile High City's namesake omelet is filled with a tantalizing mixture of sautéed peppers, onions, and chopped ham. This recipe makes one oversized omelet for two people.

2 tablespoons butter
½ cup chopped onion
¼ cup chopped green bell pepper
¼ cup chopped red bell pepper
½ cup chopped smoked ham
6 eggs
⅓ cup milk
½ teaspoon salt
½ teaspoon pepper
3 drops hot pepper sauce
½ cup grated cheddar cheese

1. In a hot skillet, melt the butter. Over medium-high heat, sauté the onion, bell pepper, and ham until the onion and bell pepper are tender, about 5 minutes. Reduce the heat to medium and remove the pan from the stove while you prepare the eggs.
2. In a small bowl, whisk the eggs and milk together; add the salt, pepper and hot pepper sauce. Return the skillet to the stove, and stir in the egg mixture. Top with cheddar cheese and let it cook until the eggs are set and the omelet is just barely browned on the bottom. Using a spatula, fold the omelet in half and serve immediately.

Makes 1 omelet.

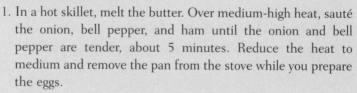

you've never tried farm-fresh eggs, you owe it to yourself to call Williams Farm and pick up a few dozen. The chickens are especially prolific in the spring and who knows, maybe you'll catch the farming itch yourself; the farm sells eggs for hatching, too. Springtime is also when the goats give birth to kids, which are available for purchase. The farm sells other unusual items, including natural raw honey, home-made soap, organic fertilizer (a positive euphemism if ever there was one!), and beautiful handspun wool and mohair yarn. Call first to arrange a visit.

Food Happenings

February: Great Chefs of the West, location varies, sponsored by the National Kidney Foundation, 3151 South Vaughn Way, Suite 505, Aurora; (720) 748–9991. One of Denver's biggest and longest-running food events, Great Chefs of the West attracts 1,000 people each year to support the National Kidney Foundation. Chefs from local restaurants go all out, serving tastings of food from lavishly appointed tables. The evening is topped off by a silent auction and raffle.

February: Suddenly Sonoma, Definitely Denver, The Historic Asbury Bell Tower Event Venue, 3011 Vallejo Street, Denver; (303) 830–2972. This tasting features wines from two dozen Sonoma County wineries. Tickets benefit the Colorado Restaurant Association Education Fund Scholarship Program.

March or April: **DAM Uncorked: A Wine Event,** Denver Art Museum, 100 West 14th, Denver; (720) 913–0039; www.denverart museum.org. Benefiting the Denver Art Museum, this annual event features live and silent auctions with a selection of wines from private collections and reserve wines from prominent vineyards. A wine tasting with wines from more than thirty-five wineries and seminars by experts in the wine and spirits industry makes this event one of the more popular fund-raising events in town.

Early May: **Cinco de Mayo,** Civic Center Park, Denver; (303) 534–8342. Cinco de Mayo celebrates the victory of the Mexican army against an invading French army on May 5, 1862, and is regarded as the beginning of Mexican independence from Europe. Colorado's Cinco de Mayo celebration is the largest in America, drawing more than 450,000 people to Denver's beautiful Civic Center Park, just west of the Colorado State Capitol. This spirited two-day fiesta features dozens of booths selling authentic Mexican food: tacos, burritos, nachos, enchiladas, churros, and much more. To cool off, try a frozen treat at the Jose Cuervo Margarita Garden. Artisans sell Mexican crafts and art, and several stages feature traditional and contemporary entertainment, including some of Mexico's top bands.

May: **Sushi, Sake, & Sumo,** Invesco Field at Mile High, Denver; (303) 592–7660. How many charitable events offer the, er, opportunity to don a sumo suit and get in the wrestling ring? Local restaurants prepare sushi, sashimi, and other menu samplings, and sake flows while the sumo wrestlers—both professional and amateur—provide plenty of entertainment. The event benefits the Generations Cancer Foundation.

Best Mexican Hamburger

A Denver institution, the Brewery Bar has been serving authentic Mexican food and oversized beers since the 1950s. Friendly, no-nonsense waitresses serve the food with lightning-fast service; my favorite is the Mexican hamburger. This fiery concoction is a fried patty of lean ground beef ensconced in a fresh flour tortilla, smothered with cheese and hot, meaty green chile. Crispy chile rellenos are popular, too; you might need to douse the chile's flames with the establishment's trademark "tiny" beer. A popular spot with

Brewery Bar II

150 Kalamath
Denver 80223
(303) 893-0971
$

the business crowd, you'll probably have to wait if you come on a weekday during lunchtime. There is no Brewery Bar I, by the way. The name was changed to the Brewery Bar II when the restaurant was relocated from its original Tivoli location in 1974. Brewery Bar III, south of Park Meadows Mall, opened last year.

Mid-June: LoDo Brewfest, Lower Downtown Denver; (303) 698–HOPS. A celebration of Colorado microbrews, this two-day event is an opportunity to sample more than thirty kinds of beer from Colorado brewpubs and microbreweries. A sampling of Colorado wineries is also presented. The festivities include a street party with food and entertainment.

June: Flavors of Denver: An Evening of Culinary Conversations, Rocky Mountain Chapter of the American Liver Foundation, 3650 South Yosemite Street, Suite 212, Denver; (303) 988-4388. This popular fund-raiser brings together a dozen and a half premier chefs from the Denver metro area to prepare their signature cuisine for a table of ten guests. Each chef designs his or her own menu and prepares a five-course gourmet dinner tableside, giving attendees the opportunity to visit with the chefs and learn more about the cuisine. The courses are paired with fine wines, and the evening includes a cocktail and appetizer reception.

June: **Greek Festival,** Assumption Greek Orthodox Cathedral, 4610 East Alameda Avenue, Denver; (303) 388–9314; www.hacac.org/culture/grkfest.html. The Greek Festival is one of Denver's largest ethnic festivals and the biggest annual event for the city's Greek community. Greek food is a main highlight of the event; sample everything from gyros and lamb sandwiches to stuffed grape leaves, souvlaki, and homemade baklava. The festival's bazaar area is a great place to pick up authentic Greek gifts, clothing, and jewelry. Traditional Greek folk dancing and music are performed throughout the three-day festival.

August: **Taste of the Nation,** location varies, Volunteers of America, 2660 Larimer, Denver; (303) 297–0408; www.sosdenver.seinecore.com. Skip lunch on the day of this event, which benefits the nonprofit organization, Share Our Strength. For that matter, you might want to plan to take a taxi home; you can eat and drink as much as you like for the duration of the party. More than seventy-five restaurants offer generous tastings from a wide variety of cuisine; several beers and 200-plus wines are poured as well. I like this event because 100 percent of ticket sales go to antihunger efforts, a testament to the generosity of the event's many sponsors and supporters.

Labor Day Weekend: Festival of Mountain & Plain . . .

A Taste of Colorado, Civic Center Park, Denver; (303) 295–6330; www.atasteofcolorado.com. Dozens of Colorado restaurants prepare all manner of cuisine for this family-oriented event that draws thousands of attendees every year. Live music, more than 200 arts and crafts booths, rides, and educational exhibits make this one of Denver's most popular weekend events. Daily cooking demonstrations are always well attended; check the event Web site for schedules and plan to arrive early. Free admission.

September: Oktoberfest, Larimer Street between

14th and 15th Streets, Denver; (303) 607–1276. Oktoberfest originated in the early 1800s in Munich, when King Ludwig I and Princess Therese exchanged their wedding vows. Today, Ludwig and Therese might be amused to see how their wedding party has evolved. The second-largest Oktoberfest in the United States is held at historic Larimer Square each year, attracting more than 300,000 people. One of Denver's longest-running events, this three-day celebration features authentic German cuisine, beer, dancing, and entertainment. Don't miss the World's Shortest Parade, usually held on Saturday, and brush up on your German before you go: "Ein bier, bitte." ("One beer, please.")

Late September or early October: **Great American Beer Festival,** Colorado Convention Center, 700 14th Street, Denver; (303) 447–0816; www.beertown.org. The Great American Beer Festival has become a truly mammoth event, showcasing hundreds of breweries and pouring a thousand different beers, for more than 20,000 beer enthusiasts. There are educational booths to help beer lovers understand the brewing process, and demonstrations for those who want to learn how to brew beer at home. After sipping suds all day, consider a stay at the historic **Hotel Teatro** at 1100 14th Street (303–228–1100), which is within skipping distance of the Convention Center.

Early October: **Denver Vineyard Harvest Party,** J.A. Balistreri Vineyards, 1946 East 66th Avenue, Denver; (303) 287–5156. Balistreri Vineyards and Spero Winery join forces to celebrate the grape harvest with plenty of good food—including a pig roast—and live music to accompany the wines.

October: **March of Dimes Signature Chefs,** 1325 South Colorado Boulevard, Suite B-508, Denver, CO 80222; (303) 692–0011; www.marchofdimes.com. A lavish buffet dinner is the cornerstone of this popular event that benefits the March of Dimes, with tastings offered by the area's top chefs, plus a silent and live auction.

Insider's Tip: For the latest updates about Denver's nonprofit events, visit www.blacktie-denver.com.

December: **Denver Cooks!,** Colorado Convention Center, 700 14th Street, Denver; (800) 422–0251 or (503) 234–1552; www.cooking events.com. Come hungry, because food samples abound at this consumer exposition that features booths from a variety of food and kitchen-related vendors. The admission price includes ongoing culinary demonstrations and seminars on a variety of topics, from kitchen design to party planning.

Learn to Cook

Art Institute of Colorado/School of Culinary Arts, 675 South Broadway, Denver; (303) 837–0825. The Art Institute of Colorado's culinary arts school has a unique advantage: an excellent student-operated public restaurant, Assignments, where students learn the real ins and outs of running a restaurant. The school's curriculum teaches competency in all the fundamental cooking skills, sanitation, safety, and food production. It also offers important courses such as computer skills, communication, and cost-control skills. Both associate's and bachelor's degree programs are offered.

Cake Crafts, 4105 South Broadway, Englewood; (303) 761–1522; www.cakecrafts.net. For candy- and cake-making supplies, Cake Crafts' selection is over the top. In addition to a full inventory of ingredients, tools, flavorings, boxes, and wrappers, the shop has hard-to-find items like candy rocks, edible glitter and gold leaf, and gum-paste flowers.

Insalata di Cipolle e Rucola
(Red Onion & Arugula Salad)

Elizabeth Montana, owner of Dream Italia (page 40), takes food lovers on amazing culinary journeys to Italy. She generously shares this simple—but fabulous—salad recipe from the Tutti a Tavola Cooking School in the town of Radda, Chianti, Italy.

2 cloves garlic, peeled

½ teaspoon salt

⅓ cup plus 2 tablespoons extra virgin olive oil

Juice of 1 fresh lemon

Freshly ground black pepper to taste

4 small red onions, peeled and thinly sliced

8 to 10 ounces fresh arugula, washed and dried

2 ounces Parmigiano Reggiano cheese, thinly slivered

1. Coarsely chop the garlic. Sprinkle with salt and use the flat of a knife blade to mash the garlic to a paste. Transfer to a small bowl and whisk in ⅓ cup of the olive oil, the lemon juice, and black pepper; mix well.
2. Heat 2 tablespoons of olive oil in a sauté pan over medium heat and cook the sliced onions until they are lightly browned. Remove from the heat and pour half of the garlic mixture over the onions.
3. On a serving dish, layer one-third of the arugula, onions, and Parmigiano Reggiano slivers. Repeat the layering with the remaining ingredients.
4. Give the remaining sauce a final whisk to blend well and drizzle it across the top of the salad. Serve at once.

Makes 4 servings.

Note from Elizabeth: Because acid ingredients like salt, lemon juice, and vinegar break down the fibers in the greens, they should be added at the very last moment in order to avoid soggy salad leaves.

Dream Italia
2035 South Adams Street
Denver 80210
(303) 868–8213
www.dreamitalia.com

The shop's upper floor has a private classroom where classes in cake decorating and candy making, and preparing wedding cakes, gum-paste flowers and other sweets are offered.

Colorado Free University, 1510 York Street, Denver; (303) 399–0093 or (800) 333–6218; www.freeu.com. If you've lived in Denver for any length of time, you're probably familiar with the CFU. No, the classes aren't free as in "without charge"; they're free as in "open to all, enjoying our personal liberty." The late founder John Hand established the school based on the idea that "a community has within it the knowledge and resources to solve its own problems." If your problem happens to be that you don't know how to cook, you're in luck. A wide assortment of informal cooking classes is taught by an eclectic group of instructors. The classes are casual and fun and often feature ethnic and seasonal classes at a variety of locations. Pick up a free catalog all over the city or register online.

Cook Street School of Fine Cooking, 1937 Market Street, Denver; (303) 308–9300; www.cookstreet.com. This cooking school offers programs for both professional and home cooks. The professional program consists of three months of study followed by three weeks of travel and education in France and Italy. Sessions begin in January, May, and August of each year. For the home cook, the school offers classes in many subjects, including sauce preparation, bread and pastry making, and basic cooking techniques. The school is located in a beautifully renovated brick building in Lower Downtown Denver, and a small shop inside offers cooking utensils and implements.

Crusted Lemon Crackers with Pistachio Boursin Cheese Rolls

Students at Johnson & Wales University's College of Culinary Arts receive an exclusive book—full of fabulous professional recipes—that is never made available to the general public. The College's Dean of Culinary Education, Jorge de la Torre, snagged one of the top-secret recipes for us and it's a treasure. This appetizer features delicate, lemon-scented crackers topped with a savory herbed cheese, and we're even given tips on how to garnish the canapés like a pro.

¾ cup flour
3 tablespoons cornmeal
1 teaspoon sugar
1 teaspoon salt
2½ teaspoons butter
⅓ cup ice water
Zest from 1 lemon
1 5.2-ounce package Boursin
    Garlic & Fine Herbs Cheese

1 tablespoon cream cheese
Finely ground pistachios for
    garnish
Thin chives for garnish
1 red bell pepper, cut into
    ¼-inch diamond shapes,
    for garnish

Dream Italia, 2035 South Adams Street, Denver; (303) 868–8213; www.dreamitalia.com. Immerse yourself in the Italian way of life when you join Dream Italia's founder, experienced traveler, and food lover Elizabeth Montana and travel in a small group on an experiential, customized tour to Italy. Learn Italian home cooking, participate in olive oil tastings and winery tours, drink cappuccino,

1. Combine the flour, cornmeal, sugar, salt, and butter in a stainless steel bowl. Blend until the mixture is crumbly. Add the water and lemon zest. Blend until a smooth dough is formed. Gather the dough into a disc and put it in a ziplock plastic bag. Chill for 2 hours.
2. Remove the dough from the refrigerator and divide into four equal pieces. Dredge the first piece in flour and roll it in a pasta machine to a thickness similar to that of pasta. Place the rolled dough on a parchment paper-lined tray. Repeat with remaining three pieces of dough. Put the trays in the freezer until the dough is frozen.

Johnson & Wales University
7150 Montview Boulevard
Denver 80220
(303) 256–9300
www.jwu.edu.

3. Preheat the oven to 300° F. Using a small, round crinkle cutter, cut the frozen dough into rounds. Spray a muffin tray with nonstick cooking spray and arrange the rounds inside the muffin cups so that the edges stand up. Bake for 6 to 8 minutes, or just until the crackers are set. Remove from the oven and cool on a wire rack.
4. Combine the Boursin and cream cheese, and form into small balls. Roll in the finely ground pistachios.
5. To serve, arrange one cheese ball on each cracker and garnish with a thin piece of chive or a red bell pepper diamond.

Makes about one dozen appetizers.

visit village markets, and experience Italy's art, history, language, design, and unimaginable beauty. During the popular Tuscany trip, you'll learn Tuscan cooking in the heart of the Chianti with the five Italian women of *When in Chianti* . . . , cooks who generously share the secrets of family recipes passed on for generations. Elizabeth also takes groups on customized trips tailored to the specific interests and passions of the participants; call or visit the Web site for more details.

Johnson & Wales University, 7150 Mountview Boulevard, Denver; (303) 256-9300; www.jwu.edu/denver. Johnson & Wales opened its Denver campus in 2000, expanding the options for students serious about a culinary career. The bachelor's degree can be obtained in baking and pastry arts, culinary arts, culinary nutrition, or food service management; the school also offers two-year associate's degree programs. Classes combine academic, laboratory, and hands-on teaching, and J&W graduates are well prepared for a variety of professions in the culinary arena.

Kathy Smith's Cooking School, 4280 East Plum Court, Greenwood Village; (303) 437-6882; www.kathysmithcooks.com. This school's mission is "the culinary education of the home cook." Owner Kathy Smith and an assortment of talented guest chefs teach participation classes and demonstrations. Following the class, students enjoy sampling the food with appropriate wines.

Mise En Place Cooking School, 1801 Wynkoop Street, Suite 175, Denver; (303) 293-2224; www.miseenplaceschool.com. *Mise en place* (MEEZ ahn plahs) is the French cooking term meaning "everything in its place." Denver's newest cooking school by the same name was founded

Best Green Chili

It's a dive in the very best sense of the word, and for hot jazz and hot green chili there's no better place than the 'Pec. Once considered to be in the seedy part of downtown Denver, El Chapultepec has survived long enough—for over fifty years—to end up right in the heart of now-trendy LoDo's renaissance. People come for the jazz and drinks, and are pleasantly surprised by the tasty Mexican food El Chapultepec serves. But it's the hearty, spicy green chili that draws as many die-hard fans as the music.

El Chapultepec
1962 Market Street
Denver 80202
(303) 295–9126
$

on the idea of teaching the organization and preparation of a meal, which in turn makes the process more efficient and creates a more enjoyable overall cooking experience. Billing itself as "a recreational cooking school," the spanking new facility located in the Ice House in LoDo is already attracting top-notch teaching talent among Denver's top chefs and sommeliers. Students can choose from two different teaching formats: the chef/instructor-led demonstration classes where students watch, listen, and learn, and the hands-on classes, where students learn by doing. Either way, students get to eat the fruits of their labor when the class is through.

Along with a huge slate of food-related classes covering everything from sushi to quick dinners to Spanish tapas, the school offers wine classes and tastings and a host of food- and wine-related events; check the Web site for a current schedule.

The Seasoned Chef Cooking School, 999 Jasmine Street, Denver; (303) 377-3222; www.theseasonedchef.com. Since 1993, the Seasoned Chef has been offering cooking classes and providing expert instruction for the novice and advanced home chef. Classes are taught by experienced culinary instructors and chefs from local restaurants with subjects ranging from basic cooking techniques and knife skills to seafood preparation, pasta and pizza making, high-altitude baking, bread making, chocolate techniques, ethnic cuisines, and wine education.

Learn about Wine

American Institute of Wine and Food, 2524 South Jasmine, Denver; (303) 333-2378; www.aiwf.org. The nonprofit AIWF was founded by Julia Child and Richard Mondavi in 1981. The group hosts events to promote its mission of enjoying good food and drink as well as "the fellowship that comes from eating together around the table." The Colorado chapter has more than 350 members and sponsors numerous food and drink events throughout the year. These include the popular "Greatest Caesar in Denver" competition in August. Non-members are welcome to attend many of the events, although members receive a discount.

International Wine Guild at the Metropolitan State College of Denver, P.O. Box 173362, Campus Box 60, Denver 80217; (303) 296-3966; www.internationalwineguild.com. If you've ever wanted to really get serious about wine, The International Wine Guild offers a two-day wine certification program covering and tasting wines from three continents; discussing old world wines, new world wines, and fortified wines; and teaching the art of wine and food pairing. Although the class material is complex, the instructors make the subject of wine appreciation accessible, interesting, and fun. Students who successfully complete the written exam at the conclusion of the seminar become members of the Guild. The Guild also offers numerous advanced professional diploma courses, as well as wine classes and tastings that are open to the public. The Guild is one of a few licensed wine vocational schools in the country.

Landmark Eateries

The Fourth Story, 2955 East 1st Avenue, Denver 80206; (303) 322–1824; $$. The Fourth Story is located on—surprise—the fourth story of the building that houses the beloved Tattered Cover bookstore in Cherry Creek. The book-filled shelves and comfortable chairs, the genuinely friendly and accommodating staff, and the nice view make this room special, indeed. Chef Tim Opiel cooks up exquisite offerings: starters like wild mushroom and goat cheese strudel with asparagus tips and white truffle butter; entrees like grilled mahi mahi accompanied by red pepper polenta; grilled shrimp, mango salsa, and tequila butter sauce; plus

TOP FIVE DENVER TEA SPOTS

The British tradition of sitting down for a hot cup of afternoon tea is alive and well in Denver. Here are a few jolly good metro area spots offering top-quality teas where you can relax to the refined sound of cups clinking saucers.

Ardelt's Victorian Garden, 1225 Logan Street, Denver 80203; (303) 861–2189; www.ardeltsvictoriangarden.com; $$. Ardelt's is housed in the 1890s home that Susan Ardelt's grandmother ran as a flower shop. Today, the shop sponsors specially-themed teas—often including live entertainment—that are as much about the food as the teas; accompaniments often include crumbly scones with Devonshire Cream and jam, delicate tea sandwiches, and desserts like lemon bars and cheesecake. Equally appealing are the over-the-top Victorian surroundings that highlight Susan's extensive collection of antiques and collectibles. Visit the Web site or call for the current schedule of tea times and events.

The Brown Palace Hotel, 321 17th Street, Denver 80202; (303) 297–3111; $$. This is a most civilized way to enjoy an elegant afternoon. The beautiful lobby of the historic Brown Palace Hotel serves formal tea every day from noon to 4:00 p.m. Tea sandwiches, pastries, and scones are available to accompany tea; reservations are required.

Cano's Collection, 235 Fillmore Street, Denver 80206; (303) 322–0654; $. This charming shop in the Cherry Creek North area serves tea and light lunch. Tea and scones are served all day. The shop also sells English foods, china, teapots, cups and saucers, and other goodies from England.

Gemini Tea Emporium, 2860 Welton, Denver 80205; (303) 292–9405; www.geminitea.com; $. A serene space in Denver's Five Points area, Gemini Tea Emporium offers more than 180 bulk teas from around the world. The proprietors will happily blend a custom tea mixture just for you, and they sell a nice selection of tea accessories as well. The smell is so intoxicating, you'll probably want to sit for a spell and enjoy the surroundings. Once you've made your selection, your tea is served in a cute little pot with an infuser so you can brew it to your liking. The seating area feels like a gallery, with its citrus walls hung with art from local galleries. The shop also serves lunch with salads, sandwiches, and homemade soup.

House of Windsor, 1050 South Wadsworth Boulevard, Lakewood; 80226 (303) 936–9029; $. This lovely shop is set in an unlikely location in a strip mall, but no matter. The homemade soups and sandwiches, as well as tea served in tea cozy–covered china pots, will soon make one forget that Wadsworth Boulevard is mere footsteps away. The shop sells lovely china and fun foods from England; pick up a package of Hob-Nob biscuits (Slogan: "One nibble and you're nobbled!") and you'll think you're snacking at Buckingham Palace.

steaks and chops; fresh pasta; and roasted chicken that provide plenty of pairing opportunities for the restaurant's extensive wine list. Desserts include the ever-popular crème brûlée and molten chocolate cake, plus more unusual offerings like crispy ginger-apple spring rolls with green tea ice cream and coconut caramel sauce. The Fourth Story serves a great Sunday brunch, too.

Mel's Bar & Grill, 235 Fillmore Street, Denver 80206; (303) 333–3979; www.melsbarandgrill.com; $$. Melvin and Janie Masters have created the warm, welcoming atmosphere at Mel's in the Cherry Creek North neighborhood. The room is beautiful, the live music is cool, and the food is consistently good. The kitchen is known for its fresh and imaginatively prepared appetizers, soups, fresh fish, chicken,

SEVEN SPLENDID DAYS OF DINING: DENVER RESTAURANT WEEK

In early March Denver Restaurant Week encourages its citizens to dine out with dozens of metro area restaurants serving three-course meals for two at the inflation-bustin' price of $52.80. There are wine specials and other activities at some participating restaurants; for more details visit www.denverrestaurantweek.com.

Best Cinnamon Roll in Denver

If your taste in cinnamon rolls runs to large, plate-sized rolls made from soft white bread dough, you are not going to agree with my choice. If you like a thick layer of white powdered sugar frosting on your favorite cinnamon roll, you won't like these, either. But if you put aside those notions and try the cinnamon rolls at Gateaux Bakery you might agree that they are the absolute finest in Denver.

Gateaux Bakery

1160 Speer Boulevard
Denver 80204
(303)376–0070
www.gateauxpastries.com
$

Each buttery bun is made from a spiral of croissant dough that manages to be nicely crisp on the outside; flaky and soft on the inside. The flavor and aroma of ground cinnamon permeate the roll, which is topped with a sweet, sticky, caramel glaze. If you want to gild the lily, you can have chopped pecans or cream cheese frosting on top. (Still longing for a good truck-stop cinnamon roll? Head north on I–25 to **Johnson's Corner** near Loveland; see page 212.)

pasta, duck, steaks, and daily specials; appropriate wines and spirits are suggested right on the menu. Some personal favorites are the housemade soups; the old-fashioned iceburg lettuce salad with blue cheese and red onions; the roasted chicken with crispy potato chips; and the roasted monkfish accompanied by a celery root sauté, crispy leeks, and topped with a parsley-flecked Hollandaise sauce. The dessert menu changes often, but the classic crème brûlée is a popular staple. The piano and bass duo that sometimes performs in the

Rocky Mountain Diner's Buffalo Meatloaf

Succulent meatloaf made from flavorful ground buffalo is served at Denver's snazziest diner. The restaurant serves it with a massive side of mashed potatoes. Ground beef can be substituted if you can't find buffalo.

1 stick (4 ounces) margarine

1 onion, diced

2 stalks celery, diced

1½ teaspoons diced fresh thyme

1½ teaspoons garlic powder

1½ teaspoons salt

1½ teaspoons freshly ground black pepper

2 eggs

½ cup milk

1 cup bread crumbs

3 pounds ground buffalo (or ground beef)

1. Preheat oven to 350° F. In a large skillet over medium heat, melt the margarine. Add the onion, celery, thyme, garlic powder, salt and pepper, and sauté until vegetables are tender. Remove from the heat and cool.

2. In a large bowl, beat the eggs. Add the milk and bread crumbs. Add the buffalo or beef to the vegetable mixture and mix well; then combine thoroughly with the bread crumb mixture.

3. Divide the mixture in half; press each half into a 9 x 5 x 3-inch loaf pan. Cover with aluminum foil; poke 12 holes in the top of the foil to let the steam escape. Bake for one hour or until the internal temperature reaches 160° F. Remove from oven and cool for 15 minutes. Slice into thick portions and serve.

Makes 10 servings.

Rocky Mountain Diner

800 18th Street
Denver 80202
(303) 293–8383
www.rockymountaindiner.com

$

Best Corned Beef Hash

Zaidy's is a busy, comfortable Jewish deli with friendly employees and coffee so stout it can take the edge off of any morning. You might have to wait for a table during the breakfast rush, but at least you can kill the time peering at the homemade *rugelach* and cakes in the glass cases up front. Zaidy's menu has dozens of offerings, but my favorite choice is the home-made corned beef hash. A generous plate arrives,

Zaidy's Deli of Cherry Creek

121 Adams Street
Denver 80206
(303) 333–5336
$

heaped with well-seasoned lean corned beef, crispy potatoes, and tender onions, bearing absolutely no resemblance to the canned stuff served at other places. The heavenly hash is served piping hot with eggs and your choice of bagel or toast. The Reuben omelet, stuffed with corned beef, sauerkraut, and Swiss cheese, is another favorite.

evenings provides the perfect musical accompaniment to the meal. The restaurant hosts regular wine dinners and tastings. Janie edits the restaurant's chatty newsletter, *Truffle Times,* which details the couple's travels and food discoveries; request a subscription at the restaurant or online.

Mizuna, 225 East 7th Avenue, Denver 80203; (303) 832–4778; $$$. If I tell you that Mizuna is famous for its macaroni and cheese, don't get the wrong impression. Owner/chef Frank Bonanno has created the ultimate version of this all-grown-up childhood favorite at the lovely

Ship Tavern Rocky Mountain Trout with Herb Butter Sauce

The Ship Tavern in the Brown Palace Hotel opened the day after the repeal of Prohibition in 1934. The chestnut-paneled restaurant has been busy ever since, serving The Brown Palace's version of casual fare—admittedly a bit more upscale than most—in a convivial setting. Rainbow Trout served with a mild lemon-butter sauce has been a menu favorite for years, and the restaurant generously agreed to share the recipe.

½ cup white wine
1 laurel bay leaf
½ teaspoon white peppercorns, crushed
1 tablespoon minced fresh herbs (parsley, thyme, chervil, tarragon)
1 cup heavy whipping cream

½ pound (2 sticks) sweet butter, diced
Salt to taste
12 boneless, skinless Rainbow Trout fillets
Salt and freshly ground black pepper to taste
¾ cup extra virgin olive oil

and perennially great Mizuna. TK's Macaroni and Cheese bathes the pasta in a rich mascarpone cheese sauce and chunks of lobster—can comfort food be any more decadent? (The TK is a nod to Thomas Keller, founder of The French Laundry, one of several stellar restaurants in Bonanno's past.) Mizuna's menu changes monthly to take advantage of

1. To make the Herb Butter Sauce, pour the white wine into a medium sauce pan, add the bay leaf, peppercorns, and herbs, and simmer until almost dry.

2. Add the heavy cream, bring to a boil, reduce heat and simmer until liquid is reduced by half. Slowly whisk in cubes of butter until fully incorporated. Remove from heat and season with salt to taste. Remove the bay leaf, tent with foil, and keep warm.

The Brown Palace Ship Tavern

321 17th Street
Denver 80202
(303) 297–3111
www.brownpalace.com
$$

3. Season trout filets with salt and pepper. Heat sauté pan and add the olive oil. Place fillets skin-side up in pan and sauté until lightly browned. Turn fillets and finish cooking on the other side until the fish is firm and cooked through.

4. To serve, place two fillets per serving on each plate. Spoon the Herb Butter Sauce over fish.

Makes 6 servings.

seasonal ingredients, starring innovative preparations of beef, chicken, chops, fish, and pasta. A six-course tasting menu changes nightly and features—well, the culinary whims of the chef. Co-owner Doug Fleischmann clearly influences the courteous, unobtrusive service. You'll want to make reservations, even during the week.

Le Central makes no bones about its moderate prices, incorporating its affordability into its name and outdoor signage. It's a casual bistro that dispels any notion of pretension, but the food is good and the atmosphere is fun, if a bit crowded at times. The menu changes daily, but a constant favorite is the mussel and clam selection, which features several preparations of the shellfish served with all the french fries you can eat. (By the way, you could justify a trip to Le Central just for the french fries, which are thinly cut from large potatoes, fried to a perfect golden brown and

Le Central Affordable French Restaurant

112 East 8th Avenue
Denver 80203
(303) 863–8094
www.lecentral.com
$

served crisp and hot.) Appetizers include a rich onion soup, escargots, and pâtés; lunch and dinner menus usually include chicken, pork, beef, lamb, and fish. The wine list is extensive, but not expensive, and the restaurant hosts regular wine tastings and events.

Sushi Den, 1487 South Pearl Street, Denver 80210; (303) 777–0826; www.sushiden.net; $$. If "location, location, location" is the old real estate adage, the exhortation for sushi should be: "fresh, fresh, fresh!" Short of making a trip to Japan, you're not going to find sushi any fresher—or better—than the sashimi, nigiri, and maki served at Sushi Den. It's been twenty years of sushi bliss since brothers Toshi and Yasu Kizaki arrived in Denver to start their own restaurant. The always-hip

Sushi Den has been packed ever since. Koichi, the youngest brother, lives in Japan and visits the fish market every morning at 4:00 A.M. to select and purchase the freshest fish. It's vacuum packed with dry ice and flown from Japan to Denver, where we can be eating a fish that was in the waters of Japan less than 24 hours earlier. Ain't life grand? Sometimes it's a long wait for a table, but there are often seats available at the sushi bar where you can watch the pros at work. Feeling adventurous? Just say, "Surprise me!" and see what comes out of the kitchen. It might be baby octopus, needlefish, or a giant geoduck clam, but whatever it is, it'll be wonderful. Those with tamer tastes might want to start with the *shake*—raw salmon sashimi, the Rocky Mountain hand roll, or any of the mouth-watering tempura rolls.

Brewpubs & Microbreweries

Brewpubs have proliferated in the Denver area in recent years. The Wynkoop Brewing Company was the first microbrewery to locate in what we now call LoDo, the revitalized Lower Downtown area of Denver. The Wynkoop began pouring its own wheat beers, ales, and stouts in the late 1980s, just as the public's appetite for handcrafted beers was gaining. When Coors Field opened in LoDo in 1995, it included the country's first major league ballpark brewpub, the SandLot Brewery. Scores of brewpubs followed, and while there have been some comings and goings as the economy sorted itself out, one thing is for sure: Denverites are still thirsty for good beer, and the brewpubs are happy to quench that thirst.

Cheshire Cat Brewery, 7803 Ralston Road, Arvada; (303) 431–9000; www.cheshirecatbrewpub.com. The Cheshire Cat Brewery, which bills itself as "Brewpub, Freehouse and Home Away From Home," is located in a handsomely restored 1891 Queen Anne-style brick house. Indeed, the warm surroundings feel quite homey, except that, unfortunately, most of us don't have a dozen beers on tap in our front parlor. Try the brewery's own "Hoppy Cat," a full-bodied dark amber ale; "Mild-Mannered Brit," a dark-colored but light-bodied ale; or the unusual "Calico," a blend of the establishment's brews, the makeup of which varies daily. The menu features sandwiches and salads, plus British specialties like sausage rolls and Bangers and Mash.

Denver ChopHouse and Brewery, 1735 19th Street, Denver; (303) 296–0800; www.rockbottom.com. The Denver ChopHouse, in a renovated old brick warehouse just a block away from Coors Field, serves seven freshly handcrafted ales on tap as well as two seasonal beers. Popular offerings are the light Honey Wheat Ale (nice with a lemon wedge) and the staff's favorite, the rich, roasty Nut Brown Ale. The bar offers a nice array of single-malt scotches and small-batch bourbons, while the lively restaurant serves huge portions of steaks, chops, and seafood. The colossal onion rings and mashed potatoes with white cheddar cheese are favorite side dishes.

A Thousand Pints of Light...

The folks at Beer at Home are eager to dispel the old notion that home-brewed beer is something that you make in your bathtub or out in the backwoods still. They'll happily teach you how to brew your own beer, and it's tough to stop in their well-stocked shop without catching the homebrew enthusiasm. Beginner kits provide all the necessary equipment and ingredients, and part of the hook is that you'll brew some reasonably good beer on your first attempt. After that, most folks hone their brewing skills to make the beer types and characteristics they prefer. Adventurous brewers can even learn to make homemade wine, mead, liqueur, and soda pop. If you *really* get into it, you can join a local homebrewers' association; "Foam on the Range" and "Hop Barley and the Alers" of Boulder are two popular ones.

Beer at Home

4393 South Broadway
Englewood 80110
(303) 789–3676; also at
1325 West 121st Avenue
Westminster 80234
(720) 872–9463
www.beerathome.com
www.beerandwineathome.com

SandLot Brewery, 2161 Blake Street, Denver; (303) 298–1587. The only microbrewery located in a major league baseball stadium, the SandLot is a lively hangout in Coors Field. All the beers served are Coors products, and several are not available anywhere else. A popular draw is the Right Field Red Ale, deep red in color, with a slightly sweet, malty

Best Bratwurst Sandwich

I'm about to reveal a secret that the men of Denver have obviously tried to keep to themselves. You'll find Bender's Brat Haus in a strip mall in Aurora, near a nail salon and a tattoo parlor. A line winds out the door of Bender's at lunchtime, a line comprised almost entirely of men. Most of the fellas are waiting for Bender's renowned homemade brats. Once inside you'll be asked if you want a single or double; I recommend you get your brat with the optional cheese, a tip I received from a plumber who was standing in line. The brat will be delivered to your table, served piping hot in a soft, fresh Kaiser roll.

Bender's Brat Haus

15343 East 6th Avenue
Aurora 80011
(303) 344–2648
$

Mustard, kraut, and relish are self-serve on a little table in the middle of the restaurant. The shop sells its links to go, and has recently started making Italian sausage, too.

taste. The Squeeze Play Wheat Ale is light in body and color. The restaurant serves better-than-average bar fare—burgers, sandwiches, and appetizers. On game days, the doors close two hours prior to the game and only Rockies' ticketholders are admitted.

Wynkoop Brewing Company, 1634 18th Street, Denver; (303) 297–2700; www.wynkoop.com. Established in 1988, the owners of the Wynkoop helped start the renaissance in Lower Downtown Denver. Today the brewery—co-founded by Denver mayor John Hickenlooper— is one of the larger brewpubs in the world. It produces nine to eleven beers, depending on the season, including its top-selling Railyard Oktoberfest Amber Ale. India Pale Ale, a classic English-style ale, is another popular choice, and designated drivers will appreciate the Tiger Root Beer made with Colorado honey. The Taster Pack allows the sampling of six different beers, a great way to get familiar with the different tastes, aromas, and qualities of the brews. The restaurant menu offers steaks, chicken, sandwiches, pasta, and a popular Shepherd's Pie.

Each year, the establishment holds the Beer Drinker of the Year Contest. Contestants submit resumes attesting to their "beeriness"; finalists then submit to two hours of beery queries from a panel of beer experts that test their knowledge of beer, how it is made, and its legend and lore. The lucky winner receives free beer at the Wynkoop for life.

Metro Denver Wine Trail

Avanti Winery, 9046 West Bowles Avenue, Littleton; (303) 904–7650. This tasting room offers an extensive stock of Colorado wines from wineries throughout the state, Colorado-made gifts, and fine cigars. Wines can be purchased here on Sunday.

J.A. Balistreri Vineyards, 1946 East 66th Avenue, Denver; (303) 287–5156. If you want to take a little getaway from the city without actually leaving the city, take a jaunt over to Balistreri Vineyards. This family-owned vineyard and winery is tucked away near the intersection of Washington and 66th Avenue, where the family has owned farmland for decades. Although the area is largely industrial now, you can see small farms interspersed between the factories, a throwback to the days when the land was primarily used for flower farming. When the United States cut flower business declined, the Balistreris shifted their efforts to winemaking. Reminiscent of European varieties, the Balistreris' wines are made using traditional methods with organic grapes, and without adding any sulfites or additives. They produced their first commercial wines in 1998, opened the tasting room in 2000, and the Balistreris began winning awards for their wines soon thereafter. The Colorado Cabernet Sauvignon and Balistreri Port are favorites, and the winery also makes a wide variety of mostly reds: Muscat, Syrah, Merlot, and several Cabernets. The tasting room is open to the public on Saturday and Sunday from 1:00 to 5:00 P.M., or at other times by appointment.

Old Town Winery, 7505 Grandview Avenue, Arvada; (303) 901-2648. Old Town's cozy tasting room in the heart of downtown Arvada is a nice spot to retire to after shopping. The winery offers wines by the glass in addition to bottles of its Chardonnay, Cabernet Sauvignon, Merlot, Sauvignon Blanc, Zinfandel, and table wines. The tasting room is open Wednesday through Friday from 11:00 A.M. to 3:00 P.M., Saturday from 11:00 A.M. to 5:00 P.M., and other times by appointment.

Spero Winery, 3316 West 64th Avenue, Denver; (720) 519–1506. Clyde Spero learned the art of winemaking from his father, who came to America at the age of thirteen from Potenza, Italy. Under the "Vino e Buono" label, the winery produces Cabernet Sauvignon, Zinfandel, Merlot, Syrah, Sangiovese, Cabernet Franc, Chardonnay, Muscat, and cherry and plum wines. The tasting room is open from 1:00 to 5:00 P.M. on Saturday, or by appointment.

Tewksbury & Company, 1512 Larimer Street, Denver; (303) 825–1880. At Writer's Square, this tasting room pours and sells the wines of Plum Creek Cellars (see page 113), in addition to offering a nice selection of fine cigars. Wines can be purchased here on Sunday.

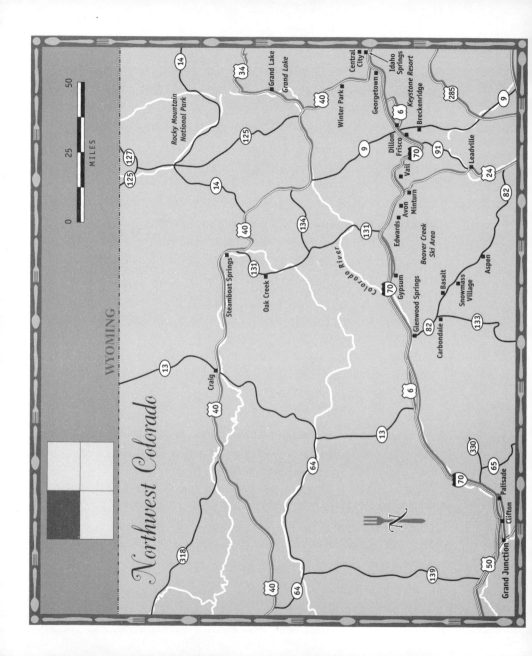

Northwest Colorado

The northwestern area of Colorado offers a wide range of experiences for the food lover. The "High Country Hollywood" towns of Aspen, Vail, and Beaver Creek are in this region, attracting the world's rich and famous year-round. Like the gold rush of the nineteenth century, skiing, snowboarding, and tourism are this era's boom, attracting locals, tourists, and part-time residents to the Rocky Mountains. The influx of money has attracted the trappings of the wealthy, too: a wide range of restaurants offering fine cuisine and wines, lavish wine- and food-tasting events and classes, and tony shops and boutiques.

This region also boasts some of the best agricultural areas in the state, with farms growing such favorites as Palisade Peaches and Western Slope apples. The surrounding mountains and cliffs, combined with good soil, warm days, and cool nights, create a microclimate that is favorable for growing a wide range of produce, including grapes. In fact, in 1991, the U.S. government recognized the Grand Valley area as a viticultural area, a grape-growing region defined by its geography, soil, and climate. Part of Colorado's growing wine country, the northwest region is home to a dozen wineries that offer tours and tastings.

Alida's Fruits, 3402 C ½ Road, Palisade 81526; (970) 434–8769 or
(877) 434–8769; www.alidasfruits.com. Alida and Robert Helmer have
grown and sold fruits and vegetables for more than twenty-five
years. The couple's spacious retail location, which began as a
humble roadside fruit stand, has expanded into a popular year-round
shoppers' destination selling a variety of fresh produce, Colorado
products, gifts, and antiques. With his overalls and straw hat,
"Farmer Bob" is a natural salesman for the business, extolling the
virtues of his products to customers, local television stations, and
anyone who will listen. Alida waits on the customers, often being
asked to fetch a few bottles of her popular Colorado Peach Syrup,
which she makes from Palisade's world-famous peaches. The shop
sells a wide variety of Colorado-produced hot sauces, salsas, herbs,
teas, dried fruit, jams and jellies, pie filling, and applesauce. In
season, farm-fresh cherries, peaches, pears, apples, squash, corn, potatoes, carrots, onions, and other produce are available. In the summertime, tour buses are a common sight in Alida's parking lot.

Enstrom's Candies, P.O. Box 1088, Grand Junction 81502; (970)
242–1655; www.enstrom.com. The next time you're stumped about
what gift to buy your boss, your father-in-law, or the "person who has
everything," don't sweat it. Just do what thousands of others do: send
a box of Enstrom's world-famous toffee. The confection, a crunchy
layer of golden almond toffee covered in chocolate and chopped

almonds, is made following the recipe Grandpa Chet Enstrom created over sixty years ago. The Enstrom family still makes this confection by hand in small batches—no small feat considering that the company produces more than a half-million pounds of the popular sweet a year. The toffee is available in one- to five-pound boxes, and Enstrom's makes other candies, too: Truffles, turtles, hard candy, fudge, and chocolates are available online and at the company's retail shops in Grand Junction (200 South 7th Street), Denver (2nd Street and University), Lakewood (14415 West Colfax Avenue), and Aspen (523 East Cooper Street).

Java Mountain Roasters, P.O. Box 1488, 1510 Miner Street, Idaho Springs 80452; (800) 568–5670; www.jmrcoffee.com. A stint in Seattle persuaded the owners of Java Mountain Roasters to open a coffee business in Colorado more than ten years ago. Today, small batches of beans are roasted right in the store, which is located on the main street of downtown Idaho Springs. The employees will happily blend a custom mixture of coffee beans to suit your taste, and while you're waiting, you can enjoy fresh coffee and an assortment of tempting pastries, scones, muffins, cookies, and other sweets. The bulk coffee can be ordered via telephone, Internet, and mail as well.

Kokopelli Herbs, Inc., P.O. Box 1512, Palisade 81526; (888) 922–4372; www.kokopelliherbs.com. Parsley, sage, rosemary, and thyme . . . Kokopelli Herbs has them all. The company specializes in dried culinary herbs and original herb blends, and in addition to the "Scarborough Fair"

quartet, the company sells dried basil, oregano, and other kitchen herbs. Garlic lovers will appreciate Kokopelli's attractive garlic braids, as well as its dehydrated elephant garlic slices, and Roasted Garlic Parmesan Sprinkle—fantastic on popcorn! The company produces a number of time-saving mixes, including Colorado Cowboy Stew and Rocky Mountain Green Chile Fixin's, as well as uncommonly flavored salsas such as smoky peach salsa and green chile salsa. Kokopelli's products are available at many Colorado retailers or you can order online or by telephone.

Palisade Pride, 119 West 3rd Street, P.O. Box 447, Palisade 81526; (800) 777–4330; www.palisadepride.com. The town of Palisade is famous for its juicy Colorado peaches and apples, and Palisade Pride will ship a gift box of perfect fruit at the height of the season to anyone in the continental United States. In nonharvest months, the company offers its premium dried Colorado fruits dipped in chocolate, plus canned peaches, glazed walnuts, and other Colorado fruit products. Order online or visit the company's storefront in downtown Palisade.

Talbott's Mountain Gold, 3782 F ¼ Road, Palisade 81526; (970) 464–5943; www.talbottfarms.com. Talbott's is known for some of the best apple cider and apple juice on the planet; the secret is the way the farm carefully blends the juice of both sweet and tart apples. The juice—which is flash-pasteurized and shipped chilled—can be ordered online, along with a large assortment of other regional foods: Colorado elk and other game meats, honey, dried fruit, gift boxes, peaches, apples, syrups, dried beans, and a line of soup, salsa, and dip mixes. But if you're planning a trip to the area, Talbott's boasts an on-site

"Peaches and Cream"

This heavenly dessert, created by Linda Quarles of Palisade, was the Grand Prize Winning Recipe in the 2004 Palisade Peach Recipe Contest sponsored by the annual Palisade Peach Festival (see page 89).

1 cup heavy whipping cream

¼ cup sugar

¾ cup powdered sugar

2 8-ounce packages cream cheese, softened

1 cup frozen raspberries with sugar, thawed

Water—see instructions

1 tablespoon cornstarch

2 Palisade peaches or enough for 1½ cups, peeled and chopped— but not diced—peaches

1. Whip the cream with ¼ cup of sugar and set aside.
2. Whip together the powdered sugar and cream cheese; fold in whipped cream. Spoon or pipe into single serving dishes. Set in refrigerator for 2 hours.
3. Strain and press raspberries through sieve for juice; add water to make this equal to 1 cup, place in small saucepan, stir in cornstarch and cook until thick. Cool.
4. Chop or slice the ripened peaches. Arrange peaches on top of the cream cheese mixture and drizzle the raspberry sauce over all.

Makes 8 servings.

cider mill where the finest apple juice is pressed fresh and you can rest your feet on the country porch while you sip a glass.

Specialty Stores & Markets

The Butcher's Block, 415 South Spring Street, Aspen; (970) 925–7554. This full-service butcher's shop offers top-quality aged beef, steaks, chops, poultry, game meats, sausages, deli meats, seafood, cheeses, and gourmet specialty items. The deli offers tasty oversized sandwiches and several different kinds of soup each day; if you're lucky, the creamy artichoke, mushroom, and chicken soup will be offered when you visit.

Carol's Oriental Food and Gifts, 2814 North Avenue, Grand Junction; (970) 245–3286. Colorado native Carol Mizushima Leinberger owns this fabulous grocery store that offers a fascinating array of Asian cooking supplies. A freezer case holds frozen fish including squid and mackerel, plus prepared foods like dumplings, egg rolls, Filipino *lupia,* Cantonese egg rolls, pot stickers, and desserts like *mochi* ice cream—frozen balls of a steamed sweet rice mixture filled with ice cream. The shop sells fresh tofu plus a wide range of different rice varieties, spices, teas, and sauces. "I try to stock the particular varieties of ingredients used in each type of cuisine," Carol says, "so, for example, in the soy sauce aisle I carry Filipino, Hawaiian, Chinese, Indonesian, and Japanese soy sauces because each one is unique." Carol has taught cooking classes for more than thirty years, offering sushi-making, Asian cooking, and customized private classes; call for a current schedule.

Confre Cellars & Fudge Factory, 785 Elberta Avenue, Palisade; (970) 464–1300; www.st-kathryn-cellars.com. I thought Confre Cellars was a fancy French name, but it turns out Confre is the combination of the down-to-earth names "Connie" and "Fred" Strothman. The couple, who also own St. Kathryn Cellars (see page 114) opened this shop in 2002 to sell their popular fruit wines and fabulous fudge. Flavors like Merlot fudge, strawberry-rhubarb, pumpkin, and a peach fudge that's offered during the peach festival are just a few of the dozens that the candy makers concoct. The wines are equally unique: Try the Concord grape wine ("goes great with peanut butter," Fred jokes), the lush white plum wine, the cherry variety made from tart pie cherries, and old-fashioned elderberry wine. If that's not enough, the shop sells assorted Colorado foods like jams, jellies, pickles, and mixes—and overflowing gift baskets.

Cookin' Cowgirl, 100 North Main Street, # 209, Breckenridge; (970) 453–8819; www.cookincowgirl.com. It's a culinary round-up at Cookin' Cowgirl, a well-stocked shop in Breckenridge's historic downtown. You'll find a huge assortment of specialty food items, including the Cookin' Cowgirl's own brand of dips, salsas, jams, a chili mix called Chili Fixin', and a tasty bruschetta spread, plus soup and bread mixes, seasonings and rubs, coffees and teas, pickled garlic, habañeros, jalapeños, oils, vinegars, and a whole lot more. The store also stocks just about every tool, appliance, or gadget a cowgirl needs for cookin' and servin': appliances, trivets, bakeware, flatware, glassware, extra cookware, linens, a good selection of cookbooks, and plenty of grilling tools for cookin' cowboys.

Culinary Corner, Mesa Mall, 2424 Highway 6 and 50, Grand Junction; (970) 245–9892. It's the Great Wall of Gadgets that makes this shop worth a leisurely visit, where you'll find everything from apple peelers to zesters. Enjoy a latte at the in-store espresso bar as you wander through aisles packed with high-end pots and pans, knives, bread bakers, coffeemakers, gadgets, aprons, cookbooks, coffee, giftware, serving pieces, and more. The shop also stocks a good selection of local and regional gourmet food items, including pickles, jams, jellies, syrups, dried fruit, and hot sauces.

Eat! and **Drink!,** The Corner at Edwards, 56 Edwards Village Boulevard, #104, Edwards; (970) 926–1393. These two synergistic shops located in Edwards offer one-stop shopping for the food lovers of Vail Valley. Eat! carries 100 to 200 cheeses, all artisanal. "Whoever raises the animals makes the cheese," says owner Pollyanna Forster. The shop specializes in farmstead cheeses from all over the United States—with a good selection of Colorado brands—and they're all available to taste before you buy, then cut to order. The sit-down area of the shop offers tapas, salads, cheese plates, charcuterie, pâtés and forty different wines by the glass. Shelves of specialty foods line the perimeter of the store with goodies like exotic rices, dried mushrooms, pasta, crackers, olive oils, truffle oils, balsamic vinegars, chocolates, conserves, and an olive bar with a dozen different olive varieties.

Right next door, Drink! is a fine wine store, carrying over 600 selections of wine from all over the world. One of the shop's most wonderful attributes is that it sells 200 different wines that are all under $15. The staff is always happy to make wine recommendations and help pair appropriate wines with whatever you're cooking.

Epicurious, Orchard Plaza, 400 East Valley Road, Unit H, Carbondale; (970) 963-8353; www.myepicurious.com. "We try to carry unusual items that are not available elsewhere," says Chris Norvell, owner of Carbondale's culinary gold mine, Epicurious. What a boon for the person who longs for a good meal at home but is too tired to cook—the shop sells homemade soups, stews, sauces, and prepared foods like meatloaf and the popular marinated flank steak. You'll also find locally smoked salmon, cured meats, organic eggs, Italian products, cheeses, pâtés, organic meats, local ground beef, free-range chicken, fresh fish, a selection of organic greens, olive oils, vinegars, and much more. Best of all, Epicurious sells locally baked brownies. Open daily.

Freshies Natural Foods Market, 34500 U.S. Highway 6, Unit B7, Edwards; (970) 926-8622. Freshies owner Delling Zing is clearly passionate about what he calls "living foods," organic, raw produce that he says, "has a vibrancy and energy that is destroyed when foods are heavily processed." His passion extends to everything Freshies sells: a wealth of fresh, organic produce, vegan foods, prepared foods, organic meats, cheeses, fruits and vegetables, sandwiches and wraps, frozen foods, grains and beans, an organic juice bar, baked products—including low-glycemic, wheat-free, and dairy-free items—and a whole lot more. Freshies is a member in a CSA Farm (see page 152), which ensures a steady supply of fresh produce during the summer and fall.

The Homesteader, 821 Lincoln Avenue, P.O. Box 770518, Steamboat Springs 80477; (800) 321–4702 or (970) 879–5880; www.home steader.net. The Homesteader stocks gourmet coffee beans and local food products such as jams, jellies, honeys, salsas, barbecue sauces, biscotti cookies, chocolates, and other candies. Stop at the shop's espresso/cappuccino bar before making your way through the hundreds of products for cooks: gadgets, cookware, kitchen appliances, dinner-ware, bakeware, Swiss raclette grills, linens, and a nice selection of cookbooks.

Ingrid's Cup & Saucer, 310 7th, Glenwood Springs; (970) 928–8973. Just half a block from the train station, this small bakery and coffee shop prepares everything from scratch. I've got a weakness for cinnamon rolls, and the toothsome buns owner Ingrid Wussow makes are stellar; in fact the shop is developing something of a reputation for having the region's best. Other temptations include muffins, scones, Danish, cinna-mon rolls, pastries, breads, cookies, coffee cakes, cheesecakes, fruit tarts, éclairs, cakes, and pies. Latte, cappuccino and espresso made from organic coffee beans are a popular accompaniment to the mouth-watering sweets. At lunchtime the bakery offers homemade soups and deli sandwiches.

Kitchen Collage of Vail Valley, 34323 Highway 6, Edwards; (970) 926–0400. Amy McDonnell and Kathy Rohlwing's shop in the Riverwalk shopping area of Edwards reflects their love of the casually elegant mountain lifestyle. The shop has plenty of gourmet food products for easy entertaining. These include flavored oils and vinegars, pastas, sauces, coffees and teas, candies, soup mixes, and seasonal items. The 4,000-square-foot store is also filled to the rafters with dishes, fine cookware, linens, and gadgets, bakeware, barware, wine accessories, bath accessories, cookbooks, stationery, candles, fondue pots and accessories, copper cookware, roasting pans, cutlery, flatware, knives, serving pieces, small electric appliances, cookie cutters, barbecue accessories, home and garden accessories, baskets, mirrors, home fragrances, small rugs, aprons, potholders, salt and peppermills, paper products, pet bowls and accessories, ceramics, tabletop dinnerware, Italian and Portuguese ceramics, glassware, wood serving pieces, casserole dishes, teapots, kettles, and coffeemakers.

Kitchen Cupboard, 207 Basalt Center Circle, Basalt; (970) 927–3634. You'll find everything but the kitchen sink at this shop—specialty foods, including salsas, mustards, preserves, oils, vinegars, baking mixes, pastas, candies, coffees, teas, and Colorado products. The shop also stocks cookbooks, linens, picnic baskets, small kitchen appliances, gadgets, cookware, bakeware, stemware, flatware, and gift items.

The Kitchen Loft, 319 East Main Street, The Miner's Building, Aspen; (970) 925–5550, extension 6. Located in the mezzanine of the Miner's Building on Main Street in downtown Aspen, this shop offers a nice assortment of cookware, dinnerware, bakeware, table accessories, linens, gadgets, and a selection of Colorado cookbooks.

Kitchen Shop of Craig, 529 Yampa Avenue, Craig; (970) 824–8148. This friendly shop sells a wide assortment of goodies for those who like to cook and eat: coffee beans, teas, hot sauces, and Colorado food products, plus dishes, linens, flatware, cookware, bakeware, coffeepots, espresso machines, waffle irons, mixers, gadgets, cookbooks, and more.

Les Chefs D'Aspen, 405 South Hunter, Aspen; (970) 925–6217. Overflowing with temptations for cooks, Les Chefs D'Aspen carries a wide selection of gourmet food products, including jams and jellies, nuts, oils, spice rubs, soups, locally roasted coffees, mulling spices, and seasonal candies. Additionally, the shop sells china, cookware, bakeware, flatware, gadgets, cutlery, baby products, cat and dog items, linens, glassware, serving pieces, small appliances, pizza stones, candles, paper goods, wooden bowls, cookbooks, soaps, floor mats, and more.

Specialty Foods of Aspen & The Cheese Shop, 601 East Hopkins Avenue, Aspen; (970) 544–6656. Partners Michele Kiley and Marco Cingolani are a dynamic duo in this well-appointed shop in Aspen. Michele—a knowledgeable cheese monger with more than a dozen years' experience in the business—fills the cheese case with a wide assortment of domestic and imported cheeses. ("One of my favorites is a washed rind sheep's milk cheese from Bingham Hill called Angel Feet," she says. See page 160 for more information.) Marco cooks Italian specialties like panini sandwiches, salads, soups, and homemade lasagna. The shop has a fresh juice bar, and the hot Lemon

Aid is great for people coming down with a cold; it combines the freshly extracted juices of ginger, lemons, and oranges with honey and a dash of cayenne. The Summer Breeze is a refreshing cooler of juiced watermelon, green grapes, and oranges. The store also stocks a good selection of specialty gourmet items like chocolates, cooking sauces, culinary oils, and vinegars.

To Catch A Cook, Village Inn Plaza at 100 East Meadows Drive, Suite #4, Vail; (970) 476–6883. Since Ursula and Larry Nisonoff bought the store in 2004, some nice additions have made their way to the shelves of To Catch a Cook. Look for caviar, foie gras, smoked salmon, and assorted cheeses in addition to a nice selection of gourmet food specialties like European candies and Colorado soup and baking mixes. When the nearby Alpenrose restaurant closed its doors, To Catch a Cook arranged to continue selling Alpenrose's mouth-watering baked goods in the shop, to the delight of locals. The shop also offers a wide assortment of top-of-the-line cookware, cutlery, glassware, tableware, tablecloths, gadgets, cookbooks, and bakeware.

Farmers' Markets

Most High Country farmers' markets begin a little later in the summer than markets in the eastern part of the state. For the most up-to-date farmers' market locations and times, call your county extension office or visit www.ag.state.co.us.

Aspen Farmers' Market, East Hopkins between Hunter and Galena, Aspen; (970) 464-7397. Saturdays from 8:00 A.M. to 3:00 P.M., from June through October.

Breckenridge Farmers' Market, Main Street Station on the Plaza, Breckenridge; (970) 453-9400, extension 2. Sundays from 9:00 A.M. to 3:00 P.M., from June through September.

Carbondale Farmers' Market, 4th and Main, Carbondale; (970) 464-7397. Wednesdays from 9:00 A.M. to 3:00 P.M., from June through October.

Dillon Farmers' Market, Marina Park parking lot, Dillon; (970) 262-3403. Fridays from 9:00 A.M., from late June through late September.

Edwards Farmers' Market, Edwards Corner, Edwards; (970) 479-1711. Saturdays from 9:00 A.M. to 2:00 P.M., from June through September.

Fruita Farmers' Market, Civic Center Library Complex, 325 East Aspen Avenue, Fruita; www.fruitafarmersmarket.com. Thursdays from 5:00 to 8:00 P.M. and Saturdays from 8:00 A.M. to noon, from June through October.

Glenwood Springs Farmers' Market, 1605 Grand Avenue, Glenwood Springs; Saturdays from 8:00 A.M. to 3:00 P.M., mid-June through mid-November.

Grand Junction Farmers' Market, Teller Arms Shopping Center, 2401 North Avenue, Grand Junction; (970) 243-2446. Wednesdays and Saturdays from 7:00 A.M. to noon, mid-April through mid- to late-November.

Grand Junction Farmers' Market Festival, Main Street between 3rd and 6th streets, Grand Junction; (970) 245-9697. Thursdays from 5:00 to 8:30 P.M., June through September.

Minturn Market, Downtown Minturn; (970) 827-5645. Saturdays from 9:00 A.M. to 2:00 P.M., mid-June through mid-September.

Oak Creek Farmers' Market, 222 East Main Street, Oak Creek; Saturdays from 10:00 A.M. to 4:00 P.M. early June through early September.

Vail Farmers' Market, Meadow Drive, Vail. Sundays from 9:30 A.M. to 3:00 P.M., from June through September.

Winter Park Farmers' Market, U.S. Highway 40 at King's Crossing, Winter Park. Fridays from 9:00 A.M. to 3:00 P.M., mid-June through mid-September.

Blue Cheese and Port Wine Fondue

The perfect appetizer or light dinner to serve après ski, this luscious fondue combines three creamy cheeses with a lightly sweet reduction of fine port wine. The recipe is provided by the Park Hyatt Beaver Creek Resort and Spa's Executive Chef, Pascal Coudouy.

1 cup port wine

1 garlic clove, halved cross-
   wise

1½ cups dry white wine

1 tablespoon cornstarch

2 teaspoons kirsch or brandy

½ pound Emmenthal cheese,
   coarsely grated
   (about 2 cups)

½ pound Gruyère cheese,
   coarsely grated
   (about 2 cups)

1 cup Gorgonzola or
   Roquefort cheese, crum-
   bled

Cubes of French bread

1. Pour the port into a heavy saucepan over medium-high heat and heat until simmering. Simmer until the port is syrupy and reduced to about ¼ cup. Remove from heat and reserve. (NOTE: *If you heat the port on a gas stove, be careful because it can flare up as it heats. If this happens, the flame will die down quickly once the alcohol is burned up.*)

2. In a small bowl, stir together the cornstarch and kirsch and set aside.

3. Rub the inside of a heavy 4-quart saucepan with the cut sides of the garlic. Add the wine to the pot and bring to simmer over moderate heat.

Park Hyatt Beaver Creek Resort and Spa

P.O. Box 1595
Avon 81620
(970) 949–1234
www.beavercreek.hyatt.com

4. Gradually add the Emmenthal and Gruyère to the pot and cook, stirring constantly in a zigzag pattern (not a circular motion or the cheese may ball up), just until the cheese is melted and creamy. Do not let it boil.

5. Stir the cornstarch mixture again and then add it slowly to the fondue, stirring constantly. Bring to a simmer; cook, stirring until thickened, 5 to 8 minutes.

6. Crumble the blue cheese into the fondue, add the port reduction, and stir until the cheese is dissolved. Transfer to a fondue pot and serve with bread.

Makes 6 servings.

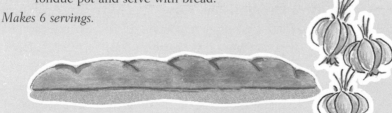

Farm Stands

Scores of roadside stands—alas, too many to mention here—spring up in Northwest Colorado during the late summer and early autumn, especially near the fruit-growing towns of Palisade and Grand Junction. I've included a sampling, but if you're traveling to the region I suggest you contact these chambers of commerce for more suggestions:

Grand Junction Visitor & Convention Bureau, 740 Horizon Drive, Grand Junction 81506; (800) 962–2547; www.visitgrandjunction.com

Palisade Chamber of Commerce, P.O. Box 729, 319 Main Street, Palisade 81526; (970) 464–7458; www.palisadecoc.com.

Clark Family Orchards, 3929 Highways 6 and 24, Palisade; (970) 464–5385. This roadside market sells fresh produce in season, including apples, cherries, peaches, pears, plums, and tomatoes. Open daily from mid-July through the end of September.

Cross Orchards Living History Farm, 3073 F Road, Grand Junction; (970) 434–9814. Cross Orchards' twenty-four-acre site was once part of a 243-acre fruit ranch that operated from 1896 to 1923. Today,  costumed interpreters offer you an opportunity to step back in time and imagine what it was like to live as a Grand Valley pioneer in the early 1900s. Displays feature vintage household effects, farmyard equipment, an assortment of horse-drawn implements and tools, and an exhibit about the Uintah Railway. Tour the orchards and stop by the country store, which sells produce grown on the farm as well as country gifts, and occasionally, fresh apple cider. Open mid-April through late October, Tuesday through Saturday.

DeVries Farm Market, 3198 C Road, Grand Junction; (970) 434–4870. This roadside market offers an abundance of seasonal produce: apples, beets, bell peppers, broccoli, cabbage, cantaloupe, carrots, cauliflower, cherries, chile peppers, cucumbers, green beans, onions, peaches, pinto beans, plums, potatoes, pumpkins, squash, sweet corn, tomatoes, and watermelon, as well as cider, honey, and handcrafted gifts. Open daily from March through December.

Mt. Garfield Fruit & Vegetables, 3371 Front Street, Clifton; (970) 434–7906. A popular summertime stop in the small town of Clifton, Mt. Garfield Fruit & Vegetables sells fresh produce including apples, apricots, asparagus, beets, bell peppers, broccoli, cabbage, cantaloupe, carrots, cherries, chile peppers (roasted chiles, too), cucumbers, grapes, nectarines, onions, peaches, pears, pinto beans, plums, potatoes, pumpkins, rhubarb, squash, sweet corn, tomatoes, and watermelon. You'll also find such specialties as cider, juices, honey, popcorn, Indian corn, and gourds. Open daily from May through mid-December.

Ron Crist Orchards, 3236 C Road, Grand Junction; (970) 434–6667. This roadside market sells fruit fresh from Ron Crist's orchard: apples,

Seared Diver Scallop with Foie Gras Flan, Mâche and Apple Salad

Miniature custards of cream and foie gras are paired with warm scallops and complemented by a tangy apple and mâche salad in this fabulous recipe from Chef Bruce Yim of Sweet Basil in Vail.

3 shallots, peeled and diced
½ teaspoon salt
1 tablespoon apple juice
2 tablespoons champagne
    vinegar
¼ cup, plus 2 tablespoons
    extra virgin olive oil
2 ounces duck foie gras

1 cup heavy cream
2 eggs
Salt and pepper to taste
4 large diver scallops
8 heads of mâche
1 golden delicious apple,
    sliced thin

1. In a mixing bowl, add one of the diced shallots, salt, apple juice, and vinegar, and mix until the salt is dissolved. Then add ¼ cup of the olive oil slowly, constantly whisking. Refrigerate until ready to use.
2. Preheat oven to 350°F. In a hot sauté pan, sear the foie gras until golden brown. Place in a small mixing bowl to cool.
3. Add cream, eggs, salt, and pepper, and whisk until smooth. Strain the mixture through a sieve. Pour the custard into 4 buttered ramekins. Place the ramekins in a metal baking pan and carefully

pour water in the pan until it is about halfway up the ramekins. Loosely cover with a sheet of aluminum foil and place in the oven. Bake for 30 to 40 minutes or until the custards are just firm. Remove and cool the ramekins on a wire rack.

Sweet Basil

193 East Gore Creek Drive
Vail 81657
(970) 476-0125
www.sweetbasil-vail.com
$$$

4. Heat a sauté pan over medium heat, add the remaining 2 tablespoons olive oil and sear both sides of the scallops until golden brown.

5. In a medium bowl, lightly toss the mâche, apple slices, and the remaining two diced shallots together.

6. To serve, arrange one seared scallop and unmold one flan next to it, making the center of the plate the junction. Put the salad on top of the junction. Spoon the vinaigrette over the salad and drizzle a little on the plate. Repeat with remaining scallops, flan, and salad.

Makes 4 servings.

peaches, pears, and nectarines. If you need a large quantity of fruit, call first and the orchard will be happy to have your order ready when you arrive. Open daily starting at 8:00 A.M., from August through mid-October.

Food Happenings

Early April: **Taste of Vail,** P.O. Box 5663, Vail 81658; (970) 926–5665 or (888) 311–5665; www.tasteofvail.com. More than a thousand people arrive in Vail to enjoy the spring skiing, taste the wines from sixty of the country's most-noted vintners, and sample the Rocky Mountain–inspired fare of the Vail Valley's world-class restaurants. This four-day event features workshops and seminars presented by wine experts, cooking educators, and guest chefs. A mountaintop food and wine-tasting picnic is held in an arena carved out of snow, and participants ride the gondola or ski in to get there. (The uncertainty of the weather adds to the fun; one year the picnic was held in a blizzard, and another year the temperature was in the 70s.) Previous events have also included a cocktail tasting, a guest chef luncheon, a lamb cook-off, and a cigar tasting. Optional nightly winemakers' dinners at local restaurants feature special menus paired with top wines. The Saturday night Grand Tasting is an extravagant culmination of the festivities, with tastings from dozens of fine wineries and over-the-top foods prepared by area restaurants.

May: **Blues, Brews, & BBQ Festival,** Beaver Creek; (970) 949–1234. This event—presented by the Park Hyatt Beaver Creek

Wild Currant Scones

If you are knowledgeable about mountain plants, bright red wild currants can be found growing in many of Colorado's high country areas during the later summer months. When I was a young girl, my mother and I once picked wild currants all afternoon while my father was fly-fishing in a nearby stream. We planned to make currant jelly with the tart red berries. After picking for hours, we had about a quart of berries, which cooked up to exactly one small jar of jelly. We learned that a better alternative is to dry the currants for baking. Once picked and washed, they can be spread out on cookie sheets and set out on a hot, dry day. (The drying process may take several days, and the trays should be brought inside at night or if it looks like it might rain.) Their texture is similar to raisins, although they are a bit more tart in flavor. Raisins or commercial currants can be substituted in this recipe for melt-in-your-mouth scones.

2 cups all-purpose flour	**4 tablespoons unsalted butter**
2 teaspoons baking powder	**2 eggs, well beaten**
1 tablespoon granulated sugar	**½ cup buttermilk**
½ teaspoon salt	**½ cup dried currants (or raisins)**

1. Preheat oven to 425° F. Lightly grease a baking sheet. In a large bowl, combine the flour, baking powder, sugar, and salt. Cut in the butter with a pastry blender or fork until the mixture resembles coarse meal. Add the eggs, buttermilk, and currants and stir until well blended. Turn the dough out onto a lightly floured board and knead for about 1 minute.

2. Divide the dough into two equal pieces. Pat or roll each piece of dough into a circle about ¾ inch thick. Cut each circle into 6 wedges. Transfer to the prepared baking sheet. Bake for 15 minutes or until lightly browned. Serve warm with butter and honey or preserves.

Makes 12 scones.

Resort and Spa Beaver Creek and Beaver Creek Resort Company—is the largest exclusively Colorado microbrew beer tasting in the state. More than thirty-five brew masters pour nearly one-hundred varieties of their finest ales, lagers, and stouts for guests to sample. Top chefs selected by *Bon Appetit* magazine go head-to-head in a mouth-watering barbecue cook-off contest. Several seminars are also offered; call ahead for seminar and tasting tickets.

June: **Food & Wine Classic,** Aspen; (877) 900–9463; www.food andwine.com. The granddaddy of all wine tastings, the Food & Wine Classic has evolved into one of the biggest events in the country for those who love to cook, eat, and drink. Celebrity chefs teach cooking classes during the day at various venues in the historic, star-studded town of Aspen. In the afternoon, the crowd moves to the huge circus tents for the Grand Tasting. Inside, representatives from hundreds of wineries pour samples of wines and share their knowledge about the grapes. A smattering of specialty food exhibitors give samples as well, but the emphasis is mainly on drink. There's just enough time for a nap before partaking in one of the optional dinners where attendees can dine with master chefs and taste extraordinary wines.

The **Hotel Jerome** and the **Little Nell** in downtown Aspen are among the most desirable hotels, usually booking up long before the event. However, if your ticket to the Food & Wine Classic zaps your checkbook, book a condominium at **The Crestwood** (970–923–2450) in nearby Snowmass Village. The rooms are comfortable and reasonably priced and Snowmass is a mere 10-minute drive from Aspen.

June: **Chili Cook-off,** Grand Lake Town Park, Grand Lake; (970) 627-8428 or (970) 627-3402. Firemen can take the heat; perhaps that's why the Grand Lake Fire Department hosts an annual chili cook-off to benefit a nonprofit organization in the community. Teams of cooks compete in this Chili Appreciation Society International (CASI)–sanctioned event, preparing red or green chili for prizes and the chance to advance to the international cook-off in Terlingua, Texas. When the judging is complete, the cooks sell samples of their lip-scorching concoctions.

June: **Culinary Festival & Pastry Competition,** Beaver Creek; (970) 845-9090. The nation's most talented pastry artists compete for a chance to win top honors and a large prize purse at the Pastry Extravaganza. *Bon Appétit* magazine sponsors top chefs who conduct culinary classes and demonstrations, and some of the area's top restaurants prepare food tastings.

June: **Chili Pepper and Brew Fest,** Snowmass Village; (888) 649-5982. After you've been sampling lip-scorching chili on a hot summer day, is there anything more welcome than a cold beer? This fun event pairs a beer fest with a chili cook-off; now *that's* what I call smart marketing. Two dozen microbreweries offer beer tastings as spectators watch the chili-making teams compete in the ICS (International Chili Society)–sanctioned cook-off highlighting three categories: Red Chili, Green Chili, and Salsa. Samples are offered once the judging is complete. Live music is featured throughout the day, and vendors offer chili pepper-themed foods, crafts, and food.

Third weekend in June: **Big Wheel 'n' Chili Festival,** Bridge Street, Vail; (970) 477–0111 or (970) 476–1000. Vail's main street, normally reserved for pedestrian use only, is transformed into a racing track during one of the village's most entertaining festivals. Chefs from Vail Valley restaurants offer tastings of their zingiest chili, vying for the title and bragging rights to the area's best. And then, another "heated" competition begins. Four-people teams relive their childhoods, racing their customized Big Wheel tricycles head-to-head down the racetrack. Roving street performers and musicians provide live entertainment during this two-day event.

July: **Grand Lake's Annual Buffalo Barbecue Celebration,** Grand Lake Town Park, Grand Lake; (970) 627–3402; www.grandlake chamber.com. Try farm-raised buffalo at Grand Lake's buffalo barbecue, an annual town tradition since 1947. The recipe for the barbecue sauce that is basted onto the slowly roasted bison is a closely held secret. The event is part of the community's annual weeklong Western Week, celebrating the town's cowboy and pioneer heritage. Other festivities include a parade, a 5K Buffalo Run, a pancake breakfast, and a barn dance.

July: **Toast of Breckenridge,** Breckenridge; (877) 359-5606; www .toastofbreckenridge.com. This three-day food, cooking, and wine festival features cooking classes and demonstrations by top chefs, plus tastings and seminars on wines and spirits. The well-worth-it weekend package includes the Grand Tasting, a progressive dinner, the lively Bloodies & Bluegrass Brunch on Sunday morning, all cooking demonstrations, and the participant's choice of three different seminars.

Late July: **Aspen Healthy Gourmet Fest,** Aspen; (970) 920–2957, extension 2; www.aspennewmed.org. This new event focusing on good, healthy food couldn't have picked a better location than the health-conscious town of Aspen. Highlights include Friday cooking classes held in private homes and at the Cooking School of Aspen (see page 95), and an organic-wine tasting seminar; check the Web site for more details and a full schedule.

Early August: **Rocky Mountain Wine, Beer, and Food Festival,** Winter Park; (970) 726–1545; www.nscd.org. Local restaurants prepare special festival dinners for several evenings prior to this popular weekend event. On Saturday morning, educational seminars provide instruction on a variety of subjects, including the subtleties of beer and wine tasting. In the afternoon, a huge food and spirit tasting allows your new knowledge to immediately be put to use. Try foods prepared by local restaurant chefs, choose drinks from more than a hundred different domestic and imported beers and 200 wines, and browse the offerings in a silent auction. The festival's proceeds benefit the National Sports Center for the Disabled.

Mid-August: **Palisade Peach Festival,** location varies, Palisade; (970) 464–7458; www.palisadepeachfest.com. The town of Palisade has been celebrating the arrival of fresh peaches for more than a century; "Peach Days" was a popular annual festival held in the late 1800s. These days, thousands of people come from all over the country to attend the daylong celebration and sample Palisade's world-famous peaches. Festivities begin with a peach-cooking/recipe contest. Later, people of all ages compete in the peach-eating contest. A local church makes home-made peach ice cream, and the Lions Club serves nonalcoholic peach daiquiris. Of course, bushels of fresh peaches, as well as locally made peach jams, jellies, and ice cream toppings, are available for purchase.

August: **Winter Park Famous Flamethrower High Altitude Chili Cook-off,** Main Street, Winter Park; (800) 903–7275. This all-day celebration of fiery foods offers the "hot prospect" of sampling scores of different types of chili and salsa. Costumed chili chefs vie for the Flamethrower title and the opportunity to represent the Rocky Mountain region in the World Chili Cook-off.

September: **Colorado Mountain Winefest,** Palisade; (800) 704–3667; www.coloradowinefest.com. Held in the charming town of Palisade, this four-day event celebrates the annual grape harvest for Colorado's wineries. The weekend begins with a golf tournament on Thursday, followed by winemakers' dinners that evening. Seminars on subjects that have included topics like grape growing and winemaking take place on Friday. That evening chefs selected by Colorado Proud prepare special winemaker dinners, pairing foods with the local wines. On Saturday participants sample the many varieties of award-winning Colorado wines, taste special foods prepared by Colorado chefs, and groove to live jazz throughout the day. The Tour of the Vineyards cycling

Grilled Colorado Lamb Chops with Mint Salsa

La Tour's owner and chef Paul Ferzacca shares his recipe for tender grilled lamb chops. With a twist on the traditional mint jelly, these chops are accompanied by a zippy salsa enlivened with fresh mint.

6 Roma tomatoes, diced
1 red onion, diced
1 Serrano chile, minced
2 cloves garlic, peeled and minced
1 bunch or 2 tablespoons fresh mint chopped

Salt and freshly ground white pepper to taste
Juice of 1 small lime
1 whole Colorado lamb rack or 16 Colorado lamb rack chops

1. Combine the tomatoes, onion, chili, garlic, and mint; season with salt, pepper and lime juice, and set aside.
2. Have your butcher clean the lamb racks to individual chops, removing any unnecessary fat and sinew.
3. Preheat grill. Season lamb racks with salt and ground white pepper. Grill to proper temperature and serve with Mint Salsa.

Makes 4 servings.

La Tour Restaurant & Bar
122 East Meadow Drive
Vail 81657
(970) 476–4403
www.latour-vail.com
$$$

TWENTY-FIRST CENTURY TURKEYS

"Shanaroba" comes from an Arabic phrase meaning "the future can be better than the past." What a fitting phrase for those who have endured one too many dry, bland, overprocessed Thanksgiving turkeys! But the future indeed looks bright, due in part to farmers like Jim Sorenson who are bringing back historic breeds of turkeys. Sorenson is the owner of Shanaroba Farm in the Roaring Fork Valley near Carbondale, where he raises heritage breeds of turkeys as naturally and as organically as possible. The handsome birds enjoy a diet of corn, squash, apples, and pumpkins, and Sorenson says the heritage breeds have a darker skin and darker colored meat. "You try one of these turkeys and you'll immediately taste the difference," he says. "They've got definite flavor."

Shanaroba Organic Farm

7299 County Road 100
Carbondale 81623
(970) 963-2134

Sorenson originally purchased a few turkeys for grasshopper control in his garden, and then discovered that the birds are gentle, surprisingly smart, and—well, delicious. Today he raises seven varieties of heritage turkeys: Black Spanish, Heritage Bronze, Buff, Narragansett, Royal Palm, Bourbon Red, and Slate.

Sorenson begins taking orders for Thanksgiving many months in advance, so it's a good idea to call early. "We always sell out," he says. The turkeys are also available from Spinelli's Market in Denver (see page 20).

event is also held on Saturday, with hundreds of bicyclists enjoying a 25-mile tour through Palisade's wine country. The Winefest concludes on Sunday when the valley's wineries are open for tours and tastings.

Mid-September: **Oktoberfest Vail,** Vail; (800) 525–3875. Experience a traditional Oktoberfest celebration in Vail's beautiful Bavarian setting. Sample traditional German cuisine from many of Vail's restaurants, complemented by the finest German beers and scores of fine European wines. Enjoy the sounds and sights of live oompah-pah music, traditional dancing, and a variety of other entertainment.

September: **Oktoberfest,** Beaver Creek; (970) 845–9090; www.beaver creek.com. Oktoberfest is a free event, open to the public and offering plenty of autumn festivities. As you might expect, you'll find an abundance of brats, beer, and pretzels, but this event also features live culinary demonstrations, food booths from Vail Valley restaurants, kids' activities, a Bavarian costume contest, an alpenhorn competition, and live music.

Mid-September: **Oktoberfest,** Main Street, Breckenridge; (970) 453–6018. German food and beer abound during this two-day festival in the charming ski town of Breckenridge. Food vendors sell German specialties like bratwurst, pretzels, and strudel, as well as good ol' American burgers and pizza. The beer flows freely, too, with Breckenridge Brewery and Paulaner as major sponsors. Oompah music and a kids' entertainment area make the event family-friendly.

October: **Apple Jubilee,** Cross Orchards Living History Farm, 3073 F Road, Grand Junction; (970) 242–0971; www.wcmuseum.org/cross orchards. With more than 22,000 trees, Cross Orchards was one of the largest orchards in Colorado in the early 1900s. Today, due to preservation efforts, many of the farm's buildings are on the National Historic Register. Each autumn, Cross Orchards hosts its Apple Jubilee to help fund the upkeep of the historic grounds and buildings. An apple-cooking contest is held to choose the best apple recipes of the region. Fresh apples are pressed into apple cider, and spicy apple butter is cooked over a wood stove in the bunkhouse, just as it was in days gone by. Both the cider and apple butter, as well as freshly baked pastries, cookies, and other treats, are for sale at the weekend event.

October: **Wine in the Pines,** Keystone; sponsored by CP of Colorado, Inc., 2200 South Jasmine Street, Denver; (303) 691–9339; www.cpco.org/ wine.htm. This popular weekend event benefits United Cerebral Palsy. On Friday evening, an optional Winemaker's Dinner pairs fine wines with an exquisite meal. More than a thousand people attend the Saturday night food and wine tasting, which also includes a silent and live auction featuring rare wines, travel packages, and sports memorabilia.

October: **March of Dimes Star Chefs,** Grand Junction and the Western Slope; 518 28 Road, Suite 103A, Grand Junction; (970) 243–0894; www.marchofdimes.com. A lavish buffet dinner is the cornerstone of this popular event that benefits the March of Dimes, with tastings offered from more than a dozen top area chefs and a silent auction.

(*NOTE*: While the event was not held in 2005, it is scheduled to continue in future years; call for details.)

December: Olde-Fashioned Christmas: A Family Celebration, Palisade Chamber of Commerce, P.O. Box 729, Palisade 81526; (970) 464–7458; www.palisadecoc.com. Santa Claus makes an appearance at this festive holiday celebration, and adults that made the "Good List" will enjoy special wine tastings at the area's wineries. Saturday's musical entertainment and parade of lights provide holiday cheer for all ages.

Learn to Cook

Cooking School of Aspen, 414 East Hyman Avenue, Aspen; (800) 603–6004 or (970) 920–1879; www.cookingschoolofaspen.com. The Cooking School of Aspen offers a full range of experiences, from serious hands-on training to cuisine-themed food adventures. Traditional classes allow students to work side-by-side with top chefs and instructors, receiving training in all aspects of the cooking process, from knife skills to the art of presentation. At the end of each class, students enjoy a sit-down meal of the dishes they helped prepare, paired with appropriate wines. The school's Culinary Adventures series whisks participants to a foreign locale to enjoy cooking classes, visit with local markets and food producers, and experience regional restaurants.

Best High Country Sushi

Despite the fact that Colorado is a landlocked state, its extensive air transportation system allows the freshest seafood to be flown in daily. At Aspen's Matsuhisa, chef Noboyuki Matsuhisa combines the freshest ingredients and flavors from around the world to dazzle the glitterati (and regular folks) in "The Hollywood of the High Country." The restaurant's spacious dining room feels very cosmopolitan, but I prefer a seat at the sushi bar to watch the chefs skillfully craft fresh fish into imaginative preparations of sushi and sashimi. Try the fiery Yellowtail Jalapeño if it's available; Broiled Black Cod with Miso is an oft-requested entree. The restaurant has plenty of offerings for nonsushi fans, too, and wine lovers will appreciate the restaurant's extensive wine list. You don't go to Aspen looking for bargains, but I should mention that Matsuhisa is not for the fainthearted of wallet.

Matsuhisa
303 East Main Street
Aspen 81611
(970) 544–6628
$$$

In addition to teaching cooking skills, the Cooking School of Aspen also houses a wine bar and tasting room, which is open weekday afternoons. A gourmet store, open every day except Sunday, sells cookbooks, gourmet ingredients, cooking utensils, and the like. Classes are held daily during summer and winter months, although the school does slow down during Aspen's off-season; call for a schedule.

Mesa State College, UTEC, 2508 Blichmann Avenue, Grand Junction; (970) 255-2600 or (888) 455-2617; www.mesastate.edu. Students in Mesa State College's Colorado Culinary Academy learn cooking and baking from scratch, plus the business aspects of running an eatery: dining room management, menu planning, food service supervision, cost controls, purchasing, marketing, and computer applications for food service. A Certificate of Occupational Proficiency and an Associate of Applied Science Degree are offered. The college's student-run restaurant, Chez Lena, provides plenty of hands-on training and an opportunity for diners to sample some truly amazing dishes. A recent menu included seafood and leek chowder, a seafood paella, and chocolate terrine with raspberry mousse for dessert. Chez Lena is open for lunch Tuesday through Friday from 11:15 A.M. to 1:00 P.M. Call (970) 255-2641 to make reservations.

Savory Inn and Cooking School, 2405 Elliott Ranch Road, Vail; (970) 476-1304; www.savoryinn.com. Is it a dream, or are you really waking up in the Paprika Room? In this spacious log cabin lodge on the banks of the Gore Creek, the twelve guest rooms are all named for spices. It's a fitting indication of the inn's passion for good food, which continues throughout the delicious breakfast and extends to the cooking classes that are hosted here for the Cooking School of Vail. Chefs and food experts demonstrate the art of preparing varied cuisines in the inn's teaching kitchen, and wine classes and winemaker dinners are regularly featured as well. The cooking classes are open to the public and the current schedule is posted online.

Beano's Cabin, 1 Beaver Creek Place, Avon 81620; (970) 949–9090; $$$. In the winter, a snowcat–aided sleigh pulls you up the snowy mountain to Beano's; in summertime a horse-drawn wagon or van transports you to the rustic cabin that feels like a sophisticated ski lodge. In a cozy atmosphere accented by river-rock fireplaces, Beano's boasts spectacular views of Grouse Mountain. The menu changes often, but usually includes homemade breads and soups, wood-fired pizzas, tenderloin of beef, Colorado rack of lamb, fresh fish, and delicious desserts like hot spice apple crumb pie and crème brûlée. If you'd like to have dinner at Beano's Cabin on a winter evening, you might want to make your reservation in September. Because getting there is half the fun, Beano's gets booked up early.

Hernando's Pizza Pub, 78199 U.S. Highway 40, Winter Park 80482; (970) 726–5409; $. Just a few minutes from the Winter Park ski area, Hernando's begins to fill up with weary skiers and hungry locals as soon as the lifts close. Its walls are covered with literally thousands of decorated dollar bills that its clientele voluntarily donate to make their mark on the place. Once you relax by the fire and have your first slice of one of Hernando's hearty pizzas, you'll begin to understand why so many people would part with so much money. In addition to a fairly traditional style of pizza, Hernando's prepares its Roma Pizza, brushed with olive oil, fresh basil, and minced garlic and layered with Roma tomatoes and mozzarella cheese. The Simone Garlic Pie is topped with olive oil, basil, extra garlic, double cheese, and black pepper. The restaurant offers a wide assortment of pizza toppings (including unusual offerings like chopped almonds and sauerkraut); we like the Supreme Pizza, which is topped with sausage, pepperoni, onions, green pepper, and mushroom. If you're in the mood for something different, the Sonoma is a fresh combination of chicken, artichoke hearts, and sun-dried tomatoes.

Keystone Ranch Restaurant, Keystone Ranch Golf Course, Keystone 80435; (970) 496–4386; $$$. This restored 1930s log homestead was a real working ranch until about forty years ago. The rustic atmosphere is still very "Bonanza," but don't let that fool you. Keystone Ranch prepares award-winning cuisine, offering a seasonal menu that highlights many regional and mountain specialties. In addition to homemade soups, fresh salads, and entrees that include steaks, poultry, and seafood, the restaurant offers specially prepared entrees and menus. A recent six-course dinner highlighted "Wild West" ingredients, featuring wild game, elk, venison, and fowl. Desserts are served by the massive stone fireplace in the living room of the old homestead, overlooking the Rockies. Reservations are required.

La Tour Restaurant & Bar, 122 East Meadow Drive, Vail 81657; (970) 476–4403; www.latour-vail.com; $$$. Paul Ferzacca may be a certified sommelier and a sophisticated chef who prepares some of the region's best contemporary French food, but he's clearly got a soft spot for kids. Consider that his restaurant, La Tour, not only has a children's menu, but instead of offering greasy chicken fingers Ferzacca cooks real food like roast chicken prepared in a kid-pleasing way, and accompanies it with sides like mashed potatoes and gravy. Attention to detail and always-terrific food put La Tour over the top, and Chef Ferzacca's passion for top-quality seasonal ingredients is reflected in his constantly changing menu. You might find sautéed rainbow trout stuffed with shrimp, topped with a chervil and tarragon *beurre blanc* sauce, or a grilled beef tenderloin and seared foie gras drizzled in a port wine sauce, served with sautéed fresh spinach, wild mushrooms, and a slice of Potatoes Anna. Desserts like a warm Lindt chocolate bomb, served with petit brandied cherries, coffee ice cream, and espresso anglaise sauce will send both adults and children out of the restaurant singing. Reservations recommended.

SIX89 Kitchen/Winebar, 689 Main Street, Carbondale 81623; (970) 963–6890; www.six89.com; $$. Mark Fischer's cooking has been described as inventive—some might even say eccentric—but since 1998 he's been cooking show-stopping food and drawing many diners to make the 30-mile drive from Aspen. Fischer was one of the first to advocate using local growers and producers, and his menu reflects the fresh, seasonal, regional products he incorporates into his cooking. A variety of small and larger plates are offered, encouraging the "sharing and grazing" that gives diners an opportunity to try a number of new tastes and flavors. The menu changes often, but the constant is that the offerings are full of innovative flavor combinations—and a few surprises. Fischer's take on bacon and eggs, for instance, pairs crisp cider-braised bacon with a fried quail egg and roasted tomato polenta.

Best Campfire Cookout

On an eighty-acre ranch a few miles outside of Winter Park, horsewoman Annie Oium and her crew throw barbecues and parties that no one in your group will ever forget. The property includes a 1906 homestead and barn set in a large wildflower meadow surrounded by breathtaking views. In the winter, Annie's crew serves dinner in the cozy, well-heated barn, which they call "Colorado's best four-stall restaurant!" In the summertime, picnic tables are set outside so that diners can enjoy the sunset. A typical cookout might include barbecued beef ribs, barbecued chicken, fresh corn on the cob, ranch beans, homemade coleslaw, warm homemade biscuits with honey butter, and homemade apple pie with caramel whipped cream. After dinner, "Washboard Annie" takes to the stage with her unique brand of song, cowboy poetry, and stand-up comedy. With her guitar, harmonica, washboard, and "stumpfiddle," (an instrument that you'll just have to see to believe), Annie will have the group belting out camp songs in no time.

Dinner at the Barn

P.O. Box 171
Winter Park 80482
(970) 726-4923
$$$

A pan-roasted fillet of Black Angus beef is served with what Fischer calls "stinky cheese tater tots," plus creamed spinach and crisp onion straws. For dessert, a pairing of Pecorino cheese with a chunk of local honeycomb is truly inspired. But then, so is the roasted chocolate and banana bread pudding served with a Marsala caramel sauce and spiced pecans. If you're feeling adventurous, book a reservation for Fischer's "Random Acts of Cooking." Fischer will have a chat with your group,

THE ULTIMATE GASTRONOMIC CHALLENGE: BEAU JO'S 14-POUND PIZZA

Are you ready for the Pizza Eating Olympics? Think you can handle the granddaddy of all pizzas? Are you ready to compete in "The Challenge," Beau Jo's invitation to dinner? If so, a twelve- to fourteen-pound, thick-crusted Mountain Pie pizza loaded with ground beef, onions, mushrooms, sausage, green pepper, and pepperoni awaits you and a hungry friend. The cost of this monster is $64.50, but if you can finish off The Challenge in an hour, you'll get the pizza for free and win $100 and a pair of Beau Jo's T-shirts and hats. Owner Chip Bair claims that seven hungry duos have successfully completed The Challenge in the thirty years the restaurant has been in operation.

Beau Jo's

1517 Miner Street
Idaho Springs 80452
(303) 567–4376
www.beaujos.com
$
Five other locations
around Colorado

Even if you're not *that* hungry, Beau Jo's pizza is delicious. The Mountain Pies are the most popular variety, starting with a hefty hand-rolled pizza crust that you can order in white, whole wheat, or cracked wheat. If you prefer thinner-crust pizza, the Prairie Pie is the way to go. The honey-based crust is delicious, and the restaurant puts honey on every table to drizzle on the leftover edges, which most diners save for dessert. (To give you an idea of how popular this practice is, Beau Jo's goes through fifteen *tons* of Colorado honey a year.) The restaurant offers your choice of sauce: Beau Jo's Pizza Sauce, Fresh Roasted Garlic and Olive Oil, Basil Pesto, and Roasted Garlic Cream Sauce, as well as barbecue sauce, picante sauce, and ranch dressing. Finally, you choose your toppings and then you order your pizza by the pound, not by inches.

and then prepare a succession of dishes according to what he thinks you might like to try. The restaurant often hosts winemaker's dinners, pairing several meal courses with appropriate wines. SIX89 is open nightly, and reservations are recommended. It bears mentioning that Fischer's new Thai restaurant, **Phat Thai** (343 Main Street, 970–963–7001), is packing in crowds and receiving accolades as well.

Ski Tip Lodge, 758 Montezuma Road, Keystone 80435; (970) 496–4950; $$$. Ski Tip Lodge is a wonderful place to go for a romantic weekend. Formerly an 1880s stagecoach stop, the inn was refurbished in 1940 into Colorado's first ski lodge. Today, it's a charming bed-and-breakfast inn that exudes charm and history. The inn's restaurant is excellent in its own right and offers a varying menu that includes homemade soups and breads; entree choices of beef, lamb, fish, wild game birds, and veal; and sumptuous desserts. The living area off the restaurant is a wonderful place to take your dessert and coffee and relax in front of the roaring fire. In the summertime, sit on the back patio overlooking the river, blanketed by a vast sky of twinkling starlight.

Sweet Basil, 193 East Gore Creek Drive, Vail 81657; (970) 476–0125; www.sweet basil-vail.com; $$$. It's one thing to be the hot new restaurant in town, and quite another to have a successful restaurant full of happy diners, year after year. Sweet Basil is that rare breed of eatery, consistently serving top-notch cuisine with a passion for quality and service that is always evident. The menu changes to reflect what's fresh and in season, but you might find entrees like the artichoke and black truffle ravioli with wild mushrooms, *haricots verts,* and lemon *beurre blanc* sauce, or a grilled Colorado lamb sirloin served with house-made herb-potato *gnocchi*. If the warm, sticky toffee pudding cake topped with whipped cream and rum sauce is listed on the menu—as the ads say, *just do it*. An extensive wine list offers plenty of bottles and wines by the glass to pair with the menu offerings, plus much-appreciated half-bottles. Sweet Basil serves a great weekend brunch, offering new takes on old favorites like an omelet stuffed with wild mushrooms, caramelized onions, and Haystack Farm goat cheese, drizzled in Romesco sauce. Reservations are recommended.

Brewpubs & Microbreweries

Backcountry Brewery, 720 Main Street, Frisco; (970) 668–2337; www.backcountrybrewery.com. If you visit the charming town of Frisco, you can't miss the Backcountry Brewery. A cornerstone of Frisco's Main Street, the brewery is housed in a massive log and stone building at the east end of town, across the street from the marina on Lake Dillon. The brewery mills its own grains and offers seven to nine handcrafted beers on tap; several are mainstays, while the others are seasonal. Backcountry's Telemark India Pale Ale, with its deep golden color and full-bodied flavor, was awarded a gold award at the 2000 Great American Beer Festival. The Wheeler Wheat is another popular brew with a pleasantly mild hoppy taste enhanced by orange peel and coriander. The restaurant menu features homemade soups, appetizers, sandwiches, Mexican specialties, burgers, and steaks. Backcountry beer is also sold at some liquor stores in Summit County, the Vail Valley, and Denver.

Breckenridge Brewery & Pub, 600 South Main Street, Breckenridge; (970) 453–1550; www.breckenridgebrewery.com. The Breckenridge Brewery & Pub opened in 1990 and is still the only brewpub in this quaint ski town. Offering handcrafted ales made on premises, the establishment has won numerous awards for its brews. Popular offerings include Avalanche, India Pale Ale, Mountain, Wheat, and Oatmeal Stout as well as a changing assortment of seasonal beers. The menu is eclectic and features traditional pub fare—appetizers, burgers and sandwiches, salads, pasta, fresh fish, and daily specials. A popular entree is the Jalapeño Shrimp—jumbo shrimp stuffed with jalapeño cream cheese and wrapped in bacon. The brewery's fresh ales are also available for take-out by the six-pack or case. The brewery has several other locations, including a popular brewpub in Denver at 2220 Blake Street (303–297–3644).

Dillon Dam Brewery, 100 Little Dam Road, Dillon; (970) 262–7777; www.dambrewery.com. Just up the road from the popular Silverthorne Outlet Stores, the Dillon Dam Brewery is a popular stopping-off place for mall-weary husbands. The brewpub offers eight beers ranging from the Slow Pitch Pilsner, a Czech-style pilsner light in body with a clean, crisp flavor, to the Old Dillon Oatmeal Stout, a dark, robust, full-bodied ale. Seasonal brews are produced, and the reasonably priced four-ounce beer samplers make it easy to try several of the pub's offerings. The restaurant menu features several entrees that make creative use of beer; try the Pilsner Chicken, finished with a pilsner-enhanced porto-bella mushroom sauce, and the Sirloin Cerveza, a beer-marinated steak topped with fried jalapeños and onion straws.

Dostal Alley, 1 Dostal Alley, Central City; (303) 582–1610. Central City was once a historic mining town. Now it's billed as "a mountain town gambling destination." Dostal Alley, the only brewpub in town, occupies an old brick building in Central City's historic district. This 4,000-square-foot casino features video poker and dozens of slot machines, but Dostal Alley's real draw is the, er, draws. Dostal's Best Bitter won the silver award in the bitter category at the 2001 Great American Beer Festival. The brewpub's dark red Powder Keg Raspberry Porter, with its raspberry aroma and flavor, is another popular pour. The restaurant menu offers a casual selection of pizzas, calzones, sand-wiches, and desserts.

Great Northern Tavern and Brewery, 91 River Run, Keystone; (970) 262–2202; www.gntavern.com. The Great Northern Tavern's in-house brews are named for spur lines of the Great Northern Railway. The Western Star Wheat is a blond, lightbodied American-style wheat beer with a balanced character of wheat and hops. The Dakota Amber Ale is a maple-hued ale with medium body and a smooth, refreshing taste. The bar, which has a daily happy hour, stocks an impressive array of single-malt scotches, and the bartenders mix a mean martini. In the restau-rant, try the beef carpaccio as an appetizer. The flaky-crusted chicken pot pie is a popular entree, while the Yukon Gold mashed potatoes and gravy are a winning side dish. The tavern has a branch in Denver at 8101

East Belleview Avenue (303–770–4741), which hosts a popular series of wine dinners; call for a schedule.

The Palisade Brewery, 200 Peach Avenue, Palisade; (970) 464-7257; www.palisadebrewery.com. Palisade Brewery features an on-site tasting pub that is open daily, serving a selection of beers on tap. Try the Red Truck IPA (an American India Pale Ale that won the Silver Medal at the 2004 World Beer Cup) or the Orchard Amber Ale made from Palisade-grown hops. During the Palisade Peach Festival (see page 89) the brewery serves Peach Pail Ale, brewed with—you guessed it—fresh Palisade peaches. Designated drivers can get silly on the brewery's delicious draught root beer. Brewery tours are available on request, and you can also purchase half-gallon jugs, six-packs, and kegs at the brewery.

Pug Ryan's Steak House Brewery, 104 Village Place, P.O. Box 2515, Dillon 80435; (970) 468-2145; www.pugryans.com. This busy Dillon brewery produces a half-dozen handcrafted beers, several of which have won major national awards. Try the dark amber, medium-bodied, and slightly sweet Kiltlifter Scottish Ale; the classically brewed, well-balanced Pallivicini Pilsner; or the eminently drinkable, unfiltered Morningwood Wheat that is typically served with a wedge of fresh lemon. (By the way, the brewery recently started offering the popular Morningwood Wheat in cans.) The steak house serves—as you might imagine—steaks, plus a number of other entrees including prime rib, chicken, pasta, ribs, and seafood.

Tommyknocker Brewery and Pub, 1401 Miner Street, Idaho Springs; (303) 567–2688; www.tommyknocker.com. Tommyknocker's is located in the historic Placer Inn in the quaint mining town of Idaho Springs. Opened around 1859, the Placer was a very busy place during the gold rush days. It housed an assay office where the miners would bring in their finds at the end of each day. After the day's activities the miners drank black coffee and ate hot bread, pork, and beans for their supper. They often shared stories about "tommyknockers," elfin creatures who were said to live in the cracks and crevices of the rock in the mines. These creatures became the focus of many stories and superstitions. Though rarely seen, they were often heard singing and working. There were two types of Tommyknockers: the mischievous ones who created problems, and the friendly ones who helped the miners find the richest ore deposits.

Today, the brewery produces a full array of microbrews. The award-winning Maple Nut Brown Ale gets its unique flavor from the addition of maple syrup. The Pick Axe Pale Ale is a classic English pale ale dominated by pleasant hop bitterness and aroma. The restaurant menu features some hearty choices, including appetizers, homemade soups and chilis, salads, sandwiches, burgers, steaks, and the stick-to-your-ribs "Bowl O' Lumpies," a steaming crock of lumpy mashed potatoes topped with melted cheddar and served with a side of gravy. Tommyknockers is also popular with the young folks for its children's menu and homebrewed soda pop in flavors like almond crème, strawberry crème, orange crème, and Key lime crème.

Amber Ridge Vineyards, 3820 G. 25 Road, Palisade; (970) 464–5314; www.amberridgevineyards.com. Winemaker Gene Corley and co-owner Lorinda Corley offer handcraft Chardonnay, Merlot, Cabernet Sauvignon, a Cabernet Franc, and additional varietals at this family-owned winery that started operations in 1998. The tasting room is open Thursday from 1:00 to 5:00 P.M. (call first to confirm) or by appointment.

Canyon Wind Cellars, 3907 North River Road, Palisade; (970) 464–0888; www.nectarwine.com. Named for its unique location, Canyon Wind Cellars is situated near the banks of the Colorado River and surrounded by towering sandstone bluffs. This creates a microclimate, which maximizes the area's warm, sunny days and cool nights; the mountain breezes that blow through the canyon help regulate the soil temperature. The winery produces Merlot, Chardonnay, and Cabernet Sauvignon. The property boasts a nice picnic area, and the owners are happy to give underground cellar tours. The tasting room is open from 10:00 A.M. through 5:00 P.M., Monday through Saturday.

Canyon Wind Cellars Tasting Room, 1500 Argentine Street, Georgetown; (303) 569–3152. This tasting room serves the wines of Canyon Wind Cellars, above.

Carlson Vineyards, 461 35 Road, Palisade; (970) 464–5554; www .carlsonvineyards.com. When a winery uses a prairie dog on its label, it's a hint that the owners know how to balance the serious business of winemaking with the importance of having some fun. Since 1982, the Carlsons have concentrated on developing and refining their regional wines, using exclusively Colorado-grown grapes and fruits. This led to a decision to label some of their wines after Western Colorado icons. They selected dinosaurs, whose fossils from the area are found in museums around the world, and the much-maligned prairie dog.

Although the labels are lighthearted, Carlson wines are definitely serious and award winning. The vineyard offers more than a dozen widely varied wines, ranging from crisp Chardonnays and velvety Merlots, to a just slightly sweet Riesling and Gewürztraminer, to absolutely remarkable tart-sweet fruit wines. The Carlson tasting room usually has several cats lounging around, and one or both of the Carlsons is often on hand to pour tastes and chat about the wine-making process. The tasting room is open daily from 11:00 A.M. to 6:00 P.M.

Colorado Cellars Winery, 3553 E Road, Palisade; (800) 848–2812. Colorado Cellars is the state's oldest winery, founded in 1978. It produces twenty-five varieties of wines and champagnes under several labels, including Colorado Cellars, Rocky Mountain Vineyards, and the Orchard Mesa Wine Company. A wonderful place to take a picnic, the winery's grounds include two gazebos and a large grassy knoll surrounded by vineyards with a panoramic view of the Grand Valley. The tasting room is open Monday through Friday from 9:00 A.M. to 4:00 P.M., and on Saturday from noon to 4:00 P.M.

Best Place to Pack a Picnic Prior to Perusing Colorado's Wine Country

Steve Thoms' family has been in the delicatessen business since 1941, so it's fair to say that he knows his knockwurst. Today, his New York-style Westside Delicatessen is a popular stopping-off point for hungry folks heading to the wine country. Choosing from all the possible combinations of sandwich-fixings is a challenge; the deli stocks a full line of Boar's Head cold cuts, thirty to forty different cheeses, and several varieties of homemade bread. The sandwiches are generous, and homemade salads are available on the side. The busy deli is open Monday through Saturday, from 7:00 A.M. to 9:00 P.M.

Westside Delicatessen
2454 U.S. Highway 6
and U.S. Highway 50
Grand Junction 81505
(970) 241–3100
$

DeBeque Canyon Winery, 3334 F Road, Clifton; (970) 523–5500. DeBeque Canyon Winery produces Syrah, Merlot, Pinot Noir, Cabernet Sauvignon, and Cabernet blends. The tasting room is decorated with a collection of western art, and the outdoor deck is a nice place to sip a glass of wine and enjoy the scenery. Tasting room hours are 10:00 A.M. to 5:00 P.M., Friday through Sunday.

Garfield Estates, 3572 G Road, Palisade; (970) 464–0941; www .garfieldestates.com. In 2000 owners Jeff Carr and Dave McLoughlin transformed thirteen acres of farmland into a vineyard and winery that produces Fumé Blanc, Rose, Merlot, Syrah, Cabernet Franc, and other varietals. The grounds boast an outdoor picnic area with stunning views of Mount Garfield. The tasting room is open seven days a week from 11:00 A.M. to 5:00 P.M.

Grande River Vineyards, 787 Elberta Avenue, Palisade; (970) 464–5867; www.granderiverwines.com. Grande River Vineyards is Colorado's largest grape producer, supplying grapes to a number of other wineries. The winery offers a full spectrum of wine types and tastes: Meritage White, Barrel Select Chardonnay, Viognier, Sauvignon Blanc, Syrah, Merlot, Meritage Red, Sweet Red, Semi-Sweet, Late Harvest Semillon, and Dessert Blush. Grande River built a band shell next to the vineyards for summer concerts, and now the winery is almost as well known as a summer entertainment venue as it is for its wines. Concert-goers pack their picnics and lawn chairs to watch the sun set and enjoy the live music with a glass of Grande River wine. The tasting room opens at 9:00 A.M. every day except major holidays; it closes at 7:00 P.M. in the summer, 6:00 P.M. in the spring and fall, and 5:00 P.M. during winter months.

Graystone Winery, 3352 F Road, Clifton; (970) 523–6611; www.gray stonewine.com. Graystone is one of the state's newer wineries, named for the gray, majestic shale bluffs surrounding the Grand Valley. Call first and make an appointment to visit the tasting room and sample the winery's Pinot Gris, Pinot Blanc, and award-winning Port.

Minturn Cellars, 107 Williams Street, Minturn; (970) 827–4065. The McLaughlin family founded this boutique winery, one of the state's smallest, in the charming town of Minturn in 1992. The winery brings in grapes from Palisade, crafting them into a variety of wines including Merlot, Cabernet Sauvignon, Cabernet Franc, and Chardonnay. During harvest season in mid-September, wine lovers can participate in the winery's annual crush and help stomp on the grapes. The back deck is a popular gathering place and picnic area and sometimes features live musicians. The tasting room, which is closed in November and May, is open Wednesday through Saturday during ski season and daily from June through October, from noon to 6:00 P.M.

Plum Creek Cellars, 3708 G Road, Palisade; (970) 464–7586. A jaunty 7-foot sculpture of a chicken (the locals call it "Chardonnay Chicken") perches outside the tasting room entrance of Plum Creek Cellars. Beginning in 1984, Plum Creek's owners Doug and Sue Phillips pioneered the effort of producing fine wines exclusively from grapes grown in Colorado. With its fifty-five acres of vineyards in the state's premier fruit-growing areas, Plum Creek has won numerous awards for its wines. It produces a wide range, including Chardonnay, Merlot, Sangiovese, Cabernet Franc, Riesling, Cabernet Sauvignon, and Riesling Ice Wine. Landscaped grounds beside the Pinot Noir vineyard and a covered patio offer quiet places to picnic. Fine art, antiques, and a stone fireplace create a warm atmosphere in the tasting room, which is open daily from 9:30 A.M. to 6:00 P.M. during summer and autumn, and from 10:00 A.M. to 5:00 P.M. during the winter and spring.

Rocky Mountain Meadery, 3701 G Road, Palisade; (970) 464–7899; www.wic.net/meadery. Rocky Mountain Meadery offers a wonderful alternative to traditional wine—honey wine, known as "mead." The oldest alcoholic drink of record, mead was consumed more than 7,000 years ago. This "drink of the gods" is produced here in Palisade, in the heart of Colorado's fruit country. King Arthur is a dry mead that pairs well with fish and wild game, while medium-dry Lancelot complements poultry dishes. Guinevere, a semi-sweet mead, is served with fruits and cheeses; Camelot is a sweet dessert wine that is delicious over ice cream. Fruit and honey meads are made from the area's abundant fruit harvest of blackberries, raspberries, cherries, and peaches. The winery also produces hard ciders from apples and peaches. The lightly carbonated ciders contain 6 percent alcohol and are refreshing on a hot summer afternoon. The tasting room is open seven days a week from 10:00 A.M. to 5:00 P.M.

St. Kathryn Cellars, 785 Elberta Avenue, Palisade; (970) 464–9288. St. Kathryn's Cellars is named in memory of winemaker Fred Strothman's mother, Kathryn. Before she died, Kathryn promised to keep an eye on the vineyard from heaven. Based on the good fortune that St. Kathryn's has enjoyed with its winemaking efforts, Fred feels certain that Kathryn is indeed watching. The winery produces Chardonnay, Merlot, Cameo Rose, and Ruby Red wines, as well as a grouping of fruit wines described as being "reminiscent of those grandma used to make." St. Kathryn's strawberry-rhubarb, blueberry, apple, and pear wines have won numerous awards and recall the pleasant aroma of fruit orchards and succulent berries. The winery has a pleasant patio and picnic area, and the tasting room is open daily from 10:00 A.M. to 5:00 P.M.

Steamboat Springs Cellars, 2464 Downhill Drive 8, Steamboat Springs; (970) 879–7501. This small winery produces handcrafted wines including Strawberry Park, Fish Creek Falls, Chardonnay, Rabbit Ears Red, and an award-winning Merlot. Although the winery doesn't have a tasting room, they pour tastings during the summer from a tent in downtown Steamboat Springs on Lincoln Avenue.

Two Rivers Winery, 2087 Broadway, Grand Junction; (970) 255–1471; www.tworiverswinery.com. This small, family-owned boutique winery produces Chardonnay, Cabernet Sauvignon, Merlot, and Riesling. Owners Bob and Billie Witham are actively involved with the vineyards, wine-making, and day-to-day operations. The winery, a handsome stone building that feels like a French country château, is positioned in the center of the vineyards and is surrounded by stunning views. The tasting room is open Monday through Saturday from 10:30 A.M. to 6:00 P.M. and Sunday from noon to 5:00 P.M.

Whitewater Hill Vineyards, 220 32 Road, Grand Junction; (970) 434–6868; www.whitewaterhill.com. Whitewater Hill grows grapes for a number of other Colorado wineries, in addition to producing its own Cabernet Sauvignon, Chardonnay, Merlot, Syrah, Shiraz, White Merlot, and other varietals. The tasting room is open during the warmer months of May through September daily from 10:00 A.M. to 6:00 P.M., and during the winter months on weekends.

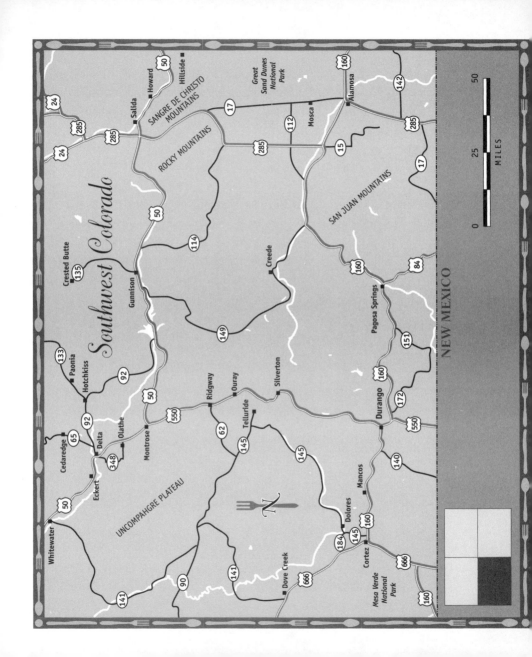

Southwest Colorado

Colorado's southwestern region is often thought of as "the real West," an area rich in history with residents known for being down to earth and friendly. Good people have inhabited the area for a long time; evidence of ancient civilizations is prevalent in many areas. The Anasazi Indian cliff dwellings at Mesa Verde National Park, for example, are reminders of a culture that grew abundant bean crops in the area. Today, Dove Creek is known as the "Pinto Bean Capital of the World."

The ski towns of Crested Butte, Telluride, and Durango are busy winter destinations, but they are equally popular with summertime visitors. The area is geographically diverse, with mountains to the west, plains to the east, and Grand Mesa, the world's largest flattop mountain, in the northern part of the region. Half a dozen wineries and numerous fruit orchards are here, taking advantage of the "banana belt" climate. For those who enjoy the thrill of the hunt, this chapter will tell you about finding wild mushrooms in the woods near Telluride and Creede, and about gathering wild pine nuts from piñon trees in the southwestern corner of the state. The "Four Corners," the intersection of New Mexico, Arizona, and Utah with Colorado, brings regional influence to the local cuisine; outstanding Mexican and Southwestern specialties are served in many area restaurants.

Made Here

Adobe Milling Co., P.O. Box 596, Dove Creek 81324; (800) 542–3623; www.anasazibeans.com. Back in A.D. 130, the Anasazi Indians lived in the "Four Corners area," now the intersection of Colorado, Utah, Arizona, and New Mexico. While the Anasazi are remembered for their architecturally advanced cliff dwellings, they also have another important claim to fame: Their spotted Anasazi beans produce 75 percent fewer gas-causing carbohydrates than pinto beans. Today, Adobe Milling grows beans at a 7,000-foot elevation, on the same land the Anasazi inhabited. The company sells a variety of other beans, including gourmet pinto beans and black turtle beans. Adobe's Cliff Dweller Bean Soup Mix, a colorful mixture of fourteen beans and spices, makes an easy, hearty meal. The firm also produces unpopped yellow and blue popcorn; products are available in retail shops or by mail or online.

Al's Alaskan Seafood, Howard; (719) 942–3382; www.alsalaska seafood.com. Howard, Colorado might not be the first place you'd think of for quality seafood, but seasoned fisherman Al Rule fishes the Alaska coast and returns with flash-frozen Copper River Wild Sockeye Salmon, Copper River Wild Chinook Salmon, and Pacific Halibut that boast a taste and texture that rivals fresh. The advanced quick-freezing technology, perfected by the Alaska seafood industry, is unique in its ability to capture the fresh caught flavor of the salmon while preserving the fish's firm texture and rich color. Al's catch is available at a number of area farmers' markets, or you can call and arrange for home delivery with a minimum ten-pound order.

Green Valley Herbal Enterprises, 1965 2150 Road, Cedaredge 81413; (970) 856–6336. www.greenvalleyherbal.com. Let's see . . . what was that new tea from Green Valley Herbal that I wanted to mention? Oh, yes—it's Remember Tea with Rosemary and Ginkgo Biloba, which is purported to help increase blood circulation to the brain. Partners Joy Beeson and Judy Aitken originally started Green Valley Herbal to avoid the financial pressures that were making them consider subdividing their farms. Eight years later, the farms are intact and the thriving company produces more than a dozen different herbal teas and several culinary herbal blends. The firm's trademark Green Valley Herbal Blend for cooking combines basil, parsley, tarragon, chives, thyme, rosemary, marjoram, and garlic. Order via mail, telephone, or online.

Hartman Gardens of Colorado, 524 North 1st Street, Montrose 81401; (970) 249–3120. Fifteen years ago, Janet Hartman began producing her homemade jams and jellies to sell at farmers' markets. Today, she has a spacious commercial kitchen right on the property where her family grows apricots, apples, and grapes. She still makes her jams and jellies the old-fashioned way, a small batch at a time from Colorado fruit and produce, with no artificial colorings or preservatives. She uses minimal sugar to maintain the natural flavors of the fruits, and in fact, one of her most popular offerings is a fresh raspberry jam that uses uncooked fruit. Several local restaurants use her jams and jellies. The company also makes flapjack and hot drink mixes, fruit syrups, and gift boxes. Call for a free brochure.

Joy's Specialty Foods, 121 Railroad Avenue, Mancos 81328; (800) 831–5697 or (970) 533–1500; www.joysinc.com. In 1981 Joy Kyzer started a small company preparing jalapeño jam from her mother's recipe. Today, the company, managed by Joy's nephew and niece-in-law, produces more than forty products. The jalapeño jam is still a best seller, but the firm has added six other spicy chile jams, including jalapeño peach jam and a mouth-searing habañero jam. Another top seller is Joy's easy dried salsa mix, to which you simply add one can of tomatoes or chopped fresh tomatoes. The company makes its own bottled salsas as well; the black bean tequila salsa is a flavorful favorite. Joy's dip mixes, meat marinades, dipping sauces, pickled jalapeño, pickled garlic, jalapeno-stuffed olives, spice mixes, and honeys are all available in the retail shop at the same address or online.

Maytag Mountain Ranch, Hillside 81232; (888) 782–9358; www.maytag mountainranch.com. The cattle that graze on the grasslands at Maytag Mountain Ranch are happy cows. They are never fed animal by-products, growth-stimulating hormones, or antibiotics. Instead they grow up pretty much the way nature intended, and the proof is in the delicious flavor of the beef. If you've ever wanted to buy "a side of beef," or perhaps, just a quarter of a side, Maytag will be happy to accommodate you. The ranch usually has availability from July to December, although it pays to plan in advance and order a few months ahead of time before everything sells out. To help you plan for the beef bonanza, the ranch says that the variety of cuts that come in a quarter side of beef usually weigh about 140 pounds, and will use about 3 to 4 cubic feet of freezer space. Along with being natural and tasty, the beef is priced significantly lower than the same cuts purchased at the grocery store. Call the number above to order.

Olathe Sweet Corn, 11 David Road, Olathe 81425; (970) 323-6874. Olathe's tender sweet corn is a well-loved Colorado treat, and the easiest way to buy it during season is at Kroger, King Soopers, and City Market stores. From mid-July through the first of September, you can also purchase it by the case (forty-eight ears) at this location.

Rocky Mountain Chocolate Factory, 265 Turner Drive, Durango 81303; (800) 367-8107 or (970) 259-0554; www.rmcf.com. When the first Rocky Mountain Chocolate Factory shop opened in Durango in 1981, it didn't take long for a crowd to gather around as store employees poured fudge and dipped chocolates right on the granite tables in the front window. Today there are more than 200 franchises around the world. People still line up to watch as apples are dipped in creamy caramel, strawberries are covered in white and dark chocolate, and fudge is spread back and forth on the candy tables. The stores also carry a huge assortment of homemade chocolates,

If you don't mind a little adventure when you shop, you'll love the challenge of finding Mountain Valley Fish & Oyster in Montrose. For starters, there's no sign on the door, just a simple wooden fish. It's in the west side of town, "across the tracks," in the warehouse area. And you can get in only on Tuesday, Wednesday, and Friday. If you need fish on Thursday, *fuggedaboutit!*

Mountain Valley Fish & Oyster

25 North Willerup Avenue
Montrose
(970) 249–8335

Mountain Valley Fish and Oyster has always been a wholesale operation, supplying fresh fish from all over the world to more than 150 restaurants on the Western Slope. Through word of mouth, locals found the place and began stopping in and begging for fresh fish; the company finally added a small retail shop to meet the demand. The offerings available each day are written on a chalkboard, and some gourmet food items such as olive oils, vinegars, and imported rice are also sold.

truffles, and caramels as well as boxed chocolate assortments, chocolate sauces, and gift baskets. Tours of the main candy factory are offered at 9:00 A.M. and 10:30 A.M., Monday through Thursday, from Memorial Day through Labor Day weekend. The tour takes about forty-five minutes and includes free tastings; sign up and get free tickets at the original **Rocky Mountain Chocolate Factory** retail store at 561 Main Avenue, Durango (970–259–1408). Chocolates can also be ordered online or by mail order.

White Mountain Farm, 8890 Lane 4 North, Mosca 81146; (719) 378–2436 or (800) 364–3019; www.whitemountainfarm.com. White Mountain Farm grows Colorado's largest crop of certified organic quinoa. A small seed about the size of millet, quinoa has been grown in the Andes of South America for centuries. It is very high in protein, expands to about three times its size when cooked, and can be substituted for nearly any grain in almost any recipe. White Mountain Farm's quinoa has a rich, delicate, nutty taste, and the farm provides free recipes with all quinoa orders. White Mountain also sells organic potatoes and other produce; call the number above to order.

Specialty Stores & Markets

Cookworks, 321 Elk Avenue, Crested Butte; (800) 765–9511 or (970) 349–7398; www.cookworks.com. Dozens of gourmet foods—jalapeño jellies, salsas, jams, mustards, olives, vinegar, salad dressings—are available at this charming shop. It sells a large assortment of cookware and baking pans, cookbooks, gadgets, and glassware as well.

The Corner Cupboard, 101 North Main Street, Gunnison; (970) 641–0313. A large assortment of Colorado-produced gourmet food prod-

Basic Quinoa

Paul New at White Mountain Farm shares the secret to cooking delicious quinoa, and it's wonderfully simple. Just rinse the dickens out of the grain before you cook it to remove the saponin, the natural bitter coating that occurs on the outside of quinoa.

1 cup black or white quinoa　　　　¼ **teaspoon salt**
1½ cups water

1. Put the quinoa into a fine strainer, and run water through it until the water is clear and no longer sudsy. If you don't have a fine strainer, rinse the quinoa in a bowl filled with water, and then pour it through a clean dishtowel.
2. In a 2-quart pot, bring the water to a boil. Stir in the wet quinoa and simmer over low medium heat uncovered until done, about 12 minutes for white, or 15 minutes for black. Quinoa is fully cooked when the germ has separated from the grain. It looks like a small white "C" shape surrounding each grain. If any excess liquid remains, pour it off and raise the heat to quickly boil off the rest. Stir in the salt.

Variations: Substitute canned or homemade stock, or fruit juice for the water; or flavor with Marmite, Vegemite, or bouillon. Adjust the salt accordingly.

Makes 4 servings.

ucts is offered at this busy store on Gunnison's main street. The shop also sells cookbooks, gadgets, tableware, cookware, gifts, and home accents.

Quinoa Griddle Cakes

Quinoa is the grain that gives these flapjacks their nutty flavor. Serve them hot off the griddle with butter and maple syrup or honey. The recipe is provided by White Mountain Farm.

2 eggs

2½ cups buttermilk or sour milk

4 tablespoons vegetable
   shortening, melted

2½ cups flour

2 teaspoons sugar

2 teaspoons baking powder

1 teaspoon baking soda

1 teaspoon salt

1 cup cooked quinoa

1. In a medium bowl, beat the eggs. Add the remaining ingredients and stir until combined.

2. Lightly grease a griddle or non-stick pan and heat over a medium-high flame. Cook pancakes until brown on bottom and bubbles form on top, about 3 minutes. Turn pancakes over and cook until bottoms are brown and pancakes are barely firm to touch. Transfer to plates.

White Mountain Farm

8890 Lane 4 North
Mosca 81146
(719) 378–2436
or (800) 364–3019
www.whitemountainfarm.com

Makes 30 4-inch pancakes.

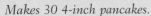

Hardin's Natural Foods, 3144 Highway 92, Hotchkiss; (970) 872–3019. A busy health food store in the small town of Hotchkiss, Hardin's offers a large assortment of organic produce and natural foods.

It's also where the locals shop for bulk grains, nutritional supplements, natural body-care products, housewares, candles, local organic buffalo and elk, Colorado products, books, kitchen gadgets, coffee and tea presses, chocolates, and more.

High Wire Ranch, 2749 M 50 Road, Hotchkiss; (970) 835–7600; www.highwireranch.com. Driving out to Dave and Sue Whittlesey's ranch, you might want to slow down in case you do a serious double-take when you see their herds. They raise more than 200 head of bison and elk at their High Wire Ranch. The animals are content to graze on the ranch's 320 acres of pastureland, and the Whittleseys don't use any added hormones or sub-therapeutic antibiotics. The company offers a wide selection of superior-quality USDA-inspected bison and elk meats, including bratwurst, summer sausage, jerky, steaks, and roasts. The meats can be purchased at the ranch or on the company's Web site and shipped anywhere within the United States.

Homestead Market, 101 Grand Avenue, P.O. Box 743, Paonia 81428; (970) 527–5655. Four years ago a group of cattle ranchers got together and decided to start their own cooperative market to sell their meat on a retail basis. Today Homestead Market is going strong, selling all-natural beef from cattle that have never received growth hormones or antibiotics. The shop also sells all-natural lamb, buffalo, elk, pork, and chicken, plus locally-made wines, jams, jellies, and salsas. A greenhouse in town supplies organic salad greens and herbs, and nearby farms provide fresh eggs and handcrafted cheeses. The market is open year 'round, closed on Sunday.

Honeyville, 33633 U.S. Highway 550, Durango; (800) 676–7690 or (970) 247–1474; www.honeyvillecolorado.com. If you're within 100 miles of Durango, you've got to drive to Honeyville to witness a fascinating sight. A working beehive is enclosed in glass, right in the store, with clear tubes leading to the outside that allow the bees to go out and return laden with pollen. The country store sells just about everything related to honey—specialty honeys, honeycomb, honey jellies, whipped honeys, honey sticks, and even honey wine. (Honeyville is the tasting room for Rocky Mountain Meadery's honey wines.) The shop also sells jams, jellies, bread mixes, pancake mixes, and dozens of other food products, and it provides free samples so you can try the products. Order online or call for a free brochure.

Farmers' Markets

For the most up-to-date farmers' market locations and times, call your county extension office or visit www.ag.state.co.us.

Alamosa Farmers' Market, on San Juan just south of Main Street, Alamosa; (719) 589–3681, extension 103. Saturdays from 7:00 A.M. to 2:00 P.M., starting in early July.

Cortez Farmers' Market, 109 West Main Street (Montezuma County Courthouse parking lot), Cortez; Saturdays from 7:30 A.M. to noon, late May through early October.

Cortez Farmers' Market II, 109 West Main Street (Montezuma County Courthouse parking lot), Cortez. Saturdays from 7:30 A.M. to noon, late June through early October.

Delta Farmers' Market, 301 Main Street, Delta; (970) 874–3616, extension 12. Wednesdays from 4:00 to 8:00 P.M., July through September.

Dolores Farmers' Market, Flanders Park, Dolores. Wednesdays from 4:00 to 6:00 P.M., June through October.

Dove Creek Farmers' Market, 101 West Highway 491, Dove Creek. Saturdays from 8:00 to 11:00 A.M., July through mid-October.

Durango Farmers' Market, 1st National Bank parking lot, 259 West 9th Street, Durango; (970) 385–9143. Saturdays from 8:00 A.M. to noon, mid-June through October.

North Fork Farmers' Market, Third and Grand, Paonia; (970) 835–7600; www.vogaco.org. Mondays from 4:00 to 6:30 P.M., late May through October.

Ridgway Farmers' Market, Ouray County Fairgrounds, intersection of Highways 550 and 62, Ridgway; (970) 626–9775. Sunday from 8:00 A.M. to noon, June through mid-September.

Telluride Farmers' Market, Downtown Telluride; (970) 728–8701. Fridays from noon to 4:00 P.M., June through October.

Uncompahgre Farmers' Market, Centennial Plaza on South 1st Street and Uncompahgre Street, Montrose. Saturdays from 8:30 A.M. until 1:00 P.M., early May through late October. Also Wednesday morning from 8:30 A.M. to 1:00 P.M., from mid-July through late September.

Farm Stands

Antelope Hill Orchards, 2238 L 70 Drive, Eckert; (970) 835–3111. You'll find fruit right off the trees at this roadside market 9 miles northeast of Delta in the small town of Eckert. In season, you can purchase apples, cherries, nectarines, peaches, pears, and plums. Open daily from June 1 to November 30.

Austin Farms, 1475 3925 Road, Paonia; (970) 527–3843. Starting in early July, this roadside market sells fresh fruit and produce—cherries, nectarines, peaches, plums, raspberries, apricots, blackberries, apples, squash, cider, eggs, honey—as it becomes available. Open Monday through Saturday in season; call for an appointment on Sunday.

Burrits Produce, 1235 2490 Lane, Hotchkiss; (970) 835–3252. Pick your own apricots, beets, bell peppers, cantaloupe, carrots, cherries, chiles, and other produce at this certified organic farm.

Dog Patch Farm, P.O. Box 1435, Paonia 81428; (970) 527–3502. Farmer Del Robinson and his family are happy to give you a tour of the

The San Luis Valley—
Potato Paradise

Colorado is the second-largest fresh potato producer in the United States, with sixty varieties grown on approximately 67,000 acres in the San Luis Valley. Some of the primary potato varieties grown here include:

Russets Russets make up most of the crop and are characterized by their even oval shape, russet brown color, net-textured skin, and few shallow eyes.

Russet Norkotahs Russet Nuggets are good for baking, mashing, and frying because of their low sugars and high solids. Their flesh can vary from a creamy white to a light golden color.

Reds Sangres are round red potatoes with a white flesh. These potatoes are best in soups and stews because slices and chucks maintain their shape during cooking and holding. They are also excellent baking and potato salad potatoes.

Yellow Flesh Yukon Gold, an American favorite, is a golden flesh potato with a creamy texture ideal for baking, boiling, and frying.

Other Varieties The San Luis Valley grows many other potato varieties including specialty varieties like all blue and fingerlings.

Provided by the Colorado Potato Administrative Committee

farm and sell you some of their fresh-picked potatoes, garlic, shallots, tomatoes, and onions. Call for directions.

First Fruits Organic Farms, Inc., P.O. Box 864, Paonia 81428; (970) 527–6122. Kris and Kevin Kropp sell many varieties of fresh certified organic fruit, plus dried fruit, apple butter, apple sauce, and a variety of jams. Call for directions.

Mattics Orchards and Veggies, 8163 High Mesa Road, Olathe; (970) 323–5281. This roadside market sells more than fifty different varieties of vegetables grown on the Mattics' farm: chiles, tomatoes, squash, eggplant, and dozens of other choices. Fresh fruit is sold right off the trees, including apples, peaches, and pears. This is the perfect place to pick a juicy vine-ripened watermelon as well. Honey, including popular flavored honeys, is available from the farm's beehives. Open daily, from early August through late October, 9:00 A.M. to 6:00 P.M.

Orchard Valley Farms, 1612-4175 Drive, Paonia; (970) 527–6838; www.blackbridgewinery.com. On the north fork of Gunnison River, scenic Orchard Valley Farms' market sells assorted vegetables, cherries, peaches, apples, pears, raspberries, blackberries, and red table grapes. Specialty food items are also offered, including local honeys, vinegars, jams and jellies, syrups, butters, mustards, and chutneys. In the popular wine-tasting area, you can sip and purchase locally-produced wines including the farm's own Blackbridge Winery offerings. Some of the farm's products are also available online. Open daily from Memorial Day to Halloween, 9:00 A.M. to 6:00 P.M.

The Polished Apple in the Apple Shed, 250 South Grand Mesa Drive, Cedaredge; (970) 856–7006 or (888) 856–7008; www.appleshed.net. Apples, apples, and more apples are sold at this roadside market; in season, you'll find premium varieties including Gala, Fuji, Cameo, Honeycrisp, and Granny Smith, as well as many standard apple varieties. Bing and Rainier cherries and peaches are available in season. The shop also sells honey, jams, cider, Colorado food products, and gifts. The deli offers sandwiches and salads, as well as a very popular homemade apple pie. Art exhibits hang in the gallery, and the shop is open year-round.

Red Mountain Ranches Orchards & Market, 1948 Highway 65, Cedaredge; (970) 856–3803; www.redmountainranches.com. This charming roadside market sells a huge variety of food products, many grown at Red Mountain Ranches' orchard. From the end of June through Christmas, you'll find fresh produce in season—cherries, peaches, more than a dozen varieties of apples, plums, and more. The orchard grows some of the grapes for Stoney Mesa Winery, so it's only fitting that the wines are sold in the store, too. A huge assortment of jellies, jams, honeys, pinto beans, popcorn, prunes, cider, honey, syrup, applesauce, apple butter, dried fruits, cooking wines, oils, vinegars, salsa, barbecue sauce, hot sauce, chocolate fruit, handcrafted gifts, homemade soaps, creams, potpourri, and teas line the shelves of the shop. Red Mountain Ranch's famous apple gift packs can be shipped anywhere in the United States and are available mid-October through Christmas; other food gift boxes are available year-round. On the Sunday of Labor

Summer Salsa Fresca

Whether your ingredients come from the farmers' market or your own garden, summertime is the perfect time to prepare fresh salsa. Serve this colorful condiment with a bowl of crispy corn chips and a pitcher of margaritas.

4 to 5 ripe tomatoes, seeds removed, chopped

1 jalapeño chile, seeds removed, finely diced

1 small onion, chopped

1 avocado, peeled, pitted, diced

4 large green chiles, seeds removed, diced

1 large clove garlic, minced

1 teaspoon extra-virgin olive oil

Several sprigs of fresh cilantro, minced

Squeeze of fresh lime

Salt and pepper to taste

Mix all ingredients in a bowl. Serve at once with corn chips, or cover with plastic wrap and refrigerate for up to 2 hours. (Skip the avocado if you want to store the salsa for more than 2 hours; without it, it will keep for 2 days.)

Makes about 1½ cups.

Day weekend, the ranch celebrates its anniversary, holding wine tastings, wagon rides, and a fruit-pie contest. Open daily from 9:00 A.M. to 6:00 P.M. from late June to the end of December. Other times, call first.

Rogers Mesa Fruit Co., Highway 92 and 3100 Road, Hotchkiss; (970) 872–2155. This tented roadside stand opens in early July and

San Luis Potato and Smoked Salmon Salad

You may never again be satisfied with plain potato salad after you taste this version, which pairs creamy Colorado Sangre red potatoes with flavorful smoked salmon in a creamy dressing enlivened with fresh dill and capers. This fabulous recipe is provided by the Colorado Potato Administrative Committee.

6-8 Colorado Sangre red potatoes, peeled if desired and cut to ½-inch cubes
½ cup sour cream
¼ cup minced purple onion
2 tablespoons chopped fresh dill

2 ounces smoked salmon, cut in thin slices
3 tablespoons fresh lemon juice
3 tablespoons capers, drained
½ teaspoon freshly ground black pepper
½ teaspoon grated fresh lemon rind

1. Cook potatoes in boiling water until tender; drain and cool.
2. Combine sour cream and remaining ingredients in a large bowl, stirring until blended. Add drained potatoes and gently toss to coat. Cover and chill.

Makes 6 to 8 servings.

generally stays open through late September, selling fresh produce as it becomes available. Cherries are usually the first crop, followed by nectarines, peaches, vegetables, pears, plums, and apples.

February: **Chocolate Lovers Extravaganza,** A.A.D.A., 120 East 1st Street, P.O. Box 173, Salida 81201; (719) 539–7347. Usually held on Valentine's Day, this decadent event includes all the chocolate desserts, pastries, cookies, and candies you can eat. The evening also features a wine and cheese tasting, live music, and a silent auction. The proceeds benefit victims of domestic abuse and assault.

April: **Durango Wine Festival,** Durango Community Shelter, P.O. Box 2107, Durango 81302; (970) 259–7462. This annual festival provides an opportunity to taste and learn about dozens of wines, which are served with specially prepared appetizers and food samples from local restaurants. Optional winemaker dinners at two local restaurants feature multi-course meals paired with appropriate wines. The event benefits the Durango Community Shelter.

Memorial Day Weekend: **Taste of Creede,** downtown area, Creede; (800) 327–2102 or (719) 658–2374; www.creede.com. The small town of Creede celebrates culinary arts and fine arts at this annual festival. Local restaurants prepare dozens of food offerings that are available for sampling and tasting, and local artists exhibit their work and demonstrate various art techniques.

June: **Telluride Wine Festival,** Telluride; (970) 728–3178; www.telluridewinefestival.com. A popular event for more than twenty years,

Telluride's four-day wine and food weekend offers folks the chance to meet winemakers, celebrity chefs, experts, and authors. The breathtaking scenery of the San Juan Mountains is a stunning backdrop for the event, which includes cooking classes, wine seminars, optional dinners, wine tastings, and winemakers' luncheons. The festival begins with an exclusive patrons' dinner on Thursday evening, held in one of Telluride's luxurious private homes. Seminars and tastings follow on Friday, concluding in a Grand Tasting in the town park in the late afternoon. The next evening, a progressive wine tasting is held downtown, as guests stroll the streets sampling more than 300 wines at various locations. The event culminates with a gourmet brunch in the town park on Sunday. All net proceeds from the wine festival are donated to charitable or educational purposes in Telluride.

July 4: **International Rhubarb Festival,** Memorial Park, Silverton; (970) 387-5770. Silverton's Independence Day celebration includes an interesting tradition that I, for one, hope catches on in the rest of the United States. After the parade ends, the Friends of the Library proudly sponsor the Annual International Rhubarb Festival at the town's Memorial Park. All sorts of delectable homemade rhubarb treats are offered, topped off with ice cream, if you like. All the proceeds benefit the Silverton Public Library.

July: **Colorado Brewers Rendezvous,** Riverside Park, Salida; (877) 772-5432. Held outdoors at the main park in Salida's historic downtown, the Colorado Brewers Rendezvous gets more popular every year. Dozens of microbreweries from the Colorado Brewers Guild gather to pour beer under the large shade trees of the park. Your admission purchase gets you a souvenir glass and a handful of tickets good for a generous pour from the various vendors.

Early August: **Olathe Sweet Corn Festival,** Olathe; (877) 858–6006 or (970) 323–6006; www.olathesweetcornfest.com. Enjoy all the "Olathe Sweet" corn on the cob you can eat at this all-day event celebrating Olathe's corn harvest. A family day full of music, food, and fun, the event features free contests and games; more than 150 food, arts and crafts, carnival, and novelty booths; and live music. The day ends with a spectacular fireworks show.

August: **Telluride Culinary Art Festival,** Telluride; www.telluride culinaryart.com. This three-day weekend-long festival highlights the culinary expertise of acclaimed local, national, and international chefs with live cooking demonstrations and food seminars. A grand tasting showcases samplings of dishes from Telluride and the Mountain Village's favorite restaurants, live music, and over 200 different wines and spirits. A progressive dinner takes participants on the gondola and through historic Telluride to sample dishes from four of the town's best restaurants. Sunday morning features a "Bloodies and Bluegrass Brunch" with a hearty brunch, live music, and Ketel One Bloody Marys.

August: **Taste of Pagosa,** Archuletta County Fairgrounds, Pagosa Springs; (970) 731–1146. This popular event is always held on a Thursday evening to kick off the opening of the Archuletta County Fair.

Olathe Corn and Shrimp Salad

This salad makes a nice summer lunch or a light dinner, and its simple preparation highlights the star ingredient—our sweet Olathe corn. Because there are just a few components, use the best of everything you can get your hands on. This is the salad to make the minute you come home from the farmers' market with fresh corn. Ask the fishmonger to sell you shrimp that is still frozen, since we rarely get fresh shrimp here and you can't always know how long those thawed shrimp have been sitting in the case.

2 tablespoons butter

6 ears Olathe sweet corn, shucked just prior to cooking

¼ cup cider vinegar

½ cup water

2 tablespoons shrimp boil mixed seasoning such as Old Bay

1 teaspoon salt

3 dozen medium frozen shrimp (about 3/4 pound), thawed in cool water

⅓ cup Balsamic vinegar

⅔ cup extra virgin olive oil

1 small clove garlic, minced

1 tablespoon Dijon mustard

1 teaspoon salt

⅛ teaspoon freshly ground black pepper

1 tablespoon minced parsley

2 tablespoons finely chopped fresh chives

Local restaurants prepare their best foods, which are appraised by a panel of judges before the "doors" of the large circus tent are opened to the public. Awards are given for best appetizer, entree, and dessert, and thousands of people enjoy sampling the food offerings and the live entertainment. Buy tickets at the door.

1. Melt the butter in a medium saucepan and remove from the heat. Cut the corn kernels off the cob into the saucepan, and use the dull side of the knife to scrape the juices from the cob into the pan. Return to the heat and simmer just until the corn loses its raw taste—about 2 to 3 minutes. Set aside and allow to cool, then transfer the corn mixture to a container and refrigerate until serving time.
2. In a saucepan, combine the cider vinegar, water, shrimp boil mix, and salt. Bring the mixture to a boil over medium-high heat. Add the shrimp and stir gently. Cover and cook until shrimp are pink and opaque, 4 to 5 minutes. Drain the shrimp into a colander. When they are cool enough to handle, remove the shells and devein the shrimp, if necessary.
3. Whisk together the vinegar, olive oil, garlic, mustard, salt, and pepper. Gently stir in the parsley and chives. Pour the dressing over the shrimp and refrigerate for two hours, stirring occasionally to distribute the dressing.
4. Just before serving, add the corn to the shrimp mixture and adjust the seasonings, if necessary.

Makes 6 servings.

August: Mushroom Foray, Creede Community Center, Willow Creek Canyon Road, Creede; (719) 658–2374. Learn all about finding and identifying wild mushrooms at this popular workshop. Larry Renshaw, president of the Colorado Mycological Society, gives a basic talk about mushrooming and then takes the group out in the field. In what feels

Best Chocolate Croissant

Don't even think about the calories. A chocolate croissant is the ultimate in self-indulgence, and that's the point. At Baked In Telluride, or BIT, as the locals call it, the chocolate croissants are flaky, buttery pastry wrapped around a center of half-melted chocolate, just begging to be dipped in a hot latte. The popular bakery, located in a century-old warehouse, is also a great spot for bagels, deli sandwiches, and pizza.

Baked In Telluride
127 South Fir
P.O. Box 575, Telluride
81435
(970) 728-4775
$

a bit like an Easter egg hunt for adults, the group searches for mushrooms and brings them back to the community center. Larry then identifies the fungi and sorts out the edible ones. The choicest mushrooms are then cooked into a gourmet meal to be savored by the group.

Late August: **Mushroom Festival,** Telluride; sponsored by Fungophile, Inc., P.O. Box 480503, Denver 80248; (303) 296–9359; www.telluride .com/mushroom.html. The mushrooms in Colorado are among the best for eating; we have many of the top gourmet mushrooms growing in our forests. The Telluride Mushroom Conference is held each year to help people expand their knowledge of edible and poisonous wild mushrooms. I should mention up front that there is some emphasis on the psychoactive varieties of mushrooms as well. Classes and discussions cover a wide variety of topics, including the cultivation of diverse mushroom species, with an emphasis on practical principles and techniques. Daily forays are held in the surrounding mountains to collect edible and poisonous species and study their field characteristics. A "Cook and Taste" mushroom feast allows participants to eat the edible mushrooms that are collected.

Saturday before Labor Day: **A Taste of Italy,** St. Joseph Great Hall, 320 East 5th, Salida; (719) 539–4300. Every year, the members of the local Sons of Italy in America chapter cook an enormous dinner of regional Italian foods for almost 500 attendees. The dinner features specialties like pasta, stuffed shells, sausage and peppers, chicken cacciatore, lasagna, meatballs, and freshly baked bread. Go early, because the food usually runs out. All the proceeds are used to provide college scholarships for local students.

Labor Day Weekend: **Salsa Fiesta,** downtown area, Creede; (800) 327–2102 or (719) 658–2374; www.creede.com. Businesses and individuals compete in this "hotly contested" event, preparing salsas to enter in four categories: red, green, fruit-based, and miscellaneous flavors. Attendees taste the salsas and vote for their favorites in each category. Previous prizewinners have included a tangy lemon salsa and a smoky peach salsa.

Mid-September: **Harvest Beer Fest,** sponsored by the Montezuma Land Conservancy, P.O. Box 1522, Cortez 81321; (970) 565–1664.

Enjoy a multitude of microbrewed beers and support a good cause at the same time. This lively annual event, benefiting the Montezuma Land Conservancy, is held at the Cortez Cultural Center at 25 North Market Street. After purchasing tickets at the door, you can meet the brewmeisters and exchange your tickets for beer samples. Plenty of food is available, too.

Mid-September: **Telluride Blues & Brews Festival,** Telluride Town Park, Telluride; (866) 515–6166; www.tellurideblues.com. The laid-back town of Telluride, with its charming downtown, out-of-the-way location, and breathtaking scenery, is a fine place for a food and drink festival. Combining the event with a world-class blues festival was a stroke of genius. This three-day celebration features more than a dozen blues acts, regional and ethnic foods, and offerings from dozens of microbreweries. Free gondola rides are given between Telluride and Mountain Village, and a special kids' area provides activities for children. Who knows, you might even spot locals Tom Cruise or Norman Schwarzkopf in the crowd.

September: **Cinders, Song & Sauvignon,** Durango; (970) 247–7657; www.durangoconcerts.com. This weekend event, held when the autumn colors in the area are at their best, begins with a concert on Friday evening. On Saturday, guests board the Durango and Silverton Narrow Gauge Railroad for a spectacular, scenic trip through the mountains. Lunch is served at the turnaround and guests can taste wines and enjoy foods from local restaurants and caterers as the train makes its way back down the mountain. The event winds down with a Sunday brunch. This is a major fund-raiser for the Fort Lewis College Concert Hall.

September: **Taste of Salida,** hosted by the Salida Chamber of Commerce, 406 West Highway 50, Salida; (877) 772-5432; www.salida chamber.org. In a large tent in scenic Riverside Park along the banks of the Arkansas River, Salida restaurants prepare their finest cuisine for attendees to sample. Salida's own Mountain Spirit Winery provides wines and several other wineries and breweries are represented as well. Live entertainment adds to the festivities.

Early October: **Applefest,** Cedaredge Area Chamber of Commerce, 245 West Main, P.O. Box 278, Cedaredge 80413; (970) 856-6961; www.cedaredge colorado.com. This two-day event celebrates the apple harvest in the scenic town of Cedaredge. Apple Lane is the place to purchase scores of apples of all varieties. Enjoy music and live entertainment and sample foods from local vendors.

November: **Annual Chateau Shavano Wine Tasting,** Salida Chamber of Commerce, 406 West Highway 50, Salida; (877) 772-5432; www.salidachamber.org. The folks from Chateau Shavano winery bring a generous assortment of their wines for this evening of tasting and toasting. Held in the lobby of the Collegiate Peaks Bank, the party includes ample hors d'oeuvres, desserts, and a silent auction. Tickets are available for purchase at the Salida Chamber of Commerce, beneficiaries of the popular event.

Friday and Saturday after Thanksgiving: **Chocolate Tasting Festival,** downtown, Creede; (800) 327-2102 or (719) 658-2374; www.creede.com. The merchants of Creede go all out for this decadent event, preparing chocolate treats and desserts to entice the attendees and judges to vote for their offering as the best. In previous years, some of the entries included a (surprisingly good!) pinto-bean fudge, peanut butter chocolate mousse, and coffee liqueur brownies. Prizes are awarded for the top choices, but the real winners are those who get to taste all the chocolate.

Learn to Cook

Now You're Cookin', P.O. Box 1970, 505 Slate River Drive, Crested Butte 81224; (970) 349–2112. Kristina Patten has been involved with food on some level—caterer, cook, restaurateur—for most of her career, so it was a natural progression for her to open her own cooking school in Crested Butte. The intimate classes she teaches in her spacious kitchen feature hands-on training for a maximum of eight students. This allows her to give each student personal attention as she teaches the ins and outs of preparing ethnic and regional specialties. When she's not teaching, Kristina moonlights as a personal chef for busy residents of Crested Butte.

Landmark Eateries

Allred's, Telluride Ski & Golf Club, 565 Mountain Village Boulevard, Telluride 81435; (970) 728–7474; www.tellurideskiandgolfclub.com;

$$$. At Allred's, it's tough to decide which is more spectacular—the view or the food. Located at the top of the gondola at over 10,500 feet, Allred's overlooks the valley and the town of Telluride. But Chef de Cuisine Ross Martin offers a menu that could make you plumb forget about what's out the window, combining French, Asian, and American influences in his fresh, seasonal cuisine. His "small plate" menu has a number of playful offerings like lamb chop lollipops, miniature seafood tacos, and a trio of petite bar burgers made of Kobe beef, foie gras, and truffles. The dinner menu offers a number of traditional steak, trout, and duck entrees, but Chef Martin also lets his culinary innovation shine with preparations like tamari-basted elk tenderloin served with roasted butternut squash-apple puree, maple glazed carrots, and a reduction of hard cider. For dessert try the Meyer Lemon crème brûlée served with a crisp sesame *tuille*. The wine cellar boasts an impressive reserve of 8,000 bottles. The restaurant is only open during the summer and winter ski season; call first to check the schedule and make reservations.

Harmon's, 300 South Townsend Avenue, Telluride 81435; (970) 728-3773; www.harmonsrestaurant.com; $$$. Located in the historic old train depot, this locals' favorite owned by Harmon Brown features a fresh, wide-ranging menu that changes often. Some favorites include the smoked trout potato pancakes with watercress and caviar, Chilean sea bass with fennel citrus salad and orange *beurre blanc* sauce, and the soy ginger-glazed rack of lamb with Japanese eggplant. Desserts vary, but the warm German crepes are delightful topped with vanilla ice cream. The mahogany bar and cozy fireplace make this a comfortable

Seasons' Green Chile Cheddar Smashed Sweet Potatoes

A heavenly combination of sweet potatoes, chiles and cheese, this is one of the most-requested side dishes at Seasons Rotisserie & Grill. Owner Karen Barger generously shared the recipe.

2 large or 3 medium red Garnett sweet potatoes
1 tablespoon olive oil
3 tablespoons butter (or to taste)
Salt and freshly ground black pepper to taste

1 cup peeled, chopped roasted New Mexico green chiles
1 cup grated aged white cheddar cheese

1. Preheat over to 350° F. Wash and dry the sweet potatoes and pierce each one several times with a fork. Rub the skins with olive oil and sprinkle with salt.

place to have an after-dinner drink and listen to a local pianist in the evening. Harmon's is also a popular gathering place for small parties and wedding rehearsal dinners.

Ken & Sue's, 636 Main Avenue, Durango 81301; (970) 385–1810. $$$. A massive, century-old bar graces the interior of Ken & Sue's, transported all the way from Chicago. People have come from a lot further away than Chicago to dine at Ken and Sue Fusco's eponymous, always-popular restaurant in downtown Durango, where the food is

2. Put the potatoes on a baking sheet in the center rack of the oven. Bake until the potatoes are cooked through and the skin is crispy, for about an hour. Remove from the oven and cool on a wire rack.

3. When the potatoes are cool enough to handle, scoop the sweet potato from its skin into a large mixing bowl. Using a large heavy spoon, coarsely smash the sweet potatoes. As you are smashing then, add the butter and season with salt and pepper. (Potatoes can be prepared to this stage and refrigerated for up to 2 days.)

4. Spread the potato mixture in a 1-inch layer in a greased casserole or baking dish. Arrange the chiles on top and sprinkle with the white cheddar cheese. Bake in a 350° F oven for 20 minutes (longer if potatoes have been refrigerated) or until the cheese is melted and bubbly. Serve at once.

Makes 6 servings.

Seasons Rotisserie & Grill

764 Main Avenue
Durango 81301
(970) 382-9790
www.seasonsonthenet.com
$$$

consistently outstanding. Some menu favorites include the field green salad with apples, gorgonzola cheese, and walnuts; a cilantro-crusted halibut; and tender lobster ravioli. The chocolate molten cake is one of the most-ordered desserts, but if you forget to order it ahead of time you can't go wrong with the strawberry crème brûlée. Ken & Sue's serves lunch and dinner every day, and a popular brunch on Sunday.

Seasons Rotisserie & Grill, 764 Main Avenue, Durango 81301; (970) 382–9790; www.seasonsonthenet.com; $$$. Winemaker Roger Roessler of

SOUTHWEST COLORADO'S NATIVE NUT

Pine nuts are the seeds from the cones of the Colorado piñon pine (*Pinus edulis*). Found in the drier mountainous regions from Colorado south and west into Mexico, three trees generally bear large nut crops every third or fourth year. The nuts may be used raw or lightly roasted, and their distinctive, buttery taste and soft texture make them popular for snacking and as an addition to pestos, breads, stuffings, salads, soups, and desserts. The best time to pick pine nuts is usually in mid- to late October. No permit is required to gather the nuts of Colorado public lands if you collect under seventy-five pounds and the nuts are for personal use only.

Sonoma's Roessler Cellars owns this contemporary bistro in downtown Durango, with a seasonal menu that focuses on simple dishes prepared with fresh, top-quality ingredients. If it's in season, start with the asparagus salad accompanied by applewood-smoked bacon, chopped, hard-boiled egg, and Maytag blue cheese dressing. True to the restaurant's name, there are a number of entrees cooked on the rotisserie; the chicken is a winner, coming out of the kitchen golden brown and crispy. Other starring entrees include the sautéed Veal Scaloppine and the double-cut pork chop, seared to perfection on the wood-burning grill. Make sure you try a side of the restaurant's deservedly famous sweet potatoes with green chile (see the recipe on page 146). One of the best items on the dessert menu is a treat you don't see much these days—apple strudel. Seasons serves the flaky pastry with butterscotch sauce and crème anglaise. The award-winning wine cellar offers an excellent selection of both bottles and fine wines by the glass, and Seasons regularly hosts wine tastings and winemaker's dinners. The restaurant also has a lovely patio for warm-weather seating. Reservations are encouraged.

Soupçon Restaurant, 127-A Elk Avenue, Crested Butte 81224; (970) 349–5448; $$$. A tiny gem of a restaurant in an old miner's cabin in Crested Butte, this perennially-pleasing charmer offers innovative French cuisine with the day's menu handwritten on a chalkboard. The half-dozen entrees change every day, but you can often find homemade soups, salads, beef tenderloin, seafood, elk, and usually, a vegetarian entree. Desserts are homemade and the wine list is small, but impressive. Soupçon offers two seatings nightly, at 6:00 and 8:15 P.M.; make your reservations two or three days ahead if you can, since it's nearly always busy. The restaurant is open during the ski season and summertime, and closed during the "off" seasons, so it's a good idea to call first for the schedule.

Brewpubs & Microbreweries

Crested Butte Brewery and Pub, 214 Elk Avenue, Crested Butte; (970) 349–5026; www.crestedbuttebrewery.com. A popular watering hole in this historic ski town, the Crested Butte Brewery and Pub, with its rough-hewn timber interior and animal mounts on the walls, feels like a rustic lodge. Co-owned by actor Tom Skerritt, the establishment produces a number of prize-winning specialty beers. The brewery's Rodeo Oatmeal Stout offers a rich aroma with a medium body, coarse black malty character with a very dry finish. Another popular pour, the Red Lady Ale, is amber in color and light in body, with a mild hop flavor. The restaurant menu features burgers and sandwiches at lunchtime; seafood, steaks, quail, trout, and other Colorado specialties for dinner. The brewmeisters are happy to give a tour of the brewery on request.

Dolores River Brewpub, 100 South Fourth Street, Dolores; (970) 882–4677. A telegraph office built in 1933 is the home of the Dolores River Brewpub. The punched-tin ceilings, original wood floors, and plaster walls add to the cozy feel of the small pub, which serves its signature beers and an innovative menu. The most popular brew is the ESB or "Extra Special Bitter," a medium-bodied caramel ale with a roasty, dry finish. The Pale Ale is assertively hoppy with citrusy character. The restaurant has a wood-fired oven for making pizzas and calzones; the homemade dough has a little fresh beer in it to make it rise. The pub's Thai Pizza is very popular; it's topped with a spicy Thai peanut sauce, chicken, sweet pep-

pers, cilantro, coconut milk, and cucumber sauce. The restaurant is also famous for its "killer salads," including a Caesar salad, a spinach salad made with local eggs, and a "Selfish" salad, said to be so good you won't want to share it with anyone else. The outdoor beer garden, with its kids' play area nearby, is the place to be in the summertime.

Main Street Brewery & Restaurant,
21 East Main Street, Cortez; (970) 564–9112.
What a delight it was to discover Rudolph
Baumel in the small town of Cortez. Rudy
founded the Red Lion Inn and the Greenbriar,

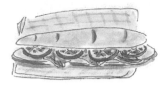

two legendary—and still immensely popular—restaurants in my hometown of Boulder. Seven years ago, he purchased an old brick building in
Cortez with original hardwood floors and a tin ceiling; it had previously
housed a pool hall and hardware store. He built a brewery on the premises, hired a German brewmeister, and now produces six German-style
lagers and ales. The establishment's Crystal Wheat is light and somewhat
fruity, an easy-drinking American-style wheat beer. The Boomer Lite
Lager is mildly hopped, light, and refreshing. Schnorzenboomer Amber
Doppelbock is dark amber in color and malty in taste. The eclectic menu
includes such German-inspired cuisine as beer pretzels, a delicious
bratwurst burrito, and a tasty brewer's plate with sausages, sauerkraut,
and mashed potatoes. Desserts include apple strudel and cheesecakes,
with a helpful menu suggestion that one accompany the sweets with a
Schnorzenboomer, "delicious and healthy."

Ska Brewing, 545 Turner Drive, Durango; (970) 247–5792; www.ska
brewing.com. In the industrial part of Durango, Ska Brewing's tasting
room caters to a select crowd of mostly locals, who come to enjoy the
company's distinctive beers and ales. The Pinstripe Red Ale is an
American-style amber ale with a slight fruity finish. Ten Pin Porter is a
robust, full-bodied porter, with a medium hop bitterness. The firm sells
brewing supplies for homebrewers; the one thing they don't offer is

CSA Farms—Share the Bounty

Community Supported Agriculture—more commonly known as CSA—is based on a simple principle: connecting people to their local food source at a fair price for the customer and a fair price for the producer. By joining a CSA you enter into a mutual partnership that provides a direct link between the production and consumption of food. Sounds lofty, doesn't it? The truth is, joining a CSA is a great way to get some of the best food and freshest ingredients you've ever eaten.

CSA members make a commitment to support the farm by buying a "share" of the farm's produce, usually in the early spring. This investment provides the farm with early-in-the-season capital to pay for seeds, water, equipment, and labor. In return, during the harvest season the farm provides healthy, just-picked produce on a regular basis for its members. Part of the fun is the surprise factor—the contents vary throughout the season, ensuring an ever-changing array of fresh produce.

To find a CSA farm near you, visit www.nal.usda.gov/afsic/csa/csastate.htm.

food. The bar serves beer only, from noon to 7:00 P.M. Monday through Friday and on Saturday from noon to 3:00 P.M.

Smuggler's Brewpub and Grille, 225 South Pine Street, Telluride; (970) 728–0919. Telluride's only brewpub, Smuggler's is just one block east of the gondola, making it a popular après-ski stop. Housed in a historic mining warehouse, the brewery produces handcrafted ales, lagers, and sodas. The restaurant menu features great appetizers, gyros, ribs, steaks, and seafood, all at affordable prices.

Steamworks Brewing Company, 801 East 2nd Avenue, Durango, CO 81301; (970) 259-9200; www.steamworksbrewing.com. A lively hangout in the college town of Durango, Steamworks brews a changing variety of handcrafted ales and lagers. The Backside Stout is a dark beer, with a mild chocolate taste and roasty overtones. Steamworks' Third Eye P.A. is a sturdy India Pale Ale with bountiful amounts of cascade hops and an alcohol content between 6.5 and 7 percent. The brewery also produces seasonal beers such as Tax Alement on April 1 and Powder Daze Porter during ski season. The food menu, with a good assortment of sandwiches, pizza, and burgers, also features especially tasty appetizers. Chili cheese fries are smothered with the restaurant's beer-enhanced chili; spicy buffalo wings and crispy beer-battered onion rings are also popular. For dessert, try the outstanding Beer Bread Pudding enlivened with Stout Crème Anglaise.

Southwest Colorado Wine Trail

Alfred Eames Cellars by Puesta del Sol Vineyards, 11931 4050 Road, Paonia; (970) 527-3269. Established in 2000, this winery is producing Merlot, Cabernet Sauvignon, and Pinot Noir. Sample the wines at the tasting room located at 510 Elk Avenue, Crested Butte; (970) 349-0881.

Cottonwood Cellars, 5482 Highway 348, Olathe; (970) 323-6224; www.cottonwoodcellars.com. Since Keith and Diana Read planted the first grapevines for Cottonwood Cellars in 1995, the vineyard has more than tripled in size. The small family-owned winery produces Cabernet Sauvignon, Merlot, Chardonnay, Gewürztraminer, Lemberger, White Riesling, and Pinot Noir. From April 1 through June 30, the tasting room and winery are open from 11:00 A.M. to 6:00 P.M., Monday through Thursday. From July 1 through September 14, they're open from 11:00 A.M. to 6 P.M. Wednesday through Saturday. If you want to visit between January and March, call first for an appointment. The winery is always closed on Sunday.

Jack Rabbit Hill, 26573 North Road, Hotchkiss; (970) 835–3677. As of this writing, Jack Rabbit Hill is the only USDA-certified organic commercial vineyard and winery in Colorado. Owners Lance and Anna Hanson carefully blend their "6 Barrel White," "Barn Red," and "Last Ditch" wines, which can be sampled at the Telluride Farmers' Market (see page 128) and at the tasting room located inside the Birds of a Feather Art Gallery, 122 East Bridge Street, Hotchkiss; (970) 835–3677. Hours of the gallery are Monday through Saturday from 9:00 A.M. to 5:00 P.M.

Mountain Spirit Winery, 15750 County Road 220, Salida; (888) 679–4637; www.mountainspiritwinery.com. Mountain Spirit Winery, located on a five-acre farmland with apple orchards and an old homestead, is surrounded by scenic 14,000-foot mountain vistas. The winery produces Chardonnay, Merlot, and Blush wines. It also produces interesting blends, including a blackberry/Chardonnay and a Merlot/raspberry combination, plus delicious chokecherry and raspberry dessert wines. The winery is open Monday, Thursday, Friday, and Saturday from 11:00 A.M. to 5:00 P.M. A nice tasting room and art gallery is located in town at 201 F Street, (719) 539-7848. This location is open Monday through Saturday from 10:00 A.M. to 5:00 P.M.

Mountain View Winery, 5859 58.25 Road, Olathe; (970) 323-6816; www.mountainviewwinery.com. This fourth-generation family orchard is now producing some lovely wines, including Merlot, Cherry Red, Chardonnay, Ash Mesa (a blend of apple and Chardonnay), plus fruit wines including apricot, apple, peach, pear, raspberry, wild plum, and Cherry Rosé. The tasting room is open year 'round Monday through Saturday, 10:00 A.M. to 6:00 P.M.

Reeder Mesa Vineyards, 7799 Reeder Mesa Road, Whitewater; (970) 242-7468; reedermesawines.com. Reeder is one of the newer wineries, but it's already receiving rave reviews for its fruity Riesling. Owners Doug and Kris Vogel also craft Merlot, Cabernet Sauvignon, Shiraz, Chardonnay, and White Merlot. The tasting room is open Friday and Saturday from 10:00 A.M. to 6:00 P.M. and Sunday from 10:00 A.M. to 5:00 P.M.

Rocky Hill Winery, 18380 South Highway 550, Montrose; (970) 249-3765. Rocky Hill Winery owners David and Marschall Fansler describe their distinctive recipe for cherry cola: "Freeze some of our cherry wine in ice cube trays. It'll take about three days to freeze solid.

Then add the ice cubes to a glass of cola and you'll have the best cherry cola you ever tasted!" The winery's cherry wine, made from tart pie cherries and sweet bing cherries, is the firm's most popular summer wine. Other offerings include Centennial Riesling, Gewürztraminer, Cabernet Franc, Black Canyon Cabernet, Ouray Black Cherry Merlot, Ski Bunny Blush, Chenin Blanc, and the new Montrose, a fruity merlot. The winery's shady picnic area is next to stream, with breathtaking views of the San Juan Mountains. The tasting room is open in mid-April through December, Monday through Saturday from 10:00 A.M. to 6:00 P.M., and Sunday from noon to 4:00 P.M.

Stoney Mesa Winery, 1619 2125 Drive, Cedaredge; (970) 856–9463; www.stoneymesa.com. Stoney Mesa is a friendly, family-run winery. Ron and Donna Neal, along with their son Bret, produce wines at one of the highest-altitude wineries in the United States. While the Gewürztraminer and Merlot are the most popular wines, Stoney Mesa's Chardonnay is beginning to win awards. The firm also produces Cabernet Sauvignon, Cabernet Franc, Sunset Blush, and Riesling. The tasting room is in an old farmhouse, part of the property's original homestead that was built in the 1880s. The room is open from 11:00 A.M. to 5:00 P.M. daily, except for Christmas, Thanksgiving, and New Year's Day.

Surface Creek Winery, 2071 N Road, P.O. Box 483, Eckert 81418; (970) 835–9463; www.surfacecreek.com. Surface Creek opened in June of 2000, instantly winning a second-place medal at the Colorado Wine

Competition for its Merlot. The winery also produces Sauvignon Blanc, Chenin Blanc, and Chardonnay. A tasting room and gallery, in the historic Eckert Odd Fellows Hall at 1297 Highway 65, is open during the summer months from 11:00 A.M. to 5:00 P.M. daily.

Terror Creek Winery, 1750 4175 Drive, Paonia; (970) 527–3484. A beautiful garden overlooks the vineyards and surrounding mountains of Terror Creek, a lovely place to bring a picnic and sample the winery's Chardonnay, Gewürztraminer, Riesling, and Pinot Noir. The tasting room is open from Memorial Day through Labor Day from 11:00 A.M. to 5:00 P.M., Friday through Sunday, or by appointment at other times.

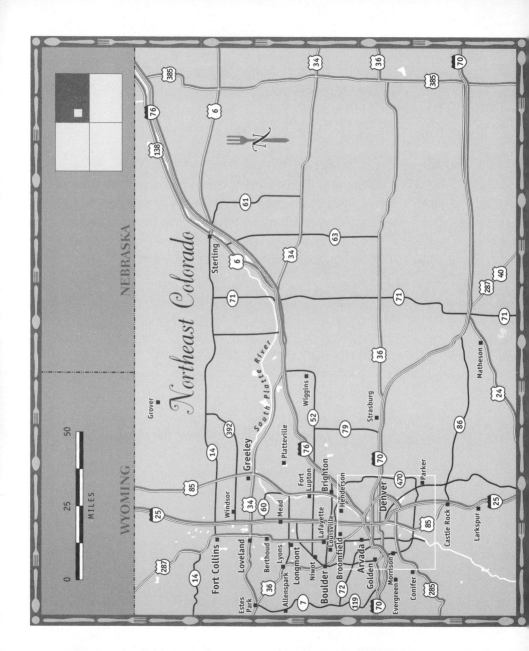

Northeast Colorado

In this region, beer lovers will find plenty of brewpubs and micro-breweries, including the state's two largest breweries, Anheuser-Busch in Fort Collins and locally founded Coors Brewery in Golden. Many food manufacturers operate in the area, and companies of all sizes produce specialty foods that run the gamut from artisan cheeses and smoked fish to toffee and tortillas.

The state's largest farmers' market is held in Boulder each summer, filling a city block and attracting thousands of visitors. Boulder is also home to three popular cooking schools, as well as the Peppercorn, an enormous "I've died and gone to heaven" store full of temptations for those who love to cook and eat.

The eastern part of the state is mostly prairie, with wide-open grasslands on the plains. Here you'll find numerous ranches and farms growing traditional crops like corn, wheat, and alfalfa. Roadside farm stands are in abundance during the late-summer months; in this chapter you'll read about many that welcome the public for "pick-your-own" autumn pumpkins and harvest celebrations.

Made Here

Bear Meadow Gourmet Foods, P.O. Box 316, Evergreen 80437; (303) 679–1949 or (800) 255–6559; www.bearmeadowgourmet.com. Ann Holloway and her mother, Rose, were always cooking up something wonderful in the kitchen. When they started experimenting with home-made mixes for a new bread machine, one thing led to another and, in 1994, a business was born. Today the company specializes in creative mixes for cooking and baking. One of the best-selling bread mixes is Durango Beer Bread, flavored with cornmeal, chile, and cheese. Mountain Morning Pancake mix is hearty with rolled oats, and the San Luis Green Chile Stew is delicious and easy; just add water and cook for a few hours. Other products include flavorful mixes for whipping up dips, cookies, and candies. Bear Meadow's products are available in local stores as well as online and by mail order.

Bingham Hill Cheese Company, 1716 Heath Parkway, Fort Collins 80524; (970) 472–0702; www.binghamhill.com. When you imagine the origin of the world's finest blue cheeses, don't you think of a musty cave somewhere in France? Astonishingly, Fort Collins' own Bingham Hill Rustic Blue recently won second place in the world championship cheese contest, beating out forty-nine other cheeses from ten countries. Owners Tom and Kristi Johnson describe handcrafting cheese as "a noble cause and fascinating challenge," which they appear to be handling nicely. Other Bingham Hill cheeses include Poudre Puff—a cheese resembling a small snowball with a white rind similar to Brie—

and Harvest Moon, a soft, ripened cheese with a washed rind and full flavor. Watch the cheese being made through the windows of Bingham Hill's small retail shop where you can buy its products fresh, or order online.

Celestial Seasonings, 4600 Sleepytime Drive, Boulder 80301; (303) 581–1202; (800) 351–8175; www.celestialseasonings. com. The aroma of herbs and mint permeates the air the minute you step inside the corporate headquarters of Celestial Seasonings. The company is known for its wide array of teas, but it is almost as famous for its whimsical tea boxes, illustrated by many well-known artists and peppered with inspirational quotes. A free company tour takes forty-five minutes; be sure to stop in the Mint Room and clear your sinuses with a mind-blowing whiff of peppermint. The gift shop offers substantial discounts on the company's teas, and the Celestial Café is a nice place to stop and have lunch and, of course, a spot of tea.

Fiona's Granola/Fiona's Natural Foods, 2695 Juniper Avenue, Boulder 80304; (303) 415–1121; www.fionasgranola.com. Boulder resident Fiona Simon produces her crispy, golden granola in small batches, using all natural ingredients like organic grains and agave nectar. The granola boasts a lot of benefits: It's high in protein and fiber, naturally sweetened, low in fat and sugar, wheat-free, dairy-free, and contains no cholesterol. But the real draw is that it's positively delicious. Flavors like Almond Cranberry and Ginger Walnut make the granola a top-seller in local stores and markets. The company also offers Swiss-style muesli in blends like Raspberry Pineapple or Almond Blueberry Peach, and granola bars that put the processed bars to shame. Order the granola bar variety pack and you can try the Chocolate Chip Peanut Butter, Cranberry Orange, Tropical Spice, and Magical Mocha flavors. Fiona's products are available at local stores and restaurants, or order online.

TheGarlicStore.com, Yucca Ridge Farm, 46050 Weld County Road 13, Fort Collins 80524; (970) 568–7664; www.thegarlic store.com. This online shop carries more than forty varieties of fresh organic garlic in season, plus garlic braids, garlic powder, crushed garlic, garlic juice, pickled garlic, garlic pepper jelly, grill sauces and marinades, salsas, pasta sauces, and spice mixes. The Web site is full of recipes, tips, and information about the health benefits of garlic and also offers garlic gadgets like garlic presses, keepers, bakers, and peelers, plus books and videos. If you'd like to grow garlic in your garden, the company offers healthy planting stock.

Is your dog tired of those mint-flavored dog biscuits? The Garlic Store also offers garlic-flavored pet treats, which "begs" the question: Is a dog with garlic breath preferable to one with dog breath? Only you can decide.

Honeysmoked Fish Company, P.O. Box 4253, Evergreen 80437; (303) 674–4636; www.honeysmokedfish.com. It's a fish story with a happy ending. As a young boy, Kevin Mason enjoyed spending time fishing with his dad on the weekends. It was a fitting introduction to a lifetime of learning about fish. As Kevin grew up, he helped out at his dad's fish market. When he was finished with school and ready for a career, he decided to partner with his father at the fish market. During slow times,

Roasted Garlic Soup

Roasting garlic eliminates the sharp flavor and renders it mellow and sweet. Garlic is the star ingredient in this soul-soothing soup recipe from Liv Lyons of TheGarlicStore (see page 162). Serve it on a chilly night with crusty bread and a glass of wine.

2 to 4 heads of garlic (not surprisingly, Liv Lyons uses 4)
8 cups chicken stock or broth
1 large sweet onion, peeled and minced

1 stalk celery, minced
1 large potato, peeled and cubed
¼ cup dry sherry
Salt and pepper to taste

1. Preheat the oven to 350° F. Remove the superfluous skin from the garlic heads and cut the base of each in order for the bulbs to rest on a flat surface. Place heads in a baking dish and cover tightly with aluminum foil. Roast for an hour or until bulbs are soft. Remove from the oven and cool on a wire rack.

2. When the garlic heads are cool enough to handle, peel the garlic and puree the cloves in a food processor or blender.

3. In a large saucepan, stir the garlic puree into the chicken broth and add the onion, celery, and potato. Cook until the vegetables are tender, about 10 to 15 minutes.

4. Puree the soup in batches in a food processor or blender until smooth. Return to the pan, and bring to a boil. Add the sherry, salt, and pepper, cook for a minute more, and serve.

Makes 6 servings.

Kevin began to experiment with different techniques and recipes for smoking fish. The fish market, with its vast inventory of fresh fish, proved to be the perfect laboratory. After years of tinkering, Kevin perfected his own technique of dripping honey onto the fire, which ignited and subsequently sealed the juices in the fish. When his father retired in 1995 after thirty-eight years, Kevin started the Honeysmoked Fish Company in the mountain town of Evergreen. Today the company produces a mellow smoked trout in addition to its mainstay, smoked salmon in variations that include original, cracked pepper, chipotle-lime, and lemon-pepper. The company's products are all natural and are carried by many local stores. They are also available for online ordering.

Lasater Grasslands Beef, P.O. Box 38, Matheson 80830; (866) 454–2333; www.lgbeef.com. On the short-grass prairie of eastern Colorado near Matheson, the Lasater family raises free-range cattle that graze and are "finished" on the range. Unlike the practices of most commercial feedlots, these cows are not given growth hormones, anabolic steroids, or low-level antibiotics. The land on which they graze is never treated with pesticides, herbicides, poisons, or commercial fertilizers.

Instead the family sees nature "as a partner, rather than a force to be overcome. We refuse to compromise when it comes to Nature—in a very real sense, she is our most valued business partner and the source of our business philosophy," says principal Dale Lasater.

In contrast to feedlot-finished cattle, grass-fed beef is lower in fat and calories, and higher in vitamins like beta-carotene and

Best Super Bowl Snack: Tortilla Chips in Bronco Colors

When the Broncos were on a serious winning streak back in 1998, the folks at EB Mexican Foods thought it would be fun to make some spirited tortilla chips in blue and orange. The townsfolk of Fort Collins loved them, and someone alerted the Denver Post about the colorful chips. When an article ran in the paper a few days later, the shop was inundated with customers; it sold 2,000 bags of chips the week before the 1998 Super Bowl, in which the Broncos were victorious.

EB Mexican Foods

400 Linden Street
Fort Collins 80524
(970) 493-6606

Fortunately, owners Christi Godinez-Gabaldon and Gary Paul Gabaldon (the fourth generation to run this family business) were already used to doing weird things to tortillas. They produce flour tortillas in unusual flavors like jalapeño, red chile, spinach-cheese, tomato-basil, and even chocolate during the holidays. The firm also produces corn tortillas (yes, those come flavored, too: yellow, white, red chile, and jalapeño-lime), taco shells, tostada shells, and, of course, tortilla chips. The company, which has been at its present location for forty-two years, has expanded the number of colors it offers, making the chips a popular choice for weddings, high school graduations, and holidays. While the company does a substantial wholesale business, the retail shop is open Monday through Thursday from 7:30 A.M. to 2:00 P.M., and on Friday from 11:00 A.M. to 2:00 P.M.

vitamin E. Lasater dry-ages its beef for fourteen to twenty-one days in a temperature- and humidity-controlled environment. The process breaks down the enzymes in the beef, naturally tenderizing the meat and enhancing its flavor. The company's beef is available online and by mail order, and its ground beef is available at local Vitamin Cottage stores.

Madhava Honey, 4689 Ute Highway 66, Longmont 80503; (303) 823-5166; www.madhavahoney.com. Taste samples of the purest high-altitude clover, alfalfa, and wildflower honey at Madhava's Sticky Wick-it Shop, a roadside retail store on Highway 66 between Longmont and Lyons. You'll also find honey sticks, creamed honeys, beeswax, and candle-making supplies. Owner Craig Gerbore has been in the honey business for nearly thirty years, and he knows his sweet stuff. Madhava's products are also sold in stores along the Front Range.

Mary Ann's Beans, P.O. Box 9576, Fort Collins 80525; (970) 482-7687; www.maryannsbeans.com. While school bus driver Mary Ann Springer shuttled her young charges back and forth to school each day, she cooked up an idea. In 1986 she started her own company with several old family bean soup recipes. She drove the school bus by day and was a moonlighting soup mix entrepreneur on nights and weekends. The company grew so quickly that Mary Ann quit her job as bus driver and enlisted help from her son and daughter-in-law, Perry and Barbara Springer. Today, the convivial couple run the busy business and keep in touch with Mary Ann, who retired in 1997. Mary Ann's perennial best seller is the White Chili mix, an assortment of three different white beans and spices. To use it, you simply add chicken and green chiles. Other popular soup mixes include the zesty Southwest Bean Soup and Colorado Beans 'n Barley. The soups are naturally low in fat, full of fiber and healthy nutrients, and contain no preservatives. The company offers many vegetarian soup mixes, as well as a green chile mix, zesty barbecue rub, and an Italian mix for dipping and pasta. The products are attractively packaged in cotton bags or glass drinking mugs. Order online or by mail.

Mountain Man Nut and Fruit Company, P.O. Box 160, 10338 South Progress Way, Parker 80134; (303) 841–4041; www.mountain mannut.com. If you work in an office building, there's a good chance you've heard the familiar intercom announcement that signals relief from the midafternoon munchies: "The Mountain Man is here!" The company's representatives offer a popular alternative to office vending machines, arriving with generous bags of candies, nuts, trail mixes, dried fruit, beef jerky, and flavored popcorn.

Owner Dave Connor says the most popular products are the candies that the company makes in its factory: giant malted-milk balls, double-dipped chocolate peanuts, and trail mixes. The company's latest creation is the Chocolate Cherry Crunch trail mix, which combines dried cherries, dark Belgian chocolate, cashews, almonds, peanuts, and peanut-butter chips. Imported candies, such as Fazer mints from Finland and English butter toffees, are also a hit. Many people are fond of the nostalgic candies the company carries, like Mary Janes and penny candies. In addition to its network of roving distributors, the company operates sixteen retail stores in the state.

MouCo, 1401 Duff Drive, Suite 300, Fort Collins 80524; (970) 498–0107; www.mouco.com. The MouCo Cheese Company originated in the early 1990s when Robert Poland and his wife, Birgit Halbreiter, began making cheese out of their home. Today, the company produces a creamy, soft-center Camembert that is delighting gourmands across the state. Birgit's father, Franz, is a master cheese maker in Germany. "My father started making Camembert cheese in Europe somewhere around 1956," she says. Robert worked for twelve years as a professional in the food industry before he and Birgit started the company. The Camembert is made entirely by hand in the company's modest factory. It is made with hormone- and antibiotic-free cow's milk, aged for two weeks in special caves, and wrapped in special French imported paper. The cheeses are available in many local stores, and may also be ordered by telephone or online. The factory is happy to give tours if you call for an appointment.

Penelope's of Evergreen, P.O. Box 2863, Evergreen 80437; (866) 972–6879; www.penelopewinejelly.com. Penelope North's mother and grandmother made their own delicious jellies and preserves, inspiring Penelope to start a company in 1989 selling her own line of old-fashioned wine jellies. The delicious jellies are mildly sweet, yet tempered by the complex flavors of the wines. The company produces them from six varietals: Cabernet Sauvignon, Chardonnay, Champagne, Merlot, Port, and White Zinfandel. Penelope's also makes scone and lemon curd mixes and several types of wine-based dessert sauces, which can be poured over ice cream, used as a topping for cheesecakes, or served over fresh fruit. Order via telephone or online.

Rocky Mountain Popcorn Company, 520 Stacy Court, Suite D, Lafayette 80026; (303) 744–8850; www.rockymountainpopcorn.com. Remember caramel popcorn? One taste takes me back to the state fair, where it was cooked in a big iron pot and the intoxicating smell made it impossible to pass by without forking over a dollar. Once you try Rocky Mountain Caramel Peanut popcorn, you'll agree that the company has taken this concoction to a whole new level. In addition to regular and caramel corn, the company has solved the dilemma of what to get the person who has everything: the Popcorn of the Month Club. The lucky recipient receives an assortment of six bags of flavored popcorn every other month for one sweet, crunchy year. The company also offers gift boxes and tins and is happy to ship anywhere.

Vern's Toffee House, 444 South Link Lane, Fort Collins 80524; (970) 493–7770; www.vernstoffee.com. Ralph Waldo Emerson said, "The reward of a thing well done is to have done it." Mary Hert, whose parents, Vern and Gert Hackbarth, started Vern's Toffee in 1976, agrees. "We just do one thing, but we try to do it very well," says Mary, who joined the company in 1984 and now owns it with her husband, Ron. Vern's is famous for its trademark crunchy almond toffee, which is covered in chocolate and coated with raw crushed almonds. A popular gift for businesses and individuals, the company does about 85 percent of its business by mail order and the Internet. Vern's Toffee is available in one- and two-pound boxes, and that's as complicated as the decision-making gets. The walk-in shop is steadily busy, especially during Christmas when Vern, who retired in 1992, comes in to help out at the counter.

A La Carte, 336 East Elkhorn Avenue, Barlow Plaza, P.O. Box 304, Estes Park 80517; (970) 586–2798; www.alacarte-estes.com. Estes Park is just a few miles from the entrance to majestic Rocky Mountain National Park, and A La Carte is the place to stop and pick up a picnic basket for the trip. (Yogi Bear has even been spotted in the shop from time to time.) This busy store sells a wide variety of jellies, preserves, salsas, spices, baking mixes, cookbooks, kitchen gadgets, a line of engraved bear and moose glassware, wine accessories, ceramic mixing bowls, pizza stones, bakeware, unusual giftware, and hundreds of other items.

Belvedere Belgian Chocolate Shop, 350 A Perry Street, Castle Rock; (303) 663–2364; www.belvederechocolates.com. Han and Johan Devriese are a couple that have something rather unusual in common. They're both professionally trained Belgian chocolatiers. Luckily for us, they decided to move to Castle Rock in 1998 with the idea of introducing their country's famous pure chocolate to Coloradoans. Rather than importing finished chocolates, they opened their own chocolate factory. Today the company produces over fifty different exquisite candies using their homeland's pure Belgian chocolate as a base. Popular filling flavors include praline, caramel, cherry cordial, nut, and marzipan. They also make traditional seashells with hazelnut paste fillings. The chocolates are all handcrafted and made without preservatives. The company has additional shops in Boulder (1634

Walnut Street; 303–447–0336), Cherry Creek North in Denver (231 Milwaukee Street; 303–771–0758) and Glenwood Springs (710 Grand Avenue, Unit 5, 970–945–2723). You can also order fresh chocolates online or via telephone.

Boulder Cheese Company, 1731 15th Street, Boulder; (303) 938–1499; www.bouldercheesecompany.com. Boulder Cheese Company's owner/cheese monger Saxon Brown gets a kick out of getting his customers to try new cheeses. His shop carries hundreds of artisan and homemade cheeses from all over the world. "The goal is not just to sell cheeses," he says. "We want to educate our customers and introduce them to new products." There are always samples available for tasting, and the shop makes fabulous cheese trays for parties. Closed Sunday and Monday.

Cheese Importers, 33 South Pratt Parkway, P.O. Box 1717, Longmont 80501; (303) 772–9599; www.cheeseimporters.com. Cheese Importers is a mostly wholesale operation, selling a fabulous assortment of cheeses to restaurants and retail shops. However, the employees are very kind, and they don't mind at all if you go into the vast refrigerated warehouse and peruse the cheese. (They'll even loan you a coat to wear.) Lining the tall shelves are hundreds of cheeses from around the world, including a large selection of completely natural cheeses, as well as raw-milk, rennet-less, flavored, aged, sheep's milk, and goat cheeses. La Fromagerie, the company's wonderful retail store, is attached to the warehouse. It carries a nice assortment of gourmet foods, cooking gadgets, candies, linens, kitchenware, cookbooks, gifts, and much more. An olive bar encourages tasting, and a deli serves soups, focaccia sandwiches, and delicious casseroles.

Colorado Cherry Company, 1024 Big Thompson Canyon Road, Loveland; (970) 667–4141 or (888) 526–6535 to order; www.colorado cherrycompany.com. If it's jam or jelly you're looking for, you'll think you've hit the Mother Lode at the Colorado Cherry Company. The quaint store sells every kind of preserve you could ever want.

The perennial bestseller is the firm's wild chokecherry flavor, but here are some of the other varieties that line the shelves: all varieties of cherry, cherry rhubarb, fig, strawberry, peach, blackberry, elderberry, crabapple, blueberry, huckleberry, plum, wild plum, pomegranate, Hopi corn, prickly pear cactus, marmalade, kiwi pineapple, cloudberry, loganberry, ginger, garlic, onion, dandelion, and horseradish. The company also makes delicious ciders made from the family's third-generation recipe, in flavors including black Bing cherry, peach, raspberry, black raspberry, and muscadine grape. There are also relishes, pickles, chutneys, olives, honeys, syrups, fruit butters, and mustards. But the pièce de résistance is the fresh homemade cherry pie, available by the slice or by the pie. It's a slice of heaven to sit outside the store at a picnic table by the Big Thompson River, enjoying a glass of cold cider and a piece of cherry pie. The shop is open daily May through October, and then on weekends until Christmas The company's products can also be ordered by telephone or online.

The Cupboard, 152 South College Avenue, Fort Collins; (970) 493–8585; www.thecupboard.net. For more than thirty years, this shop has been a mainstay for cooks in the college town of Fort Collins. A large gourmet food section supplies jams and jellies, olive oils, vinegars, hot sauces, and salsas, a wide variety of teas, coffee beans, imported chocolates and candies, cookies, crackers, soup mixes, dried pastas, Asian cooking ingredients, Colorado food products, mustards, spreads, and much more. The shop also stocks a huge array of cookware, bakeware, cookbooks, gifts, gadgets, and tableware.

The Longmont Dairy Farm Country Store, 10675 Ute Highway, Longmont; (303) 776-6456. I confess that I am old enough to remember getting milk in glass bottles, and it is sweetly nostalgic to visit the Longmont Dairy Farm Country Store and be able to buy it that way again. I'm never able to walk straight to the cooler and leave with a bottle of milk, though; there are too many other temptations. The shop sells fresh eggs, locally baked bread, cheeses, more than seventy-five spices, snacks, hot sauces, salsa, jellies, honeys, ice cream, bread mixes, soup mixes, oils, pastas, plus a nice selection of gifts.

Mocha Angelo's, 133 West Elkhorn Avenue, The Old Church Shops, Estes Park; (888) 372-6879 or (970) 577-1957. Sure, you've gone to wine tastings, beer tastings, and maybe even scotch or whiskey tastings. But is your palate ready for a hot sauce tasting? If you've never compared the subtle nuances of habañeros and jalapeños, a trip to the store's hot sauce tasting bar is in order. The shop sells over forty-

Highland Haven's Baked Orange Pecan French Toast

Owners Gail Riley and Thomas Statzell serve a scrumptious breakfast in the casually elegant setting of the Highland Haven Creekside Inn in Evergreen. This recipe—which could easily win the title of World's Best French Toast—is a treasure because you can prepare it ahead of time and bake it just in time for breakfast.

4 eggs	**¼ teaspoon nutmeg**
⅔ cup orange juice	**8½-inch bread slices**
⅓ cup milk	**¼ cup butter**
¼ cup sugar	**½ cup chopped pecans**
½ teaspoon vanilla	**Orange Syrup (recipe follows)**

1. In a medium bowl, beat together the eggs, juice, milk, sugar, vanilla, and nutmeg, until well combined.
2. Arrange the bread in a single layer in a large baking dish and top with the egg mixture, turning to coat. Cover and refrigerate for 2 hours. (The recipe can also be made up to this point the night before, and refrigerated overnight.)

five varieties of the spicy stuff, plus a host of other specialty foods: flavored dipping oils, sauces, salsas, soup mixes, gift baskets, wine accessories, coffee flavorings, Colorado jams and jellies, flavored pastas, rice mixes, European chocolates, gifts, gadgets, and much more. The in-house coffee bar is a pleasant stop for a latte, cappuccino, or Italian soda.

3. Preheat the oven to 350° F. Put the butter in a large jelly roll pan and put in the oven just until the butter is melted. Swirl it to coat the pan. Arrange the bread pieces in the pan in a single layer and bake for 20 minutes. Sprinkle with pecans and bake for 10 more minutes. Serve with Orange Syrup.

Makes 8 servings.

Orange Syrup

½ cup sugar   1 cup orange juice
½ cup butter

Combine ingredients in a small saucepan and heat over a medium-low flame, stirring until butter melts and sugar dissolves. Cook for several minutes without allowing the mixture to boil, then remove from the flame.

Makes about 2 cups.

**The Highland Haven
Creekside Inn**

4395 Independence Trail
Evergreen 80439
(303) 674–3577
www.highlandhaven.com

Peppercorn, 1235 Pearl Street, Boulder 80302; (303) 449–5847; www.peppercorn.com. The Peppercorn has a special place in my personal culinary history. I took cooking classes from owner Doris Houghland back in the 1980s when the Peppercorn was stuffed in a tiny shop, half a block away from its current location. Today the fabulous store is overflowing with cookware, a huge inventory of cookbooks, bed and bath items, and unusual gifts. The shop stocks more than 400 types of specialty food products, including hot sauces and salsas, baking mixes, imported Italian pestos and olive oils, jellies, honeys, Silver Palate products, Asian cooking ingredients, as well as scores of Colorado products. Frequently there are demonstrations and samples of various foods and products in the store. Every few years, the store has a warehouse sale full of terrific bargains, which is like the Filene's Basement of cooking sales; call for dates.

Prairie Rose Fine Tea and Bath Shop, 212 Wilcox, Castle Rock 80104; (303) 663–8846. Prairie Rose Teas has the largest selection of teas in Douglas County, which happens to be the fastest-growing county in the United States. To keep up with all that demand, the shop carries more than 180 blends of teas plus a wide assortment of British and Scottish food items: jams, jellies, Double Devon cream, Somerdale clotted creams, Carr's and Walker's shortbreads and biscuits, scones, marmalades, and biscuits. This is also a wonderful place to look for the perfect teapot to brew a spot of tea. The store sponsors high teas at various locations several times a month; call for a schedule and to make the essential reservations.

Village Gourmet, 1193 Bergen Parkway, the Market Place at Bergen Park, Evergreen 80439; (303) 670–0717. The Village Gourmet has been a fixture in Evergreen for many years, supplying locals and tourists with a surprisingly abundant assortment of Colorado specialties and gourmet foods. Popular items include coffees, teas, salsas, jams, jellies, mustards, chocolates, oils, vinegars, tapenades, spreads, baking mixes, and soup mixes. The shop also carries high-end glassware, dinnerware, cookware, kitchen gadgets, cookbooks, cutlery, and more. This is a cozy place to visit during the holidays, when the charming town of Evergreen is blanketed in snow and the busy shop hosts tastings and demonstrations.

What's Cooking, 2770 Arapahoe Road, Suite 112 (95th Street and Arapahoe Road) Lafayette 80026; (303) 666–0300; www.whatscookinginc.com. Luanne Hill was a buyer for the May Company for ten years, a career that convinced her that she loved merchandising and wanted to open her own shop someday. She realized her dream in 1995 when she opened What's Cooking in Lafayette with a well-chosen assortment of high-end products. The store stocks gourmet foods, including infused oils and imported olive oils, vinegars, peppercorns and sea salt, pastas and sauces, condiments, baking mixes, popcorns, salsas and hot sauces, soups, crackers, candies, chocolates, and much more. The shop also has a wide assortment of cookware, dinnerware, cookbooks, gift baskets, cutlery, and gadgets. The store also hosts cooking classes in its full working kitchen, where guest chefs teach classes on a wide variety of subjects (see page 200). Call or visit the Web site for a schedule.

Farmers' markets are constantly changing, so double-check times and locations. For the most up-to-date farmers' market listings, call 303–570–FARM or visit www.ag.state.co.us. Incidentally, Colorado's largest farmers' market is held in Boulder.

Aspen Park Farmers' Market, RTD Park-n-Ride at U.S. Highway 285 before Conifer. Saturdays from 10:00 A.M. to 2:00 P.M., mid-June through late September.

Berthoud Farmers' Market, Third and Mountain Avenues, Berthoud; (970) 532–5199; www.berthoudmainstreet.org. Thursdays from 3:00 P.M. to 7:00 P.M., June through October.

Boulder Farmers' Market, 13th Street between Canyon Boulevard and Arapahoe, Boulder; (303) 910–2236; www.boulderfarmers.org. Wednesdays from 4:00 to 8:00 P.M., mid-May through late September; Saturdays from 8:00 A.M. to 2:00 P.M., early April through late October.

Castle Rock Farmers' Market, 11 Wilcox Street, Castle Rock; Saturdays from 8:00 A.M. to noon, early June through September.

El Rancho Farmers' Market, Evergreen Home Depot parking lot, Evergreen. Tuesday from 10:00 A.M. to 2:00 P.M., June through October.

Estes Park Farmers' Market, 470 Prospect Village Drive, Estes Park; (970) 532–4581; Saturdays from 8:00 A.M., June through October.

Evergreen Farmers' Market, Home Depot parking lot, Evergreen. Tuesdays from 10:00 A.M. to 2:00 P.M., starting in mid-June and running through mid-October.

Fort Collins Farmers' Market, parking lot on the southwest corner of Harmony and Lemay, Fort Collins; www.fortnet.org/market. Sundays and Wednesdays, 11:00 A.M. to 3:00 P.M., early May through late October.

Golden Farmers' Market, Jackson Street between 12th and 13th Streets, Golden. Saturdays from 8:00 A.M. to 1:00 P.M., early June through late September.

Greeley Farmers' Market, 902 7th Avenue, Greeley. Wednesdays from 4:00 to 6:00 P.M. and Saturdays from 7:30 to 11:00 A.M., July through October.

LaPorte Farmers' Market, LaPorte Feed & Supply, LaPorte; (970) 494–1820. Fridays from 2:00 to 6:00 P.M., July through October.

Larimer County Master Gardeners' Farmers' Market, Old Town Fort Collins at LaPorte and Howes, Fort Collins; (970) 498–6008. Saturdays from 8:00 A.M. to noon, June through October.

Coney Island: Aspen Park's Most Famous Building

The drive up Highway 285 is a scenic one, with the road winding through the Rocky Mountains, past forests of blue spruce trees, fields of wildflowers, and . . . a giant 30-foot hot dog trimmed with mustard and relish. Right on the highway just past the Aspen Park sign, the infamous hot dog is often used by locals as a "can't miss" landmark when giving directions. The diner was located on Colfax Avenue, about 35 miles southwest of Denver, until the original owner purchased it thirty-four years ago and moved it to its present location. Today, Lisa and Taylor Firman own the fifteen-seat restaurant and serve up the kitchen's trademark hot dogs and diner fare. The most popular dog is still the Chili Cheese Dog, an all-beef dog served in a warm bun, topped with American cheese and the restaurant's secret, meat-only chili recipe. You can also order hamburgers; chicken, fish, and pork sandwiches; fries and onion rings. The diner serves a dozen flavors of milkshakes: black raspberry, cherry, hot fudge, marshmallow, vanilla, chocolate, cherry, banana, mocha, coffee, butterscotch, and pineapple. The restaurant is open year-round.

Coney Island
P.O. Box 695
Conifer 80433
(303) 838–4210
$

Larkspur Farmers' Market, Downtown Larkspur; www.colorado farmersmarket.com. Thursdays from 4:00 to 6:00 P.M.

Longmont City Park Farmers' Market, Downtown Longmont; (303) 570–3276; www.coloradofarmersmarket.com. Saturdays from 8:00 A.M. to 1:00 P.M., from May through October.

Longmont Farmers' Market, north lot of Boulder County Fairgrounds, Hover Road and Boston Avenue, Longmont; www.longmontfarmers.com. Saturdays from 8:00 A.M. to 1:00 P.M., early June through late October. Tuesdays from 9:00 A.M. to 1:00 P.M., early July through mid-September.

Loveland Farmers' Market, corner of Lincoln and 5th Streets, Loveland. Tuesdays from 2:00 to 6:00 P.M., early July through late October.

Mead Farmers' Market, Town Park, Mead. Fridays from 4:00 to 8:00 P.M., June through September.

Plum Creek Valley Farmers' Market, Southwest corner of the Castle Rock Shopping Center, 190 South Wilcox Street, Castle Rock; (720) 733–6930. Saturdays from 8:00 A.M. to noon, mid-July through early October.

Sterling Farmers' Market, southeast corner of the Wal-Mart parking lot, Sterling. Mondays from 5:30 P.M. to dusk.

Strasburg Community Council, 56841 East Colfax, Strasburg. Saturdays from 8:00 A.M. to 1:00 P.M., June through September.

Tri-County Farmers' Market, Main Street Center, 1½ blocks east of Parker Road on Main Street, Parker; (303) 621–8081; www.laughingdogfarms.net. Sundays from 8:30 A.M. to 1:00 P.M., from mid-May through late October.

Windsor Farmers' Market at Pioneer Village Museum, 116 North 5th Street, Windsor; (970) 686–0403. Thursdays from 4:00 to 7:00 P.M., mid-July through September.

Farm Stands

Anders Farm, 8443 U.S. Highway 85, Fort Lupton; (303) 857–2158. This roadside market sells a wide variety of fresh produce: beets, bell peppers, cabbage, cantaloupe, chile peppers as well as roasted chiles, cucumbers, garlic, green beans, onions, pinto beans, potatoes, squash, sweet corn, tomatoes, watermelon, and honey. Open early July through late September, daily from 8:00 A.M to 6:30 P.M.

Berry Patch Farms, 13785 Potomac, Brighton; (303) 659–5050; www.berrypatchfarms.com. This pick-your-own farm owned by Tim and Claudia Ferrell is a popular destination for school field trips. The farm grows scores of fresh vegetables and fruits, and there is always something interesting to pick or pull from the ground: broccoli stalks, fat melons, juicy tomatoes, sweet corn, squash, eggplant, zucchini, onions, carrots, cucumbers, raspberries, strawberries, and pumpkins in the fall. The farm offers children's classes in the summer and adult cooking classes in the fall; call or check the Web site for the schedule. Open in early June.

Blacksmith Ridge Farms, 5093 Nelson Road, Longmont; (303) 678-0399. Tender, just-picked stalks of bright green asparagus herald the arrival of spring at this popular farm stand, which opens in mid-May. As the season progresses, the farm offers bushels of just-picked produce: tomatoes, strawberries, spinach, corn, squash, peas, tomatoes, melons, peaches, and pumpkins. Open mid-May through late October, every day except Monday, from 9:00 A.M. to 7:00 P.M.

Eden Valley Farm, 6263 North County Road 29, Loveland; (970) 667-9225. Eden Valley's farm stand has a wealth of freshly picked fruits and vegetables, plus some more unusual varieties that delight the local cooks. It sells beets, bell peppers, broccoli, cabbage, cantaloupe, carrots, cauliflower, cucumbers, green beans, lettuce, onions, raspberries, squash, strawberries, sweet corn, tomatoes, watermelon, basil, celery, cilantro, dill, eggplant (both American and Oriental varieties), leeks, parsley, spinach, Swiss chard, cut flowers, hanging baskets, and bedding plants. From early June the stand is open Sunday through Thursday, from 9:00 A.M. to 6:00 P.M., until the end of October.

Lucky Bucky's, 5428 South County Road 3F, Fort Collins; (970) 221-5212. You're sure to find the perfect pumpkin among the thirty varieties grown at this family farm near Fort Collins. After you've gone out to the fields to pick your own pumpkin, visit the farm store, an old farm building that the family converted into a charming shop. Inside, you'll find carrots, winter squash, gourds, broom corn, Indian corn, dried flowers, handcrafted gifts, and crafts. There are sheep and goats wandering around that don't mind being petted (and fed), and the farm often hosts family activities such as a scarecrow-making area, hay-rack rides, and pumpkin painting. The farm is a popular stop for school tours. Open during October on Saturday from 9:00 A.M. to dusk, and on Sunday from noon to dusk.

Miller Farms, 9040 Highway 66, Platteville; (970) 785–6133 or (970) 785–2681. An abundance of fresh produce is grown and sold at this family farm in Platteville. Depending on what's growing, you'll find all sorts of fresh foods: lettuce, okra, cucumbers, beets, bell peppers, green beans, broccoli, cabbage, tomatoes, turnips, cantaloupe, carrots, celery, chile peppers, eggplant, leeks, onions, sweet corn, pinto beans, popcorn, potatoes, squash, pumpkins, and watermelon. Every day from late September through Halloween, the farm hosts its annual Fall Festival. Bring the family and hop on the hay wagon to be driven out to the middle of the huge pumpkin patch to pick your own. A petting zoo and a corn maze are fun activities for the younger members of your group. The farmstand is open from 9:00 A.M. to 5:00 P.M. every day, from early spring through Halloween.

Munson Farms' Stand, 7355 Valmont Road, Boulder; (303) 442–5330. When I was a kid, my family often drove to the Munson Farms' Stand for sweet corn and tomatoes. One day we arrived just as the peaches were at their finest, and that night we made a peach cobbler that still ranks in my top five of all-time favorite desserts. In summer, you'll find all sorts of fresh produce, including melons, green beans, cucumbers, and squash. In the autumn, you can pick your own pumpkin in the Munsons' fields starting in late September. You can also find autumn decorations like gourds, Indian corn, and cornstalks. The stand is open daily from 9:00 A.M. to 7:00 P.M., from early July through the end of October.

Osborn Farm, 1933 Southeast 14th Street, Loveland; (970) 669–4407. The Osborns have the oldest continually owned family farm in Colorado. It was founded in 1861, and today, Pam and Dale Osborn's sons are the sixth generation to work it. In the fall, the farm opens for pick-your-own raspberries and pumpkins and sells other autumn produce, including pie pumpkins, squashes, gourds, straw, cornstalks, and Indian corn. During the last weekend in September, the farm holds its annual Country Market, selling fresh produce as well as Pam's country and primitive antiques. There are hayrides for the kids and an antique tractor exhibit, plus live music and food. Open daily during October from 10:00 A.M. to 6:00 P.M.

Pope Farms/Pope's Pumpkin Patch, 3097 County Road T, Wiggins; (970) 483–7839. If the Great Pumpkin is anywhere in Colorado, he's most likely at Pope's Pumpkin Patch. The Popes grow fifteen different varieties of pumpkins, including the Big Moon (which can get as large as 250 pounds), the Cinderella, Lumina, baby pumpkins, mini white pumpkins, and pie pumpkins. You can walk out to the fields and pick your own pumpkin right off the vine, a memorable experience for both kids and adults. This is also the place to come for autumn decorations, including Indian corn, gourds, cornstalks, and *chile ristras*, as well as roasted chiles and sometimes, fall melons. Pope's is a popular destination for school groups. Open Friday, Saturday, and Sunday during October, or call during the week for an appointment.

Robertson Fruit Stands, 104th Avenue and U.S. Highway 85, Henderson; (303) 877–3224. This roadside stand on the way to Denver International Airport sells fresh fruit from the Robertsons' orchard in Palisade. Depending on the season, you'll find fresh-grown peaches, Bing and Rainier cherries, and apples. Robertson's own jams are often available, and include apricot, cherry, peach, and pear, as well as brandied preserves, fruit toppings, and fruit ciders. The stand is open daily starting at the end of June, from 9:00 A.M. to 7:00 P.M.

Food Happenings

January: Lafayette Oatmeal Festival, Pioneer Elementary School, 101 East Baseline Road, Lafayette; (303) 926–4352. It was 1998 when one hundred residents of the small town of Lafayette volunteered to eat oatmeal for thirty days straight in Quaker Oats' Smart Heart Challenge. The townsfolk lowered their cholesterol levels by an average of twenty-five points each, giving them not only fifteen minutes of fame, but also helping prove oatmeal's benefits in maintaining a healthy lifestyle.

Every January Lafayette celebrates National Oatmeal Month with an all-you-can-eat oatmeal breakfast with a topping bar like you've never seen. More than 140 different add-ons are available to elevate your oatmeal to gourmet status: raisins, brown sugar, fresh fruit, dried fruit, toasted coconut, dessert sauces, nuts, trail mixes, granolas, Gummi Bears, crushed cookies, and candies. Oatmeal pancakes and muffins are served as well, and a health fair and 5K run add to the healthy fun. We like the kids' workshops that help youngsters make fun things out of round oatmeal boxes; pinhole cameras and birdfeeders have been past projects. The proceeds from the event benefit various causes in the Lafayette community.

***Early February*: Chocolate Lovers' Fling,** University of Colorado Boulder University Memorial Center, Glenn Miller Ballroom, Boulder; (303) 449–8623; www.bouldercounty safehouse.org. In celebration of Valentine's Day, chefs from around the nation and the Boulder area prepare chocolate delicacies for this popular annual event that attracts more than 1,000 people. Bakers and confectioners showcase their best chocolate dessert creations—pies, cakes, candies, sauces, and more. The Chocolate Lover's Dessert Competition has categories for professionals and amateurs, with prizes awarded for the best chocolate creations in each category, plus a People's Choice award. The event benefits the Boulder County Safehouse.

***April*: Taste of the Nation,** CU Boulder University Memorial Center, Glenn Miller Ballroom, CU Campus, Boulder; (303) 652–3663. Feast at dozens of Boulder's finest restaurants under one roof, and sip spirits while you support a good cause. Taste of the Nation features special dishes prepared by Boulder area chefs, the best brews from local microbreweries, and extraordinary wines. The proceeds from the event benefit the People's Clinic and Community Food Share.

Colorado Double Crust Cherry Pie

This old-fashioned pie is packed with tart Colorado cherries surrounded by a sweet filling, encased in a perfectly flaky pie crust. Serve it warm with a scoop of vanilla ice cream.

Filling

6 cups pitted, tart fresh cherries or frozen sour cherries, thawed and drained

1 cup sugar

¼ cup quick-cooking tapioca

2 teaspoons fresh lemon juice

⅛ teaspoon ground allspice

⅛ teaspoon ground cinnamon

⅛ teaspoon almond extract

1 tablespoon kirsch

2 tablespoons unsalted butter, cut into small pieces

1. Preheat oven to 400° F. In a large bowl, toss the cherries with the sugar, tapioca, lemon juice, spices, almond extract, and kirsch.

2. Fit the bottom crust into a 9-inch pie pan, and trim around the pan edges with a sharp knife or kitchen scissors. Spoon the cherry mixture into the crust and dot with the butter pieces. Lay the top crust over the pie and trim, leaving ½-inch of overlap. Fold the top layer under the bottom layer and finish the crust edge decoratively, or press down with the tines of a fork. Using a sharp knife, cut several air vents in the top of the pie.

3. Put the pie on a baking sheet in the center of the oven, and immediately turn the oven temperature down to 350° F. Rotate the pie after 30 minutes to ensure even browning. Bake for about 1 hour or until the

pie crust is lightly browned and the juices are bubbling. Remove from the oven to a wire rack and allow the pie to sit for at least an hour before you slice it, to allow the juices to thicken.

Makes 8 servings.

Catherine's Foolproof Pie Crust

My sister's recipe combines the appealing attributes of both shortening and butter, making a crust that is flaky, yet easy to handle.

2¼ cups all-purpose flour	**⅓ cup cold, lightly salted**
1 teaspoon salt	**butter**
⅔ cup cold shortening	**⅓ cup ice water**

1. Combine the flour and salt in a medium bowl. Cut in the shortening and butter, using a pastry blender or two knives. The mixture should resemble cornmeal, but leave some pieces about the size of small peas. Add the ice water, one tablespoon at a time, using a fork to lift the ingredients and gently combine.
2. When the mixture can be shaped, divide into two portions. Shape each portion into a disk and wrap in plastic wrap. Chill for about an hour. (Bring to room temperature before rolling.)

Makes two single crusts or one double crust.

***Early June*: Haystack Mountain Goat Dairy Annual Open House,** 5239 Niwot Road, Niwot; (303) 581–9948; www.haystackgoatcheese.com. Bring the family to this working goat farm and dairy and celebrate the birth of the new "kids" on the block—that is, baby goats. Wander around the farm and taste samples of the new cheeses. Haystack Mountain is the largest goat dairy farm between Colorado and Wisconsin, producing more than 30,000 pounds of goat cheese each year. The company's products have even been featured on Martha Stewart's show. Besides the annual open house, the company grounds are open to the public on Tuesday and Sunday between noon and 2:00 P.M. The Web site has a good map, which you'll need, or call for directions.

***June*: Colorado Brewers Festival,** Downtown Fort Collins, (970) 484–6500. Over 300 kegs of Colorado beers will be poured at this weekend-long festival in Fort Collins's town square. Along with great beer, restaurants and vendors will offer food and local groups will provide live music.

***June*: 95th Street Festival of Colorado Wine,** Lafayette; (303) 926–4352. Winemaker dinners at local restaurants kick off this popular event in downtown Lafayette. On Saturday and Sunday, meet with Colorado winemakers who are on hand to pour tastings of their offerings. Wine seminars, ice sculpture exhibits, lunch events, live music, and other activities round out the weekend.

How About a Nice Bowl of Jackalope Stew?

From alligator to zebra, Dale's Exotic Game Meats is one of the biggest distributors of game meats in the country. If you've got a hankering for, say, wild boar ham, Dale's is the place to call. One of the company's more unusual items (which is saying a lot) is the canned Jackalope Stew. The concoction, which is named after the prairie's famed antler-endowed rabbit, is actually a tasty mixture of antelope and rabbit meat in gravy—a perfect gift for those out-of-town relatives who keep threatening to visit you here in Colorado. Dale's supplies

Dale's Exotic Game Meats

308 Walnut Street
Brighton 80601
(800) BUY–WILD or
(303) 659–8796
www.nativegame.bigstep.com

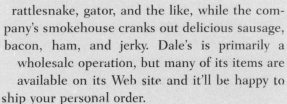

many restaurants with buffalo, elk, rattlesnake, gator, and the like, while the company's smokehouse cranks out delicious sausage, bacon, ham, and jerky. Dale's is primarily a wholesale operation, but many of its items are available on its Web site and it'll be happy to ship your personal order.

August: **The Lafayette Peach Festival,** Old Town Lafayette on Public Road, Lafayette; (303) 926–4352. In August, when Colorado's peaches are at their finest, the town of Lafayette goes crazy for the fuzzy fruits at this annual harvest festival. Feast on peach goodies like cobbler, muffins, ice cream, and smoothies, or just eat your fill of juicy fresh

Colorado peaches right off the farm. You'll also find dozens of other peachy paraphernalia, including peach candles, potpourri, soaps, and bath products. An antiques show and a juried art show are also held during the festival, which raises funds for Lafayette's community events.

August: **Boulder County Farmers' Market Farm Tour,** various locations, Boulder; (303) 910–2236; www.boulderfarmers.org. One day every summer, the family farms of Boulder invite the public to experience how they work. This is a self-guided tour of farms that are part of the Boulder County Farmers' Market. See as many farms as you like during the day. No need to follow any particular order; just pack a picnic and drive or bike to the farms you fancy.

Mid-September through Halloween: **Rocky Mountain Pumpkin Ranch Harvest Festival,** Rocky Mountain Pumpkin Ranch, 9057 Ute Highway (Colorado 66), Longmont; (303) 684–0087; www.rockymtn pumpkinranch.com. Offering a fun festival for the whole family, this Longmont farm has a pick-your-own-pumpkin patch and a fresh-produce market during the fall harvest season. A maze made entirely from hay bales is a challenge for youngsters, and the petting zoo is a good opportunity for city slickers to get up close and personal with farm animals. Tours of the farm are available upon request. Carnival rides are brought in during the weekend prior to Halloween. Mid-September through Halloween, daily from 9:00 A.M. to 6:00 P.M.

October: **March of Dimes Signature Chefs,** The Onmi Interlocken Resort, 500 Interlocken Boulevard, Broomfield; (303) 692–0011; www.marchofdimes.com. A lavish buffet dinner is the cornerstone of this popular event that benefits the March of Dimes, with tastings offered from two dozen of the area's top chefs plus a silent and live auction.

Learn to Cook

Cooking School of the Rockies, 637 South Broadway, Suite H, Boulder; (303) 494–7988; www.cookingschoolrockies. com. Whether you're a home cook or an aspiring chef, the Cooking School of the Rockies has a comprehensive schedule with classes to meet every need. Home cooks can study basic techniques, food and wine pairing, ethnic specialties, pastry techniques, bread making, vegetarian cooking, and entertaining ideas. The school's professional division offers three different programs for career chefs. The six-month Culinary Arts program is designed to efficiently train students in the art of restaurant cooking. The Chef Track, a twenty-four-week, part-time, evening program, is designed and taught by sixteen top Colorado chefs. For those who want to learn the fine art of baking desserts, the Pastry Arts program is an intensive four-week class covering the essential techniques of making pastry and baking.

The school also offers the France Food and Wine Experience, a fantastic weeklong stay at a seventeenth-century chateau. Students begin the day at the local market choosing fresh ingredients for the evening meal and have a hands-on class to learn the cooking techniques. The classes are supplemented by visits to wineries and artisan food producers, wine lectures, and more.

Peggy Markel's Culinary Adventures, P.O. Box 54, Boulder 80306; (800) 988–2851 or (303) 413–1289; www.cookinitaly.com. I figured out what I'm going to ask Santa for next year, and he won't be able to fit it in his bag. Peggy Markel orchestrates fabulous weeklong trips to Italy for people who love to cook and eat. Sign me up! The Tuscany trip, which is offered the most frequently, is a heavenly week at a villa that was formerly a fourteenth-century monastery. A small group of about fifteen people enjoy the relaxed atmosphere and cooking lessons at the state-of-the-art kitchen on the property. Professional chef Piero Ferrini instructs students in Italian while Peggy translates; language differences fade away as he demonstrates how to prepare dishes like *Pollo al Rosmarino e Salvia* (rosemary and sage chicken). The group enjoys an excursion every day, perhaps to a local bakery, herb farm, vineyard, or market. Peggy also takes groups to groups to Morocco, Sicily, and Elba. Call for a complimentary brochure.

Savory Palette Gourmet Retreats, 81 Cree Court, Lyons; (303) 823–0530; www.expressionretreats.com. Cookbook author, teacher, gourmet chef, and entrepreneur: Deborah DeBord has combined her passions into a highly successful business, designing retreats for those who love to cook and enjoy fine food. During your stay in a comfortably furnished cabin in the woods near Estes Park, Deborah will guide

Judi's Granola

I have been teased all my adult life about being from Boulder. People assume that I must be a Birkenstock-wearing, tree-hugging, liberal granola-eater. I knew we had to have a granola recipe in this book, in honor of my fellow Boulderites! This recipe, prepared by Judi Schultze of the Inn on Mapleton Hill in Boulder, is one of her most popular breakfast requests. It's not only delicious, it's also low-fat and healthy, something all Boulder people will surely appreciate.

2 cups rolled oats (do not use quick or instant)
⅛ cup wheat germ
⅛ cup shredded coconut
¼ cup roasted, unsalted sunflower seeds
⅛ cup brown sugar
⅛ cup canola oil
¼ cup honey
Generous splash of pure vanilla extract
Dash of salt

1. Preheat the oven to 350° F. In a mixing bowl, combine all the ingredients thoroughly with a fork. Spread in a 9 x 12-inch metal baking pan. Bake for 15 minutes.
2. Remove from oven, stir, spread in pan again, and bake for another 5 minutes or until golden brown and the whole house smells wonderful! Let cool totally before storing in an airtight plastic container.

Makes about 2½ cups, or 4 to 5 servings.

The Inn on Mapleton Hill

1001 Spruce Street
Boulder 80302
(800) 276-6528 or
(303) 449-6528
www.innonmapleton hill.com

Owners Judi and Ray Schultze serve a complete breakfast for guests every morning, and Judi has written a wonderful cookbook of some of her most-requested recipes, which she sells at the inn.

Italian Food:
Two Palate-Pleasing Perspectives

You like-a Italian? Two of Colorado's top Italian restaurants are within a few miles of each other, offering vastly different interpretations of our state's most popular cuisine.

At one end of the spectrum is the perennially popular restaurant, **The Blue Parrot** (640 Main Street, Louisville 80027; 303–666–0677; $). Louisville has long been known as a destination for Italian food, and four generations of the Colacci family have run The Blue Parrot, which first opened in 1919. Although it burned down in the 1980s, the family rebuilt it, right down to the trademark neon sign out front.

The menu offers a variety of Italian dishes, including ravioli and lasagna, but it's the spaghetti that reigns supreme: homemade, thick, perfectly cooked noodles that are squiggly and uneven and hold the delicious sauce just right. You'll have to decide whether you want a giant meatball or a link of Italian sausage on the side; neither is remarkable, but either choice will be just fine. Your waitperson will bring a pitcher of spaghetti sauce to the table, which you'll probably use up. (For a real treat, hit The Blue Parrot for breakfast, and order eggs, Italian sausage, thick Italian toast, and a side of spaghetti. You won't need to eat again until dinnertime!)

In neighboring Lafayette, **Rezzo** (211 North Public Road, Lafayette 80026; 303–666–2154; $$) has been attracting a lot of attention for its innovative, more modern preparation of Italian cuisine. Chef James Mazzio—who was named one of the top new chefs by *Food & Wine* magazine back in 1999—consulted with Rezzo, bringing his creative interpretation to such favorites as spaghetti, meatballs, and lasagna. The steamed Prince Edward Island mussels cooked in a garlicky white wine broth and the spinach salad are stars unto themselves; most of the menu items can be ordered individually or in family portions. Be sure to save room for the homemade *panna cotta* for dessert.

you in learning new culinary techniques and processes while you prepare menus designed especially for you. Do you need to cook a diet that is gluten-free? Diabetic? Vegetarian? Or perhaps you want to learn how to cook on a grill? Or cook Italian? It's up to you. Deborah will guide you through the processes, perhaps starting with basic knife techniques, working through cooking without recipes, and concluding with ideas about table settings. At the end of the class, enjoy your meal with a glass of wine and bask in the serenity of the property. A culinary library is nearby for browsing, and the hot tub is always warm.

School of Natural Cookery, P.O. Box 19466, Boulder 80308; (303) 444–8068; www.naturalcookery.com. Boulder's well-known natural cooking school first opened its doors in 1983 with classes for home cooks; in 1991 the school expanded its curriculum to include a professional program. In both programs, students study vegetarian food preparation techniques and philosophy and learn how to cook intuitively, without recipes. Classes for home cooks focus on four main areas: Grains, Beans, Vegetables, and Sauces; Soups, Tofu, Tempeh, Desserts, and Meal Composition; Improvisation and Knife Skills; and Ethnic Dishes. Most meals are prepared without animal or dairy products. Call or visit the Web site for a brochure and schedule.

Stir It Up Cooking School, P.O. Box 1486, Boulder 80306; (303) 494–2665; www.stiritupcooking.com. Carol Wiggins teaches small, hands-on classes for kids, teens, singles, and couples in her South Boulder home. Couples and singles, enjoy learning techniques for preparing ethnic cuisines like Japanese, Mediterranean, and Thai—

often taught by guest chefs. Carol's popular gingerbread house decorating classes are a fun family activity during the holidays. Participants learn how to use a decorator bag, assemble the house, and create beautiful scalloped roofs, painted trees, and other toothsome details. The school also teaches a Junior Chefs' program for kids ages seven to eleven and a Saturday Chefs program for young people twelve to fifteen years old; a recent menu from the Oriental cooking class included Tasty Chicken Stir Fry, Chinese Fried Rice, and Mango Pudding. Week-long summer camps for 7- to 15-year-olds teach techniques for making popular offerings like sushi, spring rolls, baked chicken, lasagna, desserts, and homemade ice cream.

A Taste of Class, 1159 Eagle Drive, Loveland; (970) 669–5653; www.tasteofclass.com. Guest chefs teach cooking classes on a variety of subjects in the spacious demonstration kitchen of this gift basket shop owned by Eileen Heusinkveld. Along with the always-popular Wilton cake decorating classes, the shop offers decidely gourmet workshops; past subjects have included food and wine pairing, Southwestern foods, sushi making, Greek cooking, bread baking, South Asian cuisine, and tortilla making. Most classes are held on weeknights or Saturdays, and a current class schedule is always posted on the store's Web site.

Vegetarian Cooking Classes, 33001 Alpine Lane, Evergreen; (303) 674–0955; www.vegancooks.com. "There are all kinds of ways to make vegetarian foods beautiful, delicious, enticing, and nutritious," Vicki Johnston declares. And if you attend her cooking

The Next Best Thing to Sunday Dinner at Grandma's

In the charming small town of Berthoud between Loveland and Longmont, the Wayside Inn serves "supper" in a comfortable dining room that makes you feel like one of the family. The specialty—hands down—is the pan-fried chicken. Hot, crispy, golden brown, and not greasy, it's the most-ordered entree at this restaurant which has been serving it since 1922. There are plenty of sides to go with the chicken: salads, homemade soups (cream of chicken is a staple, as is a soup du jour), cottage cheese (with peaches if you wish), mashed potatoes, baked potatoes, french fries, and vegetables. Finish your meal with a slice of homemade pie or a dish of ice cream.

The Wayside Inn
505 Mountain Avenue
Berthoud 80513
(970) 532–2013
$

classes, she'll share her secrets with you. Vicki began immersing herself in the study and art of vegetarian cooking in the 1970s; she has been teaching her popular classes in her spacious home kitchen in Evergreen for over ten years. Although she grew up with "a meat and potatoes diet," she experienced greater health and energy when she switched to a vegan diet.

Her menus emphasize the use of whole foods rather than processed foods, and she teaches basic cooking techniques, cooking with seasonal foods, food theory, and food categorizing. Whole grains are used rather than processed flours; natural sweeteners instead of sugar; vegetable proteins instead of meat. A popular bean class teaches students how to make pâtés, spreads, dips, sauces, soups, and casseroles from the high-protein legumes. Desserts are prepared with natural sweeteners, and cookies are made without eggs or butter, using ground nuts and oils instead. The classes are small and intimate, held in Evergreen and other Front Range locations; call for a current schedule.

West Pawnee Ranch Bed & Breakfast, 29451 Weld County Road 130, Grover; (970) 895–2482; www.westpawneeranch.com. This popular bed-and-breakfast is a working ranch located 4 miles from the Pawnee National Grassland. Every March, owners Paul and Louanne Timm invite Beverly Cox, author of *Spirit of the Earth: Native Cooking from Latin America,* to instruct cooking classes at the inn. After a brief history lesson about Latin American culture and foods, Beverly teaches students how to prepare specialties like Guatemalan black bean tamales, Yucatán-style pork ribs, tomato and jalapeño salsa, quinoa griddle cakes, and prickly pear pineapple tossed with mescal and honey. Call for a schedule.

What's Cooking, 2770 Arapahoe Road at 95th Street, Suite 112, Lafayette; (303) 666–0300; www.whatscookinginc.com. A variety of classes are taught in the spacious demonstration kitchen of this cooking store (see page 177). Guest chefs demonstrate subjects such as basic knife skills, preparing ethnic cuisine, and how to best pair wine and food. Of note is that popular instructor Mei Hamilton regularly teaches healthy Chinese cooking here, emphasizing easy preparation methods and authentic, delicious flavors.

Learn about Wine

West End Wine Shop, 777-C Pearl Street, Boulder; (303) 245–7077; www.westendwineshop.com. This friendly wine shop hosts a variety of wine tastings at area restaurants several times a month, gearing the popular events to the seasons and a special theme. Previous events have focused on topics such as "Wines from France," "Wines of the Southern Hemisphere," "Great Wine Values," and "Hard-to-Find Wines." In the sit-down tastings, the restaurant chef prepares the food to match the wines from a particular winery. Wines are tasted with each course, followed by a discussion of how the attributes of the wine pair with the food. The shop also hosts "walk-around" tastings, in which food is served buffet-style and wines from a number of wineries are served. Tasters sample the foods and wines, learn from discussions, and jot down their impressions on tasting sheets.

Landmark Eateries

Chautauqua Dining Hall, 900 Baseline Road, Boulder 80302; (303) 440–3776; www.chautauquadininghall.com; $$. The Chautauqua movement started as a way to bring culture—classes, lectures, concerts—to rural communities across the nation. One of the first Chautauquas opened in Boulder in 1898, in a breathtaking location at the base of the Flatirons. Today Boulder's Chautauqua is on the National Register of Historic Places, one of the few remaining such organizations in the nation. The Chautauqua Dining Hall is certainly doing its part to add to the area's culinary enlightenment, serving wonderful meals year-round in the beautifully restored dining hall. Executive Chef Bradford Heap uses top-quality organic and local ingredients whenever possible, preparing even the basics with flair and creativity. Consider a salad: Heap might pair local goat cheese and pears with baby field greens and top it with balsamic vinaigrette and spiced pecans. Or try roasted chicken: Under Heap's hand it's cooked under a brick until the rosemary-rubbed skin is crispy and brown, served with old-fashioned mashed potatoes and a silky gravy enlivened with three different types of caramelized onions. Children are truly welcome here and have their own menu; at breakfast real Green Eggs and Ham—green-tinted scrambled eggs served with juicy ham and home fries—will draw a smile from even the smallest of diners. Brunch on the lovely porch is not to be missed, but be sure to make reservations.

Flagstaff House, 1138 Flagstaff Road, Boulder 80301; (303) 442–4640; www.flagstaffhouse.com; $$$. Since 1951 the Flagstaff House has been wowing diners with its fine cuisine and spectacular nighttime views of the lights of Boulder below. The menu changes daily, but a wide selection of beef, local game, and fresh fish is always among the offerings. Appetizers might include pheasant breast, fresh oysters, or a selection of caviars. Entrees are often based on seasonal ingredients, such as Colorado buffalo filet mignon, porcini mushroom–stuffed organic chicken breast, ahi tuna, and Nantucket Bay scallops. Several of the desserts are worth ordering ahead of time—the Hot Liquid Valrhona Chocolate and Almond Cake and the Bailey's and Valrhona Chocolate Soufflé are extraordinary. The wine cellar is abundant, boasting more than 20,000 bottles, and the restaurant often hosts winemaker dinners. One more interesting note: The Flagstaff House sells a number of prepared entrees and foods, plus some of its more novel serving items—two-part martini chilling glasses, Yixing Chinese tea pots, and hand-painted German cordial glasses—online at www.shopflagstaffhouse.com.

The Fort, 19192 Highway 8, Morrison 80465; (303) 697–4771; www.the fort.com; $$$. We had friends in from New York, and they wanted us to take them to a real Colorado restaurant. We chose The Fort, which turned out to be a stroke of brilliance. The adobe restaurant is a replica of Bent's Fort and sits on a ridge in the foothills near Morrison; when we arrived, a campfire was blazing near a full-sized teepee in the courtyard. We settled in at the bar with Hailstones, a sort of primitive mint julep served in a Mason jar. It's made from ice, mint, sugar, and a whiskey called Taos Lightning. Our friends tried the goodies on the Historians' Platter, tentatively at first, and then with gusto: Boudies, hearty frontier sausages re-created from an old French fur-trappers' recipe; Rocky Mountain oysters; guacamole; bison tongue; and peanut butter–stuffed jalapeños. Our waiter seated us at a table by the window with a magnificent view of the Denver city lights. We ordered Gonzales Steak, a grilled New York strip with a pocketful of Hatch chile inside (see recipe, page 204); a hearty soup called The Bowl of the Wife of Kit Carson; and grilled bison filet mignons. When our entrees

The Fort's Buffalo Gonzales Steak

Founder Sam Arnold shares the history of this steak recipe, one of The Fort's most famous:

"On April 1, 1964, Elidio Gonzales, the gifted Taos madero (woodcraftsman) who hand-carved The Fort's Spanish Colonial–style doors and Padre Martinez chairs, came to Denver to give wood-carving demonstrations. When he called me from town for help, hopelessly lost among Denver's one-way streets, I was tempted to repeat to him what he'd told me in late October when, after a heavy snowfall, I'd harangued him for being three months late finishing all of The Fort's doors: "People in Hell are always wanting ice water!" The old adage about always wanting what you couldn't have had taken all the wind out of my sails, and we'd waited another month for the doors to arrive. Now Elidio needed my help. I drove to town and led him back to The Fort, pondering how I could teach him a little April Fool's Day lesson. The solution came to me when he asked for a steak with chiles.

"This is no Mexican restaurant!" I thundered. "We don't have any chile here," I fibbed as I cut a pocket into a thick sirloin and stuffed it with chopped green chiles. "Oh, you damned gringos, you don't know what's good", he replied. "All you eat is meat and potatoes!" I grilled the steak, placed it before a grumbling Elidio, and watched him take a bite. "April Fool, Elidio!" I shouted. "April Fool to you, too!" he replied. "You're the biggest fool for not having this on your menu! Here try it!" I did, and the Gonzales Steak has been one of our most popular dishes ever since. Elidio passed away a few years ago, but his furniture and his steak live on.

–Samuel P. Arnold

12 green Anaheim chiles,
    roasted and peeled
    (canned will do, but fresh
    are best)
Salt
4 cloves garlic, peeled and
    chopped

½ teaspoon Mexican leaf
    oregano
4 10- to12-ounce, thick-cut
    buffalo (bison) strip steaks
2 teaspoons vegetable oil
Freshly ground black pepper
4 teaspoons butter (optional)

1. Slit the chiles to remove the seeds; chop 2 of them into fine dice and mix with the salt, garlic, and oregano. (New Mexicans traditionally like to leave a few of the seeds in the dish. The seeds give it life, they say.)
2. With a very sharp knife, cut a horizontal pocket into each steak. Stuff the chopped chiles into the pocket. Brush the meat and the remaining chiles with the salad oil. Grill the steaks on both sides to the desired doneness. If using buffalo, watch carefully so as not to overcook! Because it contains less fat than chicken, buffalo cooks much faster than beef and is best medium-rare.
3. Salt and pepper the meat. Grill the remaining whole-roasted chiles to get a nice patterning of grid burn on them. Lay them across the steak as a garnish.
4. A teaspoon of brown butter on the steak as a special treat is heaven. To make brown butter, simply melt the butter in a sauté pan over medium-high heat and allow it to turn golden brown.

The Fort

19192 Highway 8
Morrison 80465
(303) 697–4771
www.thefort.com

Makes 4 servings.

(NOTE: *The Fort sells top-quality restaurant-grade buffalo steaks through its online Fort Trading Company, www.forttradingco.com or via telephone, 877–229–2844.*)

arrived, we passed our plates around and shared; our friends said they had never eaten so well.

Sam Arnold, who owns the restaurant with his daughter, Holly, stopped by our table to say hello. In addition to being a well-known restaurateur, Sam is a cookbook author, chef, and historian of foods of the Old West. He regaled us with a few stories and tall tales as we shared an ice cream sundae topped with malt powder and a pinch of gunpowder—a real Colorado meal at a real Colorado restaurant.

The Fort is open daily for dinner; reservations are suggested. The restaurant often sponsors wine and spirit dinners; call for more details.

Frasca, 1738 Pearl Street, Boulder 80302; (303) 442–6966; www.frasca foodandwine.com. $$$. It's true that Frasca's owners—master sommelier Bobby Stuckey and chef Lachlan Mackinnon-Patterson—trained with Thomas Keller at the French Laundry in Yountville, California. But that fact is fading in importance as the restaurant matures and the partners' distinctive talents and vision shine through in both the kitchen and the wine cellar. From the Riedel crystal glassware to the Plugra butter served in classic quenelle shape (that we wanted to eat with a spoon), to the little bowl of faintly pink *fleur de sel*, the art is in the details at Frasca. The serving sizes are restrained, encouraging diners to try an appetizer, a first and second course, and a dessert. A few favorites: the smoked meat platter to start, with a sampling of thinly sliced smoked prosciutto, speck and Oldani Filsette, and skinny fresh breadsticks; handmade cannellini bean *agnolotti* with zucchini and bacon vinaigrette; and a mind-numbingly good banana sundae with chocolate and pistachio ice creams, bananas, warm butterscotch custard, chocolate sauce, and toasted almond crumble. Frasca offers a three-course fixed-price dinner on Monday evenings that is a bargain; call to make reservations. One final note: Mackinnon-Patterson was named one of *Food & Wine* magazine's top new chefs for 2005.

John's Restaurant, 2328 Pearl Street, Boulder 80302; (303) 444–5232; www.johnsrestaurantboulder.com; $$$. A tiny gem of a restaurant in Boulder, John's has been one of my favorite eateries for more than twenty years. Chef/owner John Bizzarro prepares consistently good, creatively prepared, fresh cuisine in his relaxed, unpretentious restaurant housed in a beautiful old cottage tucked away on Pearl Street. The menu changes daily, but it always includes appetizers, pastas, fresh fish, fowl, and beef. One of my favorite touches is that each entree comes with a small cup of the soup of the day. All of John's desserts are made in his kitchen, and the restaurant offers a well-selected wine list as well as beers from local microbreweries. Open for dinner Tuesday to Saturday; reservations suggested.

The Kitchen, 1039 Pearl Street, Boulder 80302; (303) 544–5973; www.the kitchencafe.com. Kimbal Musk and Hugo Matheson are the chefs and owners of Boulder's hottest bistro, The Kitchen, serving breakfast, lunch, and dinner to a grateful crowd of diners. The duo strives to cook with free-range, natural and organic ingredients, preparing an innovative lineup of menu items that is constantly evolving and changing. Here are a few recent highlights: an endive salad tossed with prosciutto, chunks of Parmesan, and drizzled with saba dressing; organic roasted chicken served with soft polenta, *haricots verts,* and topped with a creamy balsamic Bordelaise sauce; and for dessert, a comforting banana bread pudding studded with milk chocolate. Along with consistently great food, the restaurant has a unique philosophy about bringing the community together. There are several popular communal tables where you can sit, eat, and chat with other people, and Monday evenings are dubbed "Community Night," where all diners pay a fixed price for family-style dining; be sure to make reservations for this popular event.

Brewpubs & Microbreweries

Although they're not microbreweries, it's worth noting that both Anheuser-Busch Brewery and Coors Brewery are located in Northeastern Colorado. **Anheuser-Busch** is in Fort Collins (2351 Busch Drive, Fort Collins; 970–490–4500; www.anheuser-busch.com). Tours of its brewery take about an hour and fifteen minutes and are available Thursday through Monday from 10:00 A.M. to 4:00 P.M. (Those hours are extended during the summer; call the tour office at 970–490–4691 for times or to book large groups.)

At Colorado's own **Coors Brewing Company** (311 Tenth Street, Golden; 303–279–6565), free tours are offered Monday through Saturday on a first-come, first-served basis. Tours begin at the visitors' parking lot at the corner of 13th and Ford Streets and run from 10:00 A.M. to 4:00 P.M. every twenty to thirty minutes. The entire tour takes about an hour and a half, and you can sample the company's brewery-fresh beers at the end of the tour.

Coopersmith's Pub & Brewing Company, 5 Old Town Square, Fort Collins; (970) 498–0483; www.coopersmithspub.com. A friendly, casual brewpub in the Old Town area of Fort Collins, Coopersmith's usually has about a dozen of its own handcrafted beers on tap. Two ales, the Punjabi Pale Ale and the Poudre Pale Ale, are year-round favorites, while the refreshing Mountain Avenue Wheat is a popular pour in the summertime. The brewery also offers a variety of seasonal beers, which might include bocks, weizens, Oktoberfest beers, Christmas ales, barley wine, fruit beers, and hard cider. A Sampler Pack is available with either four, five, or six tasters of beers. The pub restaurant has a wide-ranging menu; try the crispy coconut shrimp, excellent burgers and steaks—including a top sirloin with garlic portobello-mushroom sauce—the Highland Cottage Pie, and Bangers & Mash. The bar also has a nice selection of wines and single-malt scotches. Kids are welcome at the friendly brewpub, which makes its own root beer, cream soda, and ginger ale and also provides a children's menu.

Estes Park Brewery, 470 Prospect Village Drive, P.O. Box 2161, Estes Park 80517; (970) 586–5421; www.epbrewery.com. At Estes Park's visitors' center, one of the most-asked questions is, "Can you tell us how to get to the brewery?" Tourists and locals flock to the pub to quaff the microbrewery's deliciously drinkable beers. A light and easy-drinking ale called Stinger Wild Honey Wheat is tied for the distinction of most popular beer here. The brewmeister adds 120 pounds of honey to each batch, which gives the beer a sweeter profile and also raises the alcohol content because the yeast ferments some of the honey. The Longs Peak Raspberry Wheat, the other most-requested brew, is a light

No one had ever heard of Harry and Charlotte Schmidt's *bieroch* sandwich, but word got around quickly enough. When the German couple opened a small bakery in Loveland in 1980, they made many of the "old country" specialties they had both grown up with: German breads and rolls, pastries, bear claws, cinnamon rolls, tortes . . . and *bieroch*. Harry's grandparents had made the tasty German krautburger for years.

"They don't contain sauerkraut," he explains. "It's a combination of cooked cabbage, ground beef, and seasonings, baked inside a special dough. The round buns are topped with sesame seeds and look like a hamburger bun." The rest, as they say, is history. Today

Schmidt's Bakery and Delicatessen

808 14th Street South West
Loveland 80537
(970) 667–9811

Schmidt's includes a delicatessen, bakery and full-service restaurant, and Harry estimates that he has made "about ten million" *bieroch*.

The delicatessen has scores of cold cuts, the bakery's fresh breads, and homemade salads to choose from. The *bieroch* is still the most popular sandwich, but the Reuben sandwich and the multilayered Dagwood sandwich are close seconds. The deli also stocks gourmet foods such as mustards, pickles, candies, pasta, jams, jellies, and ground coffee.

In the sit-down restaurant, the German Streudel is a delicious breakfast treat with sausage, eggs, and imported cheese baked in a flaky puff pastry. European omelets are another specialty. The Greek omelet features spinach, feta cheese, and tomatoes, and the French omelet is filled with marinated chicken, Swiss cheese, and mushrooms.

raspberry-flavored wheat ale. India pale ale lovers rave about the Renegade, a bitter, somewhat darker ale with a pronounced hoppy flavor. The brewery also received a lot of press for its Samson Stout, a commemorative ale created in honor of Samson, the magnificent bull elk, which was poached illegally in Estes Park several years ago. The restaurant has a fairly standard menu with American pub fare: sandwiches, burgers, pizzas, appetizers, steaks, pasta, and brats. An outdoor deck has a fantastic view overlooking Longs Peak.

Gordon Biersch Brewing, 1 West Flatiron Circle, Suite 428, Flatiron Crossing Mall, Broomfield; (720) 887–2991; www.gordonbiersch.com. German-style lagers are the only beers brewed at this popular microbrewery at the Flatiron Crossing Mall—an unusual distinction that results in some deliciously drinkable brews. The Pilsner is quite popular, with a golden color and clean, crisp taste. The Marzen is a quintessential Oktoberfest beer, auburn in color, well balanced, slightly malty, and smooth. Dunkles means "dark" in German, a fitting name for this mahogany-colored beer, smooth and full-bodied with a slightly nutty flavor.

The restaurant serves food that is several notches above typical pub fare. Crispy fried artichoke hearts and cornmeal crab cakes are tantalizing appetizers, while entrees include pizzas, pasta, stir-fried chicken or beef, roast chicken, old-fashioned meatloaf, steaks, and fresh fish. The Banana Split Cheesecake, baked in a chocolate-cookie crust and topped with toasted almonds and fresh-berry sauce, is a delicious way to end your meal. Tours of the brewery facilities are available on request.

Colorado's Famous Truck Stop

It was November of 1998 when *Travel and Leisure* magazine selected Johnson's Corner for serving one of the "Top Ten Best Breakfasts in the World." Joining a roster that included restaurants in Provence and Barcelona, the truck stop was praised for its oversized, sugary cinnamon rolls and Johnson's Corner was put in the national spotlight. Forty-five miles north of Denver, just off highway I–25, Johnson's Corner is a full-service truck stop that has been open since 1951. Serving bountiful breakfasts and truckers' portions of stick-to-your-ribs lunches and dinners, the restaurant is open 365 days a year, twenty-four hours a day. Tuckered-out truckers and tourists alike appreciate the hot coffee, home-style meals, and friendly service.

Johnson's Corner
2842 Southeast Frontage Road
Loveland 80537
(970) 667–2069
www.johnsonscorner.com
$

Left Hand and Tabernash Brewing Co., 1265 Boston Avenue, Longmont; (303) 772–0258; www.lefthandbrewing.com or www.tabernash.com. Left Hand Brewing and Tabernash Brewing merged in 1998, making it one of Colorado's largest handcrafted breweries. Business tactics aside, there's a whole lot of good beer coming out of the company. The Left Hand Sawtooth Ale is an English-style Extra Special Bitter, well balanced with significant hop character, medium body, and a pleasant maltiness. The Tabernash Weiss is an unfiltered German-style wheat beer, with a cloudy, golden appearance and refreshing spicy-fruity taste. Left Hand's Black Jack Porter is a London-style beer; although slightly sweet at the first taste, it finishes with a distinctive roasty flavor. The tasting room is open Monday through Saturday from noon to 6:00 P.M., and you can taste beers or purchase them by the pint, half-gallon, or bottle. Tours are available on Saturday between noon and 3:00 P.M., or by appointment.

Mountain Sun Pub and Brewery, 1535 Pearl Street, Boulder; (303) 546–0886; www.mountainsunpub.com. Proprietor Kevin Daly describes his comfortable neighborhood pub as "the quintessential Boulder place." With its relaxed atmosphere, eclectic clientele, and Grateful Dead posters decorating the walls, it certainly earns the distinction. Unlike most brewpubs, Mountain Sun's bar has twenty-one draft handles, with twelve dedicated to the establishment's home-brewed beers; the remainder are quality draft beers from other breweries. The beer sampler is a good way to taste all those beers; the pub's own Colorado Kind Ale, Java Porter, and Raspberry Wheat are popular pours. Mountain Sun also brews its own root beer. The restaurant menu offers a wide selection of reasonably priced sandwiches, salads, soups, vegetarian entrees; everything is made from scratch. The brewery opened a second location, Southern Sun, at 627 South Broadway, (303) 543–0886.

New Belgium Brewing Company, 500 Linden Street, Fort Collins; (970) 221–0524; www.newbelgium.com. One of Colorado's favorite breweries, New Belgium is the creator and maker of the popular Fat Tire beer. The company attributes the beer's success to its well-balanced, smooth character; scientifically speaking, this is a result of the well-balanced hops and malt ratio. That may be true, but most of us just know Fat Tire as the beer we love to drink. The brewery makes six staple beers, including the also-popular Sunshine Wheat, plus special releases and new, unusual products. The company's new La Folie, for instance, is a wood-aged beer that takes three years to age properly; when finished, it goes well with Stilton and other stinky cheeses. In fact, Belgian beers tend to pair well with food, an advantage that the company tries to highlight with beer-and-food pairing dinners that it hosts at various Colorado restaurants.

The brewery offers guided tours at 2:00 P.M. on weekdays. On Saturday, the tours are held at the top of the hour from 11:00 A.M. to 4:00 P.M. The thirty-minute tours include free tastings of the company's products; a recently expanded tasting room is also open Monday through Saturday from 10:00 A.M. to 6:00 P.M.

O'Dell Brewing Company, 800 East Lincoln Avenue, Fort Collins; (970) 498–9070; www.odellbrewing.com. Since 1989, O'Dell Brewing has been handcrafting beers in the college town of Fort Collins. The company's 90 Shilling is its top-seller, an amber ale that is smooth, medium bodied, and well balanced. Another favorite, Easy Street Wheat, is an unfiltered American-style wheat beer. Visitors are welcome, and the brewery hosts regular tours from 10:00 A.M. to 3:00 P.M. Monday through Friday, and at 2:00 P.M. on Saturday. The tasting room is open Monday through Friday from 10:00 A.M. to 6:00 P.M. and Saturday from noon to 5:00 P.M.

Rockies Brewing Company, 2880 Wilderness Place, Boulder; (303) 444–8448; www.boulderbeer.com. "Hazed and Infused" is one of the

A Tale of Two Cities: Boulder's Dushanbe Teahouse

In 1987, the mayor of Dushanbe, Tajikistan, visited Boulder and offered to present the city with a teahouse to celebrate the establishment of sister-city ties. For the next four years, more than forty Tajikistan artisans worked to create the decorative elements of the stunning structure. Today, the Boulder Dushanbe Teahouse is a magical place to sip delicious teas, relax, and marvel at the surroundings. Outside, one of the largest rose gardens in Boulder surrounds the garden-patio seating area. The restaurant offers a full menu of appetizers, salads, and entrees, with offerings from Bali, Tibet, and Thailand, plus several fabulous desserts including gingerbread, apple crumble, and a luscious chocolate truffle sampler. English-style afternoon tea is offered each day between 3:00 and 5:00 P.M.; make reservations at least twenty-four hours in advance.

Boulder Dushanbe Teahouse

1770 13th Street
Boulder 80302
(303) 442–4993
www.boulderteahouse.com
$

Workshops and classes are offered regularly in subjects like brewing the perfect pot of tea, blending your own herbal teas, and preparing a formal tea ceremony; call or visit the Web site for a current schedule. The teahouse also hosts the Rocky Mountain Tea Festival every summer. The three-day event features seminars and tastings, a retail tea bazaar, a Saturday night four-course tea dinner with tea used in each dish, and a children's teddy-bear tea party on Sunday afternoon.

most popular beers at this Boulder microbrewery, an amber-colored brew left in its natural, unfiltered state and "infused with hoppy goodness," according to the bartenders. The Single Track Copper Ale is another widely haled ale, a refreshing, crisp, full-flavored beer with a clean finish. The pub menu is full of surprises. Munch on the Chips and Gravy—crispy, thick-cut potato chips served with a side of gravy—my kind of stuff. Fish and chips is a popular entree offering, as is the Porter Bratwurst, marinated in the pub's own porter beer. For dessert, the deep-fried Snickers Sundae features the chewy candy bar, wrapped in a flour tortilla; fried until it's crispy and golden brown on the outside, oozing and melted on the inside; and served with ice cream, chocolate, whipped cream, and a cherry. Whew! The Porter Milkshake is another interesting and delicious dessert—porter beer mixed with vanilla ice cream. During the summer, request a seat on the brewpub's patio with its gorgeous view of the Flatirons. Brewery tours, held Monday through Friday at 2:00 P.M., last about an hour.

Rockyard Brewing, 880 West Castleton Road, Castle Rock; (303) 814–9273; www.rockyard.com. A friendly brewpub in Castle Rock, Rockyard Brewing always has half a dozen of its regular beers on tap plus a couple of specially made seasonal brews. One of the most-ordered beers is the Double Eagle Ale, a light-colored, full-bodied beer with a smooth taste, similar in style to a German Helles beer. Another favorite is the Redhawk Ale, which won a silver medal in the World Beer Championships; it's amber in color, full-bodied, complex, and somewhat malty, similar to an English ale.

The restaurant menu has plenty of creatively prepared cuisine. A hearty snack that goes perfectly with a pint of ale is the artichoke-ale dip, made with Redhawk ale and served in its own bread bowl with tortilla chips. The Caribbean andouille sausage and shrimp pasta is a popular entree. The pub has "happy hour" every weekday from 3:00 to 6:00 P.M., with reduced prices on house brews. If you think you're going to be really thirsty, the brewery also sells a 64-ounce refillable "Growler" or a 2.25-gallon "Party Pig" to go.

Northeast Colorado Wine Trail

Augustina's Winery, 4715 North Broadway, B-3, Boulder; (303) 545–2047. Proprietor Marianne Walter—owner, winemaker, and marketing department for her one-woman company—will welcome you warmly to her small winery located just north of Boulder. Several of her firm's wines are made with favorite Colorado activities in mind. A "backpacking wine," for instance, has a bouquet reminiscent of the outdoors; a "porch wine" is a slightly sweet white, perfect for drinking outside on a warm summer evening; and her "theater wine," a Chardonnay, is one that she pours at the Nomad Theater in the nearby town of Niwot. Her "Wine Chick" label includes a Rosé, a red, and a Cabernet-Merlot blend. The winery's selection changes, but in addition to her mainstays she usually offers a small batch of cherry wines every year. The tasting room is open during the summer on Saturday and Sunday from noon to 5:00 P.M., or call at other times for an appointment.

Book Cliff Vineyards, 5501 Aztec Court, Boulder; (303) 499–7301; www.bookcliffvineyards.com. Book Cliff opened in 1999 and is quickly becoming well known for its award-winning Ensemble—a Bordeaux varietal blend—and Viognier wines, as well as Cabernet Sauvignon, Chardonnay, Merlot, and a Black Muscat grape dessert wine. Book Cliff is a regular fixture at the Boulder Farmers' Market (see page 178), where you can sample the latest offerings.

Boulder Creek Winery, 6440 Odell Place, Boulder; (303) 516–9031; www.bouldercreekwine.com. One of our state's newest wineries offers handcrafted traditional varietals including Merlot, Chardonnay, Cabernet Sauvignon, and Cabernet Franc, as well as a special release Reserve Blend of premium red varieties. The tasting room is open during April and May and October through December on Saturday and Sunday from 2:00 to 5:00 P.M., and from June to September Wednesday through Sunday from 1:00 to 6:00 P.M.

Creekside Cellars Winery and Italian Deli, 28036 Highway 74, Evergreen; (303) 674–5460; www.creeksidecellars.net. What a treasure Creekside Cellars is, located right on the main street—Highway 74—that runs through Evergreen. The Donahue family produces award-winning wines including Chardonnay, Bianco, Viognier, Rosé, Rosso, Syrah, Cabernet Franc, Cabernet Sauvignon, Merlot, and several port wines. The tasting area is adjacent to a terrific Italian deli, where we ordered a huge antipasto platter (be sure to ask for some of the cheese-stuffed marinated peppers), homemade soup, and freshly baked focaccia to accompany the wines we tried. In warmer months the outdoor deck is a lovely perch, right over Bear Creek.

Medovina, 308 Third Avenue, P.O. Box 629, Niwot 80544; (303) 845–3090; www.medovina.com. I can't think of a more romantic drink than Medovina's Stringing Rose mead, created with hand-picked rose petals gently steeped, blended with honey and fermented. The fruity Paonia Peach mead is made from organic peaches blended with honey, and Medovina also produces a less sweet Classic Mead, the medium sweet Melissa, and Harvest Apple Honey Wine (a blend of honey wine and apple cider). Call first to visit the meadery, or sample the wines at the Boulder Farmers' Market (see page 178).

Redstone Meadery, 4700 Pearl Street, Unit 2-A, Boulder; (720) 406–1215; www.redstonemeadery.com. As of this writing, Redstone was the only meadery in the country producing a draft mead. The meads are: Nectar (sparkling meads), Mountain Honey Wine, and Redstone Reserve. Visitors to the tasting room enjoy free samples. As well, the Meadery offers a free half-hour tour Monday through Friday at 3:00 P.M. and on Saturday at 12:30 P.M.

Spruce Mountain Meadery, 1218 Yarnell Drive, Larkspur; (719) 351–4909; www.sprucemountainmeadery.com. According to the wine-makers at Spruce Mountain, mead is "the stuff of legends, believed to bring power and victory to warriors, as well as harmony and poetry to lovers." Sounds like as good an excuse as any to sample one of Spruce Mountain's offerings: Traditional Mead, Spiced Mead, Fruit Mead, or a sparkling mead called Ambrosia. The meadery also offers bottles with customized labels for those who want mead as a part of a wedding or other important celebration. A "Spring Fling" revelry and tasting is held each May, and the meadery is happy to arrange private tours and tastings, but be sure to call first to make arrangements.

Trail Ridge Winery, 4113 West Eisenhower Boulevard, Loveland; (970) 635–0949; www.trailridgewinery.com. If you're driving through Big Thompson Canyon from Estes Park or Rocky Mountain National Park, Trail Ridge Winery will be on your way into Loveland. After all those souvenir shops, the winery's tasting room might be a welcome

respite; stop and sample Trail Ridge's offerings, which are produced from Colorado grapes, apples, and cherries. The firm makes Riesling, Gewürztraminer, Chardonnay, Merlot, Cabernet Franc, Lemberger, fruit wines, Never Summer White, and other special blends. The tasting room is open seven days a week during summer months, from 10:00 A.M. until 5:00 P.M. During spring and autumn, it's open Wednesday through Sunday from 10:00 A.M. to 5:00 P.M.

Valley of the Wind Winery, 411 North Railroad Avenue, Loveland; (970) 461–1885; www.valleyofthewind.com. Patrick and Geri McGibney own one of Colorado's newest wineries located in the foothills west of Loveland. The tasting room is open Thursday and Friday from 4:30 to 8:00 P.M. and Saturday from 2:00 to 8:00 P.M.

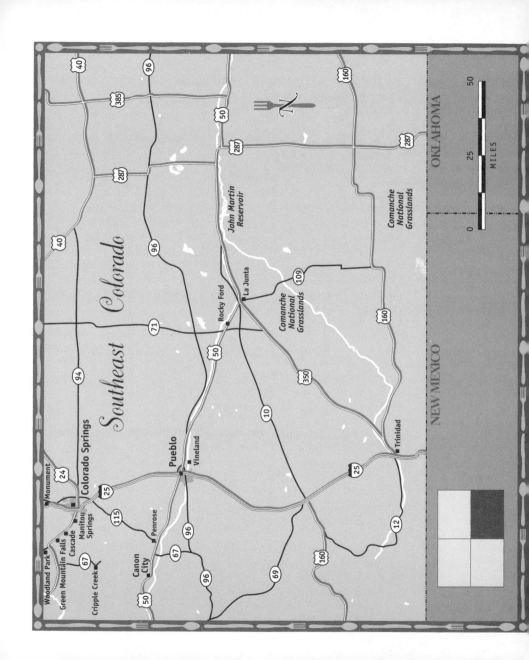

Southeast Colorado

This area includes Colorado Springs, the state's second-largest city, which is rich in history, architecture, scenery, and good food. Situated near the base of Pikes Peak, the area is a destination for many travelers; food lovers will find attractions like Cave of the Winds and Garden of the Gods secondary in appeal to the sizable number of candy stores, cider stands, ice cream shops, and excellent restaurants located nearby. The historic Broadmoor Hotel is a sparkling gem set in the foothills, with several top-flight restaurants and a gourmet kitchen shop inside.

In the 1800s, the Santa Fe Trail wound through southeastern Colorado, between Independence, Missouri, and Santa Fe, New Mexico. Many of the historic towns that are still in existence in this area were original settlements. The small town of Penrose has been a successful apple orchard community for many years. Back in 1935, the neighboring towns of Canon City, Florence, and Penrose decided to host an event to bring together their residents. Penrose's Apple Day Celebration is still in existence today; read on to find out why it's such a well-attended event.

The region is also a thriving farming area. Pueblo's climate is ideal for growing peppers, and the Pueblo chile pepper is considered by many to be the very finest. The Chile and Frijoles Festival held every September is a celebration of the spicy cuisine of the region. Rocky Ford is synonymous to most Coloradoans with the word "melon." The sweet cantaloupe, honeydew, and muskmelon start arriving in stores toward the end of the summer, from the town known as the "Watermelon Capital of the World."

Made Here

DiNardo's Cider Mill and Farm Market, 1400 Royal Gorge Boulevard, Canon City 81212; (719) 275-2727. Twin brothers Albert and Mario DiNardo have been making their own brand of delicious, all-natural cider for years. In addition to the #1 seller—cherry cider—the boys make apple, boysenberry, blueberry, blackberry, loganberry, Concord grape, and strawberry cider. In the springtime, they offer bedding plants; in the summertime, they sell homegrown produce including fresh corn and vine-ripened tomatoes; in the autumn, they have fresh fruit from local orchards; and during December, they sell Christmas trees. The market is stocked year-round with locally produced jams, jellies, pickles, baking mixes, and more.

Michelle Chocolatiers & Ice Cream, 122 North Tejon, Colorado Springs 80903; (719) 633-5089; www.michellecandies.com. If visiting Michelle's brings on a bout of nostalgia, it may be because the shop is one of the rare holdovers of the candy shops and ice-cream parlors that were so popular in the last century. That old-fashioned flavor comes from a long history; Michelle's was founded in 1952 by the Michopoulos family of Colorado Springs. Today the company is still family-owned and even employs several fourth-generation Michopoulos'.

The firm is well known for its handmade chocolates, all created in Colorado Springs; there are dozens of soft, chewy, crispy, or nutty centers to choose from, plus English toffee, fudge, cherry cordials, peanut brittle, and coconut crisp. Old-fashioned ribbon candy is made during the holidays, and hand-dipped Easter eggs appear in the glass cases during the springtime, some as large as fifteen pounds!

The company also sells its own line of ice-cream toppings, which leads us to the next battalion of temptations at Michelle's. Gourmet ice creams come in more than forty different flavors; a few favorites include espresso, rocky road, Dutch mocha chip, and cherry Bordeaux. The ice cream parlor also specializes in fantastical sundae creations; the "Believe It or Not" sundae was featured in *Life* magazine. The colossal creation consists of a Neapolitan–ice cream base layered with cake, ice cream, more cake, more ice cream, whipped cream, nuts, and cherries; this monster feeds twenty-five people!

Michelle's has two other stores, one at the Citadel Mall in Colorado Springs and another in Greenwood Village (6880 South Clinton Street, 720–482–8390). All three stores have restaurants that serve breakfast, lunch, and dinner daily. Candies can also be ordered online.

Nettie's Colorado Candies, 109 Colorado Avenue, Pueblo 81004; (719) 543–4631. Since the 1940s, Nettie's has been a beloved candy company in Pueblo, producing a full line of handcrafted chocolates. Glass cases are seductively arranged with irresistible fudges, truffles, chocolate creams (with sixteen different kinds of centers), peanut brittles, caramels, caramel/chocolate/nut "critters," jelly beans, and a surprising assortment of sugar-free candies. A half block down the street, you'll find **Nettie's Gourmet Shoppe** (119 East Abriendo, Pueblo; 719–562–4316). There owner Aileen Warfield says she sells all the other gourmet goodies that were tempting her every year at specialty food shows. You'll find a wide array of jams, jellies, soups, rices, gourmet foods, coffee beans, teas, oils, vinegars, and more. Looking for a gift and can't make up your mind? Both shops are happy to make up a gift basket with assorted Nettie's products.

Patsy's Candies, 1540 South 21st Street, Colorado Springs 80904; (719) 633–7215 or (888) 472–8797; www.patsyscandies.com. Tired of your kids rolling their eyes when you begin a story with "Back when I was a kid . . . "? The perfect antidote is a trip to Patsy's old-fashioned country store, where candy is made fresh daily and there are often free samples of fresh candy to be had. Patsy's old-fashioned taffy is—dare I say it?—even better than the saltwater taffy I remember from my childhood candy store.

Since 1903 the Niswonger family has been cooking up crowd-pleasing candies and confections, and the almond toffee is still the company's most popular offering. The crunchy, almond-laden, golden center is dipped in a thick layer of smooth milk chocolate and generously coated with more freshly ground almonds. The company ships

Thelma's Washboard Cookies

These crispy little cookies, with their fork tine impressions, are reminiscent of an old wooden washboard. This recipe, submitted by Thelma Eastham, first appeared in the cookbook, Castle Cookery, published by the Manitou Springs Historical Society in 1978. The book was used as a fund-raiser to help pay for the ongoing restoration of the forty-six-room Miramont Castle, built in 1895 and purchased by the society in 1971. The castle museum, which houses a nice tea room serving sandwiches, homemade desserts, sundaes, and ice-cream sodas, is located at 9 Capital Avenue in Manitou Springs.

2 cups brown sugar	4½ cups all-purpose flour
1 cup vegetable shortening	1½ teaspoons baking powder
2 eggs	1 teaspoon baking soda
1 cup sweetened flaked coconut	¼ teaspoon salt
1 teaspoon vanilla extract	¼ cup hot water

1. Preheat the oven to 350° F. Grease a large cookie sheet. In a large bowl, cream together the brown sugar and shortening until thoroughly mixed. Add the eggs and stir until well combined. Add the coconut and vanilla and stir well.

2. In a separate bowl, combine the flour, baking powder, baking soda, and salt; stir well.

**Miramont Castle Museum/
The Manitou Springs
Historical Society**

9 Capital Avenue
Manitou Springs 80829
(719) 685-1011

3. Add the dry ingredients in 3 parts to the sugar mixture alternately with the hot water. Beat the batter until smooth after each addition.

4. Form the dough into walnut-sized balls and arrange on the baking sheet. Flatten with a fork that has been dipped in cold water. Bake for 8 minutes or until light brown. Remove to a wire rack.

Makes about 10 dozen 2-inch cookies.

all its chocolates next-day UPS with an ice pack so you can enjoy them at home just like you were right there in the shop. Your kids will probably be telling their kids about Patsy's Candies someday.

Peppers Plus, 2115 Santa Fe Drive, Pueblo 81006; (719) 546–3137; www.farmerfixins.com. Can you say "Zippy Pickle Snackers" fast ten times? The potent pickles, canned in dill brine with garlic, jalapeño and Pueblo chile, are a popular offering from this third-generation farm family, along with similarly savory Zippy Tomatoes, Zippy Asparagus Mix, and Hot Mama Zucchini. Garlic From Hell is a fiery combination of garlic and jalapeño peppers, while Sweet Daddy Beets combine fresh homegrown red beets with a touch of jalapeño pepper. The farm even cans pumpkin with cinnamon and clove spices in its popular Pumpkin Delight. Popcorn and homegrown pinto beans are available in jars or bulk; order Peppers Plus products by telephone or online.

Pueblo Chili Company, 39651 South Road, Vineland 81006; (719) 948–4556; www.pueblochilico.com. In the small town of Vineland, about twenty minutes from Pueblo, the Pueblo Chili Company grows all manner of chile peppers, from the milder cubanelle to the hotter jalapeño to the downright fiery habañero. "The climate in Pueblo is just right for growing peppers," explains owner Joe Pantaleo. "Our chile peppers are thick and meaty and noticeably more flavorful than peppers grown in other parts of the country." His company specializes in chile products; the latest offering is a fire-roasted chile that is dehydrated.

The resulting product tastes "better than frozen," Joe promises, and it's easy to store and ship. The firm also sells dried red chile peppers. If you're in the area, stop by and purchase some of the company's famous bulk sausage, seasoned with its homegrown Pueblo chiles.

Specialty Stores & Markets

Cheyenne Gourmet, Broadmoor Hotel, 1 Lake Avenue, Colorado Springs; (719) 577-5823. This is a store that is serious in its commitment to cooks. Every day at 11:00 A.M. and 2:00 P.M., a cooking demonstration takes place in the shop. As the aromas drift out the door, the shop soon attracts a crowd to watch Broadmoor chefs or store employees teach the fine art of cooking. The store stocks a large gourmet food inventory, with chutneys, oils, vinegars, pestos, crackers, cookies, candies, preserves, pretzel dips, olives, salsas, bean dip, tortilla chips, pretzels, baking mixes, soup mixes, fudge mixes, hot spiced cider mixes, salsa mixes, and much more. This is the place to come for a chocolate fix; the store carries a number of local and imported brands. Is it caffeine you crave? The shop stocks teas, tea accessories, and the Broadmoor's own blend of coffee. You'll also find cooking gadgets, picnic baskets, glassware, copper pieces, pot racks, butcher-block tables, cookbooks, gifts, and more. The store employees will gladly assemble a gift basket for you; just ask.

The Gourmet's Pantry, 4510 Oro Blanco Drive, Colorado Springs; (719) 597-4545. This aptly named shop is a treasure trove for people who love to cook and eat, offering a butcher shop, fresh seafood, deli meats and cheeses, unusually shaped Italian pastas and sauces, imported crackers and chocolates, olives, plenty of unusual ingredients for ethnic cuisines, and a good selection of cheeses—more than 200 kinds, in fact. The staff often sets out samples of the store's wares to tempt shoppers; the last time we visited we nibbled on Belgian semisweet chocolate and caramel apple butter—and both ended up in our shopping bag.

Joe Tomato Italian Delicacies, 3000½ North Elizabeth, Pueblo; (719) 584–3007. *Mama mia!* This Italian market has so many good things to choose from, you won't know where to start. A full deli is stocked with meats and cheeses; the "Dutch Lunch" is a popular luncheon plate that consists of three meats, three cheeses, bread, peppers, onions, and sliced tomatoes. There are scores of cut and whole cheeses to choose from: Italian asiago cheese, goat cheeses, and local and imported varieties. There are plenty of fresh produce, grocery items, imported pastas, sauces, olive oils, vinegars, herbs and spices, jams, jellies and preserves, pickled garlic and asparagus, as well as regular pickles, and too much more to mention. The store is open every day except Sunday.

Mollica's, 985-A Garden of the Gods Road, Colorado Springs; (719) 598–1088; www.restauranteur.com/mollicas. This family-run Italian market, deli, and restaurant has been owned by the Mollica family since 1987. Hands down, Mollica's specialty

is the homemade Italian sausage;
five different varieties are made
fresh daily from the recipe that was
handed down from Jerry Mollica's grandfather. Besides
the sausage, the market sells homemade and imported pastas, including
flavored pastas like tomato and spinach. There are also shaped pastas
like spaghetti, fettuccine, linguine, ravioli, lasagna, and tortellini, and
several kinds of homemade sauces to go with them. The deli offers a full
selection of imported meats and cheeses, plus a large assortment of
olives, peppers, olive oils, vinegars, and other specialty food items. In
the restaurant, you can sip a glass of wine and feast on homemade
Italian dishes, including the famous sausage and pasta. Finish your meal
with an espresso or cappuccino and one of the shop's outstanding can-
nolis. Mollica's is open Monday through Saturday.

R.S.V.P., 515 Main Street, Canon City; (719) 275-0294. Suzanne
Wilson and her mother started R.S.V.P. twenty-six years ago. Her mom
passed away in 1993; "I still miss her every day," confesses Suzanne,
who continues to run the successful business solo in downtown Canon
City. The shop sells a little bit of everything related to cooking: specialty foods like salsas, pasta, pasta mixes, cookie mixes, teas, coffees,
candies, syrups, and jellies, as well as cooking utensils, china, crystal,
baskets, gifts, cookie jars, and much more.

Seabel's, 105 West C Street, Pueblo; (719) 543-2400. Seabel's is in a
neat old building in downtown Pueblo, part of the downtown Historic
Arkansas River Project. The store is filled to the rafters with goodies:

bread and scone mixes, pastas, pasta sauces, bakeware, salsas, chips, honey, sauces, jams, jellies, oils, vinegars, olives, cookies, candies, snacks, mixes, cookware, gadgets, foods, coffees and teas, and gifts. If you're stumped for a gift, the shop makes up fabulous gift baskets. Seabel's has another location at 22 South Tejon in Colorado Springs (719–473–6709).

Serranos Coffee Company, 582 Highway 105, Monument; (719) 481–9445. An unassuming coffee shop in a strip mall just west of I–25 between Denver and Colorado Springs, Serranos has that wonderful aroma of fresh-ground coffee beans that would be plenty enough reason to pull off the highway. When you see the slab of homemade pecan rolls in the glass case, however, you know that your car will never drive down this particular piece of road again without involuntarily pulling over to Serranos. In addition to fresh coffee and pastries, the shop offers dozens of varieties of whole and ground coffee beans. Take a pound of the shop's own Monument Hill blend with you or have it shipped anywhere in the United States.

Sparrow Hawk, 12 East Bijou Street, Colorado Springs; (719) 471–3235. If you're tired of lugging around a picnic basket, come to Sparrow Hawk for an ingenious invention—a picnic backpack. You'll find all sorts of other marvelous things in the shop, too—jams, jellies, teas, coffee beans, spices, imported herbs, salsas, baking mixes, soup mixes, teapots, cookbooks, aprons, cookware, coffees, dishes, gift items, gadgets, cookie jars, cutlery, cookie cutters, and a surprising inventory of pot racks. Sparrow Hawk is closed on Sunday, except during the holidays.

Spice of Life—An Ingredients Emporium, 727 Manitou Avenue, Manitou Springs; (719) 685–5284; www.geocities.com/spice_of_life_colorado/. If you need a caffeine boost the next time you're in Manitou Springs, stop at Spice of Life and try the shop's signature Hill Climb Shot. The concoction's moniker refers to the stamina required to sprint in the area's annual Pikes Peak Hill Climb, and once you've finished the generous cup of dark coffee combined with two shots of espresso, you'll be off and running. Part cafe, part espresso bar, and part gourmet specialty shop, Spice of Life offers a nice selection of spices, coffees, gourmet foods, gifts, and hard-to-find ingredients. Owners Michael Cornejo and Doug Lewis create many of their own spice blends, including *zaatar*, an Israeli mix used for marinating and seasoning, a Cajun spice mix for gumbo, and a salsa mix based on Michael's grandmother's recipe. The cafe sells breakfast items and sandwiches, too; an artichoke and cheddar scramble is a popular breakfast offering.

Wooden Spoon, Pueblo Mall, 3541 Dillon Drive, Pueblo; (719) 542–4783. If you're a coffee connoisseur, you'll find more than a hundred coffees and teas in this fun shop that caters to Colorado cooks. The store has an abundance of gourmet food products, too—salsas, chips, honey, sauces, jams, jellies, oils, vinegars, specialty pastas, pasta sauces, olives, cookies, candies, snacks, bread and scone mixes—plus a great assortment of bakeware, cookware, gadgets, and gifts.

Farmers' Markets

For the most up-to-date farmers' market listings call (303) 570–FARM or visit www.ag.state.co.us or www.coloradofarmersmarket.com.

Canon City Farmers' Market, Veterans Park, Canon City; Wednesdays from 7:30 A.M. to 1:00 P.M., mid-June through early October.

Colorado Springs Farmers' Market, Memorial Park at East Pikes Peak Avenue and Union Boulevard, Colorado Springs. Mondays and Thursdays from 7:00 A.M. to 1:30 P.M., July through early October.

Colorado Springs Farmers' Markets, three locations: 24th Street and West Colorado Avenue, and 4515 Barnes Road, and Colorado Avenue

How to Pick a Great Watermelon

1. Look the watermelon over and choose a firm, symmetrical watermelon that is free of bruises, cuts, and dents.

2. Lift it up. The watermelon should be heavy for its size. Watermelon is 92% water, which accounts for most of its weight.

3. Turn it over. On the underside of the watermelon, there should be a creamy yellow spot from where it sat on the ground and ripened in the sun.

Tips provided by the National Watermelon Promotion Board

and Cimino, Colorado Springs; Saturdays from 7:00 A.M. to 1:30 P.M., mid-June through late September.

Pueblo Farmers' Market, Midtown Shopping Center, Pueblo; (719) 583–6566. Tuesdays and Fridays from 7:00 A.M. to 1:00 P.M., early July through late September.

Trinidad Farmer's Market, 134 West Main Street, Trinidad; Saturdays from 8:00 A.M. to noon, late June through mid-October.

Woodland Park Farmers' Market, West on U.S. Highway 24 from Colorado Springs, north on Fairview at parking lot, Woodland Park. Fridays from 7:00 A.M. to 1:00 P.M., late June through early September.

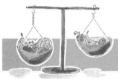

Farm Stands

Country Roots Organic Vegetable Farm, 29342 Everett Road, Pueblo; (719) 948–2206; www.countryrootsfarm.com. This roadside stand sells a huge variety of organic produce grown at Country Roots' farm: beets, carrots, chile peppers, cucumbers, garlic, onions, pumpkins, salad mix, squash (summer and winter), watermelon, a wide variety of heirloom tomatoes, cantaloupe and honeydew melons, and herbs. You can also purchase naturally raised chickens, free-range eggs, and green and dry crafting gourds. Open Saturday from 9:00 A.M. to 5:00 P.M., from early June through late October, or call for an appointment at other times.

Gary Hanagan Farm Market, 25388 Road 24.5, La Junta; (719) 384–5067. There's not a sign or a roadside stand, but people seem to find out about the Hanagans and make their way to the family farm. Starting in late July, the shed on the side of the house will begin to fill up with produce from the farm, and people will start dropping by, often bringing a picnic and making a day of it. You're welcome to come pick your own vegetables from the fields; chiles are a popular pick and the Hanagans are happy to freshly roast them for you in one of their three chile roasters. You'll find plenty of produce at the farm as it ripens: cantaloupe, beets, bell peppers, cucumbers, sweet corn, tomatoes, green beans, honeydew, okra, onions, black-eyed peas, pinto beans, potatoes, pumpkins, squash, watermelon, and many more varieties. The Hanagans also sell cider, dried beans, honey, handcrafted gifts, dried flowers, and gourds. The farm has a market at 807 East Olive in Lamar, Colorado, too. Open late July until late October.

Knapp's Farm Market, 29742 Highway 71, Rocky Ford; (719) 254–6265. You'll find a variety of vegetables at this farm market: beets, bell peppers, chile peppers (fresh and roasted), cucumbers, green beans, onions, pinto beans, squash, sweet corn, tomatoes, and, of course, Rocky Ford's world-famous melons. Open daily from July through October, 8:00 A.M. to 7:00 P.M.

Pantaleo Farms and Produce, 39651 South Road, Pueblo; (719) 948–4556; www.pantaleofarms.com. The Pantaleos' family farm stand sells exclusively Colorado-grown fruits and vegetables. Depending on the season, you'll find all sorts of fresh produce—apples, apricots, asparagus, beets, bell peppers, cabbage, cantaloupe, carrots, celery, cherries, chile

Best Company Picnic

If you have the thankless, fraught-with-so-many-things-that-could-go-wrong task of planning the company picnic, take heart. Flying W Ranch has it all figured out, from the delicious menu and beautiful setting to the small details like parking and restrooms. This working cattle ranch has been providing western cookouts and entertainment on its property since 1953. The ranch offers picnic lunches and dinners that are time-tested crowd pleasers. A typical menu might include barbecued Colorado beef, baked potatoes, Flying W beans, chunky applesauce, homemade biscuits with honey-butter, old-fashioned spice cake, and cold lemonade. All of the activities and games—tug-of-war, sack races, volleyball, horseshoes, a baseball field, and even a dunking tank for getting even with the boss—are provided.

Flying W Ranch

3330 Chuckwagon Road
Colorado Springs 80919
(800) 232–3599
www.flyingw.com

peppers (fresh and roasted), cucumbers, eggplant, garlic, green beans, honeydew, lettuce, nectarines, okra, onions, peaches, pears, pickles, pinto beans, plums, popcorn, potatoes, pumpkins, radishes, spinach, squash, strawberries, sweet corn, tomatoes, turnips, and watermelon, as well as handcrafted gifts. The stand usually opens in late July or early August and closes in late October.

The farm also hosts an event each autumn called "The Great Pumpkin Patch by Moonlight." Usually held during the second weekend of October, the farm offers free hayrides, a pick-your-own pumpkin

Mile-High Watermelon Pyramids

Rocky Ford, Colorado, is called the "Watermelon Capital of the World," and this stunning summer dessert features juicy watermelon in a layer of decadent stacked fruit, cakes, and fresh caramel sauce. The recipe is used with permission from the National Watermelon Promotion Board and was created by chef Harry Schwartz.

8 1-inch thick slices watermelon

4 1-inch thick slices pound cake

4 1-inch thick slices peeled kiwifruit

1 recipe quick caramel sauce (see below)

Dark and white chocolate shavings for garnish

1. Cut 4 4-inch by 4-inch and 4 2-inch by 2-inch squares of watermelon. Cut 4 3-inch x 3-inch square slices of pound cake. Cut 4 1-inch by 1-inch squares of kiwifruit.

2. On each of 4 dessert plates, place 1 slice of the largest watermelon

patch, a Halloween costume contest, corn maze, pony rides, bonfires, and food. Call for a schedule.

Phil's Market, 41999 U.S. Highway 50 East, Pueblo; (719) 948–4102. You'll find a proliferation of peppers at Phil's, plus seasonal fresh produce: apples, bell peppers, cabbage, cantaloupe, carrots, chile peppers, (fresh and roasted), cucumbers, green beans, onions, peaches, pears, pinto beans, popcorn, potatoes, pumpkins, squash, sweet corn, toma-

squares. Then, on each square place a slice of pound cake, then place a smaller watermelon square. Top each with a slice of the kiwifruit.

3. Drizzle the warm caramel sauce over the pyramids and then garnish with the chocolate shavings. Serve immediately.

Makes 4 servings.

Quick Caramel Sauce

4 tablespoons butter
1½ cups brown sugar

1 teaspoon vanilla
¼ cup heavy cream

In a 1- or 2-quart saucepan over medium heat, melt the butter and brown sugar, and then stir in the vanilla and cream. Bring to a simmer and adjust the heat to maintain a slow simmer. Simmer 5 minutes and serve immediately.

Makes about 1¼ cups.

toes, watermelon, cider, honey, and more. Open daily, mid-July through late October.

Smith's Corner, 18975 Highway 50, Rocky Ford; (719) 254–6550 or (719) 254–6960. It's melons, melons, and more melons at this roadside market located in the world's melon capital, Rocky Ford. You'll also find fresh produce like sweet corn, tomatoes, beets, bell peppers, cherries, plums, chile peppers (roasted chiles, too), pears, cucumbers, green

Should an Anti-food Event be Promoted in a Food Lovers' Guide?

The holidays are over, the wrappings have been discarded, and the tree is out on the curb, but one dilemma remains: What to do with the insipid fruitcake that Aunt Mabel sent? That very plight inspired the Annual Great Fruitcake Toss, now a well-attended affair held in Manitou Springs in early January, just as the fruitcakes are starting to get good and "aged." Zealous competitors come armed with brick-solid fruitcakes that they project with homemade catapult devices in distance trials, hoping to win prizes and, of course, glory. There is also a special event for the ugliest fruitcake. Held at Memorial Park at the 500 block of Manitou Avenue, the event is sponsored by the Manitou Springs Chamber of Commerce and Visitors Bureau and the proceeds benefit a local food bank. For more information call (719) 685–5089 or (800) 642–2567.

beans, onions, peaches, pinto beans, popcorn, potatoes, pumpkins, squash, watermelon, and honey. Open daily from mid-July through mid-October, from 8:00 A.M. to 7:00 P.M.

Third Street Apples, 935 3rd Street, Penrose; (719) 372–6283. Eleven miles east of Canon City, an old-fashioned apple orchard offers memories in the making. Bring the family to pick your own apples from the twenty-eight different varieties the farm grows. Well-known apples like Jonathan, Golden and Red Delicious, McIntosh, Rome, and Granny Smiths are grown here. You'll also find more unusual varieties: a fairly new type, good for cooking and eating, called Lura Red; "Jonalicious";

Fuji; and several varieties of antique apples including Red June, Grimes Gold, Yellow Transparent, and Ben Davis. Owners Lance and Gail Tyler have picnic tables on the property; you're welcome to bring a picnic lunch, pick apples off the trees, and make a day of it. The couple also sells picked apples, plus pumpkins and fresh vegetables in season. The farm is open early September through late October, Wednesday through Sunday, from 9:30 A.M. to 5:00 P.M., or call first to visit at other times.

Vic Mauro Produce, 35455 Ford Road, Pueblo; (719) 947–0655. A family farmstand with fresh produce that attracts a summer crowd, Vic Mauro Produce has plenty to choose from: apples, apricots, beets, sweet corn, tomatoes, potatoes, bell peppers, broccoli, cabbage, lettuce, okra, cantaloupe, carrots, cauliflower, cherries, fresh and roasted chile peppers, cucumbers, eggplant, garlic, grapes, green beans, onions, peaches, pears, pickles, pinto beans, popcorn, pumpkins, radishes, squash, watermelon, cider, eggs, honey. Open early June through late October, daily from 8:00 A.M. to 6:00 P.M.

 Food Happenings

January: **A Salute to Escoffier,** Broadmoor Hotel, 1 Lake Avenue, Colorado Springs; (800) 634–7711 or (719) 634–7711; www.broad moor.com. This three-day weekend of eating and drinking honors the legendary French chef, George Auguste Escoffier, author of the book, *Le*

Guide Culinaire, who is largely credited with bringing the culinary arts to a professional level. The event begins with a welcome reception Friday evening that includes hors d'oeuvres paired with appropriate wines. A variety of cooking demonstrations, wine seminars, and tastings are offered on Saturday. The highlight of the day, however, is "A Salute to Escoffier" Grand Buffet featuring more than a hundred culinary offerings prepared by the award-winning culinary team at the Broadmoor. After finishing the evening with dessert, coffee, and dancing, it's a good thing the hotel rooms are only footsteps away. Participants ease into the third day with the Broadmoor's traditional Sunday brunch. Proceeds from the event benefit the Education Fund of the Colorado Restaurant Association and The Broadmoor's Culinary Training Program and Scholarship Fund.

February: **Chocolate Indulgence,** Pueblo Convention Center, sponsored by the YWCA 801 North Santa Fe Avenue, Pueblo; (719) 542–6904. Bakers, pastry chefs, and candy makers pull out all the stops at this sinfully good event that happens around Valentine's Day. Sample dozens of chocolate dessert creations, from mousses to pies to cakes and much more. The event raises money for the YWCA's crisis shelter and for programs to help domestic violence victims.

February: **Mumbo Jumbo Gumbo Cook-off,** sponsored by the Manitou Springs Chamber of Commerce, 354 Manitou Avenue, Manitou Springs; (719) 685–5089. Around Mardi Gras, local cooks prepare their very best versions of the New Orleans specialty—gumbo, a stew traditionally prepared from shrimp, tomatoes, peppers, and okra. Judging conveniently takes place around lunchtime, when samples of the tasty gumbo go on sale. Vote for your favorite in the People's Choice competition; amateur and professional trophies and prizes are awarded as well. The event is held at Soda Springs Park and benefits the Manitou Springs Chamber of Commerce.

March: **Colorado Springs Dance Theatre Wine Fest,** Colorado Springs Dance Theatre, 7 East Bijou Street, Suite 209, Colorado Springs; (719) 630–7434; www.csdance.org. This two-day event brings together food and wine lovers in support of the Colorado Springs Dance Theatre. Wine aficionados will appreciate the Grand Tasting held Friday night, when local restaurants provide food offerings, which are accompanied by tastings from a number of wineries. Top winemakers present educational seminars during the day on Saturday. The festival culminates on Saturday evening with a sumptuous dinner and live auction.

April: **Gourmet Sampler,** Holy Cross Abbey, sponsored by Habitat for Humanity, 702 Greenwood Avenue, Canon City; (719) 275–7781 or (719) 372–6756. Each year, Canon City's best restaurants prepare their specialty dishes and offer tastings for the Gourmet Sampler, which is held in the events center of the town's beautiful Holy Cross Abbey. A special wine tasting room allows attendees the opportunity to sample wines from several vineyards. The event benefits Habitat for Humanity.

Memorial Day Weekend: **Hot Time Chili Cook-off,** sponsored by the Cripple Creek Chamber of Commerce, P.O. Box 650, Cripple Creek 80813; (719) 689–2889. This three-day event attracts serious chili cooks from all over the United States to participate in the cook-off, which is sanctioned by the International Chili Society. Winners advance to the

Betty's Eminently Edible Golden Fruitcake

To offset the hate mail I'm sure to receive for sensationalizing the Annual Great Fruitcake Toss (see page 240) I respectfully submit my mother's famous fruitcake recipe. This is a moist cake that contains the perfect ratio of cake to fruit—just not any of the offensive-to-some candied citrus peel. Even die-hard fruitcake boycotters like this cake—try it and see!

1½ cups dried apricots, quartered

⅔ cup water

¾ cup butter

¾ cup sugar

4 eggs

1½ cups flour, plus ½ cup of flour

½ teaspoon salt

½ teaspoon baking soda

1 cup dried cherries

1 cup slivered almonds

1½ cups golden raisins

½ teaspoon grated lemon peel

2 tablespoons rum

1. Preheat the oven to 275° F. In a small saucepan, cover the apricot pieces with water and heat over low-medium heat until simmering. Cook uncovered several minutes, until the apricots are tender. Remove from the heat and cool.

2. In a large bowl, beat the butter and sugar together until creamy. Add the eggs, one at a time, beating well after each addition.

3. In another bowl, combine the 1½ cups of flour with salt and baking soda and stir well. Add to butter mixture.

4. In the bowl that held the flour mixture, combine the apricots, cherries, almonds, raisins, lemon peel, and ½ cup of flour. Add to the batter and stir just until blended.

5. Spoon the batter into 2 buttered and floured 4-inch by 8-inch loaf pans. Bake for about 1½ hours. or until pick inserted in center tests clean. Cool cakes in pans on rack. While cakes are still warm, spoon the rum over each. Wrap tightly in plastic wrap or foil and refrigerate or freeze.

Makes 2 fruitcakes.

World Championships, so the stakes are high. Teams of cooks prepare their most delicious red chili (official rules state that beans are *not* allowed!) along Bennett Street in downtown Cripple Creek. After the judging, the cooks sell samples of their chili creations; the proceeds benefit the Cripple Creek Chamber of Commerce.

Early June: **Colorado Wines Festival,** sponsored by the Manitou Springs Chamber of Commerce, 354 Manitou Avenue, Manitou Springs; (719) 685–5089. Wine lovers who want to learn more about our state's wines will enjoy this event that focuses exclusively on Colorado's own vintners. The event kicks off on Friday evening with a Colorado wine and food dinner pairing held at a local restaurant. On Saturday meet the makers and try the wines at an all-day tasting held at Soda Springs Park. Selected cheese makers and specialty food vendors will provide samples to accompany the wines.

June: **Otero Museum Chuck Wagon Bean Supper,** Otero Museum, 218 Anderson, P.O. Box 223, La Junta 81050; (719) 384–7500. More than 250 people show up for this annual dinner to support the Otero Museum and . . . eat beans. That's right, the centerpiece of the dinner is an old-fashioned baked bean recipe that never fails to please the crowd. The beans are accompanied by homemade side dishes, cornbread, and a tasty beef stew. After dinner, coffee is served with homemade pies baked by local volunteers. A country-western band plays and everyone dances or wanders around the museum's extensive displays of historic artifacts from the area. The event benefits the Otero Museum Association.

July: **Good Old Summertime Ice Cream Social,** sponsored by the Manitou Springs Chamber of Commerce, 354 Manitou Avenue, Manitou Springs; (719) 685–5089. Sinton Dairy provides the ice cream for this old-fashioned ice cream social in Soda Springs Park. Many people bring a picnic and enjoy the shade under the trees before indulging in a huge bowl of ice cream; after dessert, there's a concert to enjoy. The Manitou Springs Chamber of Commerce sponsors the event.

July: **Pikes Peak or Bust Street Breakfast,** Weber Street and East Pikes Peak Avenue, Pikes Peak or Bust Rodeo, P.O. Box 2016, Colorado Springs 80901; (719) 635–3547; www.pikespeakorbustrodeo.org. At this very popular event, sponsored by the Sertoma Club, Fort Carson volunteers cook fabulous flapjacks for thousands of local supporters and tourists. Since 1950, the Street Breakfast has been the official send-off of the Pikes Peak Range Riders. The smell of pancakes fills the air, starting at the "Rise and Shine" hour of 5:30 A.M.; breakfast is served until 9:30 A.M. Come early, because promptly at 9:00 A.M., scores of horse-drawn vehicles and mounted Range Riders ride out of town.

August: **Watermelon Day/Arkansas Valley Fair,** Rocky Ford Fairgrounds, Rocky Ford; (719) 254–7483. In 1878, Senator George Swink shared his bountiful crop of watermelons with the train passengers who stopped at the Rocky Ford Depot. I wonder if Swink would be surprised to know that his generous tradition continues today. Every year visitors who show up at the Arkansas Valley Fair on Watermelon Day are given a free Rocky Ford watermelon.

Best Italian Sausage

If the homemade Italian sausage at Gagliano's tastes like you remember it from the Old Country, perhaps it's because the family still uses the same eighty-year-old recipe that Joe and Carmella Gagliano brought over from Sicily. It was 1923 when the couple started the business in Pueblo, and today owners Tony and Josephine Gagliano continue the tradition of excellence. The perfectly-seasoned sausage is the shop's big draw; and during the holiday season the staff will make 1,000 pounds a week to ship to customers all over the country. The shop also carries meats, homemade pasta sauce, meatballs, lasagna, Italian cookies, imported olives, anchovies, and olive oils plus Italian housewares like pasta makers and pizzelle irons.

> **Gagliano's Italian Market**
>
> 1220 Elm Street
> Pueblo 81004
> (719) 544–6058

Late September: **Harvest Festival,** The Winery at Holy Cross Abbey, 3011 East U.S. Highway 50, P.O. Box 1510, Canon City 81215; (877) 422–9463; www.abbeywinery.com. The Winemaker's Dinner is a fitting way to begin this festive weekend held on the grounds of the Winery at Holy Cross Abbey during grape harvest season. A local chef prepares a fine meal that is complemented with appropriate wines from the Abbey winery. (Reservations are required for this event only.) On Saturday and Sunday, wine tastings are supplemented by a lavish buffet. Area growers sell locally grown produce, and local artists display and sell their interpretations of the historic monastery at the abbey.

Third weekend in September: Chile and Frijoles Festival, sponsored by the Greater Pueblo Chamber of Commerce, P.O. Box 697, Pueblo 81002; (800) 233-3446; www.pueblochamber.org. In the past, more than 20,000 people have attended this annual weekend event celebrating the harvest of the Pueblo region's *Mira Sol* chile pepper. Along Union Avenue in front of the historic Vail Hotel building, a dedicated group of local farmers roast thousands of bushels of just-picked chiles. The fragrant smell from the chiles is intoxicating, and one of the festival's most delicious treats is a simple one: buy a freshly made flour tortilla from one of the vendors, top it with a freshly roasted pepper, roll it up, and eat it. *Bueno!* Other local specialties include "red beer," beer spiked with tomato juice, and "sloppers," messy but delicious open-faced cheeseburgers smothered in green chili.

A cooking contest among town locals means "heated" competition for the title of best red chili, green chili, frijoles, and salsa; there is an amateur and a professional division. Vendors in an open-air market sell *chile ristras*; wonderful Mexican food; and beans, melons, and other regional produce and foods. Musicians play throughout the day, and a piñata full of goodies is hung up for the kids to break. The festival begins Friday evening and continues through the weekend.

First Saturday in October: Apple Day Celebration, Downtown Penrose, sponsored by the Penrose Chamber of Commerce, 210 Broadway, P.O. Box 379, Penrose 81240; (719) 372-3994. Back in 1935, the towns of Canon City, Florence, and Penrose decided to host an event so folks in the neighboring towns could get to know one another. In a stroke of genius, someone suggested that the apple-growing town of Penrose offer free apple pie for everyone who came to the celebration. A tradition was born.

The daylong event begins with a festive parade through town. When the parade is finished, the longstanding tradition is upheld as free slices of apple pie are dished up to every person who wants one. (Residents of Penrose volunteer to make the pies each year, which are always outstanding.) Then, it's on to the pie contest, in which local cooks present their best pies as judges choose the grand champion and top prizewinners in both a senior and junior division. Still hungry? Local vendors serve plenty of food and drink as the warm-up for a spirited baseball game begins. Finally, in the evening, a celebration dance is held in the school gym.

***October*:** **March of Dimes Signature Chefs,** March of Dimes Chapter Columbine Division, 421 South Tejon, Suite 236, Colorado Springs 80903; (719) 473–9981; www.marchofdimes.com/colorado. The March of Dimes puts the "fun" in "fund-raiser" with its annual dinner that features a mouthwatering variety of gourmet dishes, personally prepared by the area's top chefs. Music and a lavish silent auction round out the evening, and the funds raised support the work of the March of Dimes.

Learn to Cook

Marway's Cake and Wedding Supplies, 2508 East Bijou Street, Colorado Springs; (719) 633–1991; www.marways.com. "We carry everything for the home candy maker and cake decorator," declares Marla Soukup, owner of Marway's Cake and Wedding Supplies. To help cooks learn those skills, the shop gives candy-making and cake-decorating classes. In a spacious classroom that can seat sixty people, adults learn beginning or intermediate cake decorating, fondant making, advanced flower making for wedding and specialty cakes, and candy making. In the autumn, the store hosts baking demonstrations, and during the holidays, there are free candy-making demonstrations.

The kids' classes are popular, too, especially the candy-making ones. Children age four and older can learn how to make simple molded candies, taking home the molds, the recipes, and of course, their own creations. Cake-decorating classes are popular with children seven years and older, and a basic cooking class teaches children ten and up how to prepare a meal, set a table, and have nice manners. The shop is a popular venue for kids' birthday parties, which include a cooking class and a birthday cake. Call or visit the Web site for a current schedule of classes.

The store, which opened in 1975, is stocked with a dazzling array of candy-making supplies: plastic molds, chocolate, candy coatings, filling ingredients, thermometers, and coating paintbrushes. There are scores of cake-decorating supplies, too: decorating equipment, cake boards, boxes, flavoring, pans, columns for wedding cakes, and cake stands that can be rented.

Nutritional Bread Baking Supplies, 7455 Winding Oaks Drive, Colorado Springs; (719) 528–7098; www.whispermill.net. Phyllis Stanley teaches the lost art of bread baking at her Colorado Springs shop. "Did you know that the Front Range is ranked number 1 in the United States in terms of health consciousness?" she asks. "Once people try homemade breads, especially those made from freshly ground wheat, they'll never go back to store-bought." In addition to the bread-baking classes,

Best Runzas

The nostalgic Drive-In in Colorado Springs, at the same location for nearly 60 years, serves a tasty rendering of the original "hot pocket." *Runzas* are traditional German-Russian buns stuffed with a tasty filling of meat, cabbage, onions, and spices. According to owner Chris Bettendorf, *runzas* are also known as *bierochs*, and were sort of a precursor to the hamburger. Served hot from the oven, a *runza* makes a perfect quick lunch or snack, and as long as you're at the Drive-In you might as well enjoy a delicious hand-mixed shake or malt from the old-fashioned ice-cream fountain menu.

The Drive-In
2309 North Weber Street
Colorado Springs 80907
(719) 733–0618
$

Phyllis teaches cooking with a pressure cooker, holiday baking and other special interest subjects. (Risotto, pizza, nuts, and sourdough-bread making have been popular past topics.) Her store, which has been in business for more than fifteen years, sells equipment and supplies for virtually every aspect of bread making, plus a host of other appliances and supplies. Call or visit the Web site for a class schedule.

Pikes Peak Community College, 5675 South Academy Boulevard, Colorado Springs; (719) 576–7711; www.ppcc.cccoes.edu. Pikes Peak Community College offers an Associate of Applied Science Degree in Culinary Arts, which is accredited by the American Culinary Federation. This two-year program prepares students for work as second cooks or station supervisors in all preparation areas of a professional kitchen, and

Colorado Peach Pecan Sour Cream Coffee Cake

Phyllis Stanley, owner of Nutritional Bread Baking Supplies, shares her recipe for a sweet, moist coffee cake that features fresh, ripe Colorado peaches. Phyllis grinds her own wheat into flour to bake this flavorful cake and says, "I've found that people overwhelmingly, prefer the taste of freshly ground flour and, of course, it has many more nutrients than white flour." If you don't yet own a flour mill, you can substitute regular flour.

¾ cup butter, softened
½ cup sugar
½ cup maple syrup or honey
3 eggs
2¾ cups freshly ground flour
    (wheat, spelt, or kamut) or
    all-purpose flour
1½ teaspoons baking powder

1½ teaspoons baking soda
16 ounces sour cream
2 teaspoons vanilla extract
¾ cup dark brown sugar
1 cup pecans, chopped
1 teaspoon cinnamon
2 cups peeled, chopped fresh
    Colorado peaches

the curriculum includes plenty of hands-on training, plus related work experience and apprenticeships. The school also offers one-year programs in Culinary Arts, Baking, and Food Service Management.

Pueblo Community College, 900 West Orman Avenue, Pueblo; (719) 549–3071; www.pueblocc.edu/dept/cua.htm. The school offers an Associate of Applied Science (AAS) Degree in Hospitality Studies, designed for students who hope to enter the food service industry at a

1. Preheat oven to 375° F. Grease and flour a 10-inch tube pan or Bundt pan.
2. In Phyllis' baking classes she makes this coffee cake in a Bosch stand mixer equipped with whisks. The batter can also be made with an electric mixer. In a large bowl, combine the butter, sugar, and maple syrup or honey. Add the eggs, one at a time, mixing well between additions.
3. In a separate bowl combine the flour, baking powder, and baking soda. With the mixer running, add the flour mixture slowly to the butter mixture. Add the sour cream and vanilla and mix just until blended.

Nutritional Bread Baking Supplies

7455 Winding Oaks Drive
Colorado Springs 80919
(719) 528–7098
www.whispermill.net

4. In a small bowl combine the brown sugar, cinnamon, and pecans. Add the peaches and stir gently. Fold the peach mixture into the batter and pour it into the prepared pan.
5. Bake for 60 to 65 minutes, or until a toothpick comes out clean. Carefully turn the pan over onto a serving plate or cake stand and remove the pan. For a lovely presentation, sprinkle with powdered sugar.

Makes about 12 servings.

skilled or supervisory level. The Certificate Program in Culinary Arts prepares students for employment in the food service industry at a functional level, such as cook's helper, host/hostess, cashier, waiter/ waitress, or short-order cook. The curriculum includes food preparation, baking, cost controls, sanitation and safety, menu planning, and customer service. The college also offers cooking classes for home cooks; recent catalog offerings included courses in cake decorating and candy making.

The Black Bear Restaurant, 20375 Ute Pass Avenue, Green Mountain Falls 80819; (719) 599–4776; $$–$$$. Chef and owner Victor Matthews offers an eclectic menu of both casual and fine cuisine at The Black Bear, serving everything from hot wings and burgers to lacquered duck and Kobe beef. Regardless of a food's pedigree, Matthews always strives to use fresh, organic products from Colorado growers and producers in his constantly changing repertoire. The Chef's Menu option is perfect for diners who are content to place themselves in Matthews' competent hands and leave all the decision making to him. Any number of courses will follow, creatively prepared with the freshest ingredients and guaranteed to provide you with at least a couple of new culinary experiences. A recent Chef's Menu included red caviar crostini accented by fresh thyme and honey mascarpone; asparagus and artichoke salad; smoked lobster and truffle bisque; a blue marlin "martini"; wild mushroom risotto; filet mignon "Margherita" prepared with buffalo mozzarella and grilled tomatoes; and Bananas Mozambique, a dessert based on a West African recipe with homemade cardamom yogurt.

By the way, Matthews makes a darned good Chicken Fried Steak, too.

The Broadmoor's Penrose Room, 1 Lake Avenue, Colorado Springs 80906; (800) 634–7711 or (719) 634–7711; www. broadmoor.com; $$$. For an elegant, romantic dinner, it's hard to beat the Penrose Room in the Broadmoor Hotel. The views of Colorado Springs and Cheyenne

Mountain are spectacular, and the service is sophisticated, but not stuffy. Live music accompanies dinner, and when the couples sway on the dance floor, it feels as if you've got a role in a 1940s movie.

The restaurant serves contemporary French cuisine, with a menu that emphasizes traditional favorites. Start with sautéed escargots, a lobster cocktail, sweetbread crepes, or a crispy Caesar salad prepared tableside. For dinner, in addition to nightly specials, you'll find chateaubriand, grilled Colorado lamb, flambéed tournedos of beef, and English Dover sole. Save a little room, because the restaurant really shines with its desserts. Bananas Foster and cherries jubilee are prepared tableside, or try a dessert soufflé in your choice of chocolate, lemon, Grand Marnier, or raspberry. The restaurant carries an award-winning wine selection and an extensive menu of cognacs, Armagnacs, single-malt scotches, and ports. Jackets are required for gentlemen, and reservations are recommended. The Penrose Room serves dinner from 6:00 to 10:00 P.M. nightly.

High tea is served 2:00 to 4:00 P.M. daily, from May to September. (Other months, check availability.) Reservations are required for tea.

The Cliff House Dining Room, 306 Cañon Avenue, Manitou Springs 80829; (719) 685–3000; www.thecliffhouse.com; $$$. The historic Cliff House at Pikes Peak in Manitou Springs has long been an integral part of the life of this small town located near Colorado Springs and the base of Pikes Peak. Originally built as a boarding house in 1873, The Cliff House has been open to guests longer than Colorado has been a state. Past guests include Thomas Edison and Theodore Roosevelt, and the inn has survived flash floods and fires. Today the

The Penrose Room's Butternut Squash and Green Pea Risotto

Colorful and bursting with flavor, this risotto can be served as a side dish or a light brunch or lunch. Executive Chef Siegfried Werner Eisenberger's exquisite recipe has been adapted for home cooks.

1 large acorn squash

1 tablespoon brown sugar

2 tablespoons fresh squeezed orange juice

Salt and pepper to taste

2 tablespoons honey

3 tablespoons olive oil

½ teaspoon minced garlic

Half of a medium onion, diced

1¼ cups Arborio rice

¼ cup dry vermouth

3 cups chicken broth

½ pound fresh peas, cooked

¼ cup peeled, finely diced tomato

Juice of 1 lemon

3 basil leaves, sliced finely into chiffonade, plus 8 basil leaves for garnish

2 ounces Parmigiano Reggiano cheese, grated

2 ounces toasted pine nuts (garnish)

1. Preheat the oven to 350° F. Slice the acorn squash into 4 rings, removing the seeds and reserving the end sections. Combine the brown sugar, orange juice, salt, pepper, and honey. Brush the mixture on both sides of each squash ring. Arrange the squash rings and the end pieces on a parchment lined baking sheet and bake

until tender. Cover the squash rings with foil and keep warm. Peel the end sections and cut the squash into ½-inch dice; reserve.

2. Heat the olive oil in a large saucepan over a medium flame. Add the onion and garlic and sauté for about 5 minutes, or until the onion is softened but not browned. Add the rice and cook for 3 minutes, stirring so that each grain of rice is coated with the oil. Add the vermouth and continue to cook until most of the vermouth evaporates. Add 1 cup of the chicken broth and stir with a fork until it is absorbed by the rice. Continue to add the chicken broth a half cup at a time and stir the mixture until all of the broth has been added and absorbed by the rice. This will take approximately 25 to 30 minutes. The rice should be creamy and have a tender texture.

The Broadmoor's Penrose Room

1 Lake Avenue
Colorado Springs 80906
(800) 634-7711 or (719) 634-7711
www.broadmoor.com
$$$

3. Add the reserved diced squash, peas, diced tomato, lemon juice, and basil chiffonade to the risotto. Stir gently, and fold in the Parmigiano Reggiano cheese.

4. To serve, arrange a squash ring in the center of each plate and spoon some of the risotto into the center of each ring. Garnish each portion with 2 basil leaves and sprinkle with toasted pine nuts.

Makes 4 servings.

restored hotel boasts sweeping porches, panoramic views, and an elegant dining room. Executive Chefs David Sieverts and Scott Savage incorporate fresh Colorado ingredients with classic French cooking techniques into unforgettable meals served in an elegant setting.

Breakfast is no ordinary affair here; even the standard "Bacon & Eggs" is served with a potato galette and fresh fruit. But the real star is the golden brown Grand Marnier battered French toast, served with butter and real maple syrup. At lunch and dinner the Cliff House Salad is a refreshing starter of organic greens, Balsamic vinegar-marinated apples, artichoke hearts, tomatoes, and a zesty herb vinaigrette. The dinner menu changes periodically, but some intriguing recent offerings included a Colorado cheese plate, Bacon-Wrapped Grilled Buffalo Tenderloin, and Ginger-Marinated Tenderloin of Pork. Save room for the crème brûlée or one of the kitchen's other sumptuous desserts. The inn often sponsors cooking classes, too; call for a schedule.

Conway's Red Top, 1520 South Nevada, Colorado Springs 80906; (719) 633–2444; $. The plate-sized hamburgers at Conway's are legendary. "Colorado's biggest burger" is about half a pound of perfectly cooked ground beef, which falls over the edges of a 6-inch bun and is served with crispy lettuce, sliced tomato, and onion. For smaller appetites, Conway's will serve you a "half" burger, which is still about a third of a pound of beef on a bun. Chili burgers, served open-faced and smothered with red chili, are another popular option, as are burgers dressed up with bacon and barbecue sauce.

Other notable specialties include the chicken sandwich, steak sandwich, chicken salad, and homemade soups. The soda fountain has wonderful milkshakes, sundaes, and sodas, and a fun kids' menu is available for little folks. There are libations for grown-ups, too; Conway's recently started serving beer and wine. There are four other Red Tops in the Colorado Springs area plus one in Pueblo, all open seven days a week for lunch and dinner.

Juniper Valley Ranch, 16350 South Highway 115, Colorado Springs 80926; (719) 576–0741; $$. In a restaurant that looks like a frayed-at-the-edges ranch house, Juniper Valley Ranch serves an old-fashioned, family-style, country dinner. The restaurant, which is about 15 miles south of Colorado Springs on the way to Canon City, has been in operation since 1951, serving a timeless menu that is as well loved today as it was fifty years ago.

To begin, you have your choice of cherry cider or curry consommé. You don't need a menu, because there are just two choices of entrees at the Juniper Valley Ranch: pan-fried chicken or baked ham. Side dishes are laid out on the table just like at Grandma's house for Sunday dinner. There are mashed potatoes and gravy, homemade biscuits with apple butter, okra casserole, cole slaw, homemade salads, and assorted vegetables. The dessert varies each night, but might feature a cherry, peach, apple, or rhubarb cobbler; bread pudding; custard; cake; or ice cream sundae. The restaurant is open for dinner Wednesday through Saturday, and for Sunday afternoon supper, during the summer months only. Call for reservations.

The Margarita at PineCreek, 7350 Pine Creek Road, Colorado Springs 80919; (719) 598–8667; www.margaritapinecreek.com. It was 1976 and we stopped at The Margarita on our way back from Taos, New

Ancho Chili Roasted Duck Breast with Orange Cider Chipotle Glaze and Grilled Tomatillos

Chef Eric Viedt shares his recipe for succulent duck with a decidedly south-western flair. Smoky chipotle chiles in adobo sauce and ancho chili powder are available in the Latin American section of specialty markets and the ethnic section of some major grocery stores. This recipe has been adapted for home cooks.

- 2 cups fresh-squeezed orange juice
- 1 cup apple cider (or substitute apple juice)
- 1 to 2 tablespoons of canned chipotle chiles in adobo puree (use more or less depending on your heat tolerance)
- 1 tablespoon chopped fresh cilantro
- 2 to 3 tablespoons butter
- ¼ cup lime juice
- ¼ cup apple cider vinegar
- 1 teaspoon salt
- 1 tablespoon brown sugar
- ½ cup olive oil
- 8 to 10 tomatillos husked, cleaned and quartered
- 1 bunch scallions, washed and trimmed
- Olive oil for grilling
- 4 duck breasts with skin/fat still intact, trimmed and scored
- 2 tablespoons ancho chili powder

1. In a small saucepan set over medium-high heat, combine the orange juice and apple cider and heat until boiling. Cook until the mixture is reduced to about 1 cup. Add chipotle and cilantro and remove from the heat. Allow to cool for a minute and then whisk in the butter until it is all incorporated. Keep warm.

2. In a medium bowl combine the lime juice, apple cider vinegar, salt, brown sugar, and olive oil. Whisk until well blended and marinate the tomatillos at room temperature for 1 hour. Preheat the grill to medium heat while the tomatillos are marinating. Remove the tomatillos from the marinade with a slotted spoon and arrange on the grill. Cook until tender and slightly charred, turning occasionally with tongs. Remove to a warm platter. Brush the scallions with olive oil and grill until tender and slightly charred. Add to the platter and cover with foil; keep warm.

The Margarita at PineCreek

7350 Pine Creek Road
Colorado Springs 80919
(719) 598–8667
$$$

3. Preheat the oven to 350° F. Heat an ovenproof sauté pan over medium heat and sear the duck breast, fat side down, until most of the fat is rendered (spoon out the fat occasionally while cooking) and the skin is crispy. Flip the duck over and dust with the ancho powder. Put the pan in the oven and roast for about 7 minutes to finish cooking.

4. Remove the duck breast from oven and spoon the orange-cider sauce over it. Arrange the tomatillos around the duck and garnish with the grilled scallions. Serve at once.

Makes 4 servings.

Mexico. We were hot and tired, and our kind waiter led us out to the shady patio and poured iced tea for us. Soon we were served a fresh salad, a cup of homemade soup, Southwestern chicken enchiladas, and ice cream for dessert. The breezes were cool, the atmosphere was peaceful, and owner Pati Davidson stopped by to make sure everything was all right. We felt absolutely revived.

For over thirty years, The Margarita has been a welcome oasis to many, consistently delivering attentive service and splendid cuisine. Ordering is simple: There are usually three entree choices every night; two are Continental, and one is Southwestern or Mexican. All dinners include an appetizer, the entree and accompanying sides, and dessert; once you've made your selections, you have only to sit back, relax, and enjoy yourself. The menu changes nightly, but everything is made from scratch, right down to the salad dressings. The outdoor patio is a lovely place to enjoy lunch or dinner during the warmer months. A musician plays the harpsichord on Saturday evenings, and other live musical entertainment is provided from time to time. Lunch is served Tuesday through Friday, and dinner is served Tuesday through Sunday.

Sencha, 331 South Nevada Avenue, Colorado Springs 80903; (719) 632–8287; www.sencha-restaurant.com; $$. Sencha's Executive Chef Brent Beavers has flourished in Colorado Springs with a loyal clientele that has responded enthusiastically to his creatively prepared food. Describing his unique brand of cooking as "world fusion cuisine," Chef Beavers works with local growers and ranchers to obtain the freshest and most flavorful fruits, vegetables, and meat raised in a natural and sustainable manner. The inspired menu changes frequently, but might include entrees like free-range chicken breast stuffed with shoestring potatoes; a house blend of cheeses and green chiles over farm vegetables topped with chipotle cream; or grilled all natural pork porterhouse with honey-roasted butternut squash and black tea pomegranate sauce. Desserts change daily, but the restaurant is best known for its incredible Chocolate Strata, a flourless chocolate torte of walnuts layered with chocolate mousse and chocolate ganache, wrapped in a chocolate shell adorned with an elegant gold design. Adventurous diners will enjoy the restaurant's Chef's Tables, a fixed-price meal of four courses paired with small estate wines. The extensive wine list offers a terrific opportunity to sample new wines by the glass, and Sencha offers cooking classes and wine events throughout the year.

Steel City Diner and Bakeshop, 121 West B Street, Pueblo 81003; (719) 295–1100, $$. Richard Warner and Mary Oreskovich met at the Culinary Institute of America in Hyde Park, New York, and brought their culinary expertise to the grateful people of Pueblo, Mary's hometown. Their restaurant is located in Pueblo's historic Union district, and the attached bakery has a magnetic draw for shoppers in need of a coffee and a piece of Mary's Peach "Melba" Cake. But the restaurant is where Richard and Mary's talents really shine. They are committed to cooking with organic produce, responsibly raised beef, and sustainably fished seafood, and the quality of their ingredients shows in every bite. The menu changes often, but a variation of Richard's Maryland-style crab cakes, packed with crab and nicely seasoned, is usually a staple. The menu might feature Colorado lamb, grilled salmon with braised greens, or a homemade pasta like wild mushroom ravioli. A well-rounded wine list is supplemented by Colorado microbrews and Thomas Kemper root beer. Mary oversees the desserts and temptations abound: Malted milk chocolate crème brûlée and crispy chocolate-banana wontons with rum custard and candied hazelnuts were two recent examples of her creative work in the pastry kitchen. The restaurant serves lunch Tuesday through Saturday and dinner Wednesday through Saturday.

Brewpubs & Microbreweries

Blick's Brewing, 625 Paonia Street, Colorado Springs; (719) 596–3192. Mike Blickenstaff opened Blick's Brewery in December of 1996. The company currently brews two beers, which are sold locally as well as being available for sampling in the brewery's tasting room. The Misty Flips Red Ale is reddish amber in color with a malty flavor and dry finish. The Blind Side Pale Ale is a golden, medium-bodied, pale ale. The tasting room is open Tuesday through Friday from 2:00 to 8:00 P.M., Saturday from noon to 5:00 P.M., and by appointment at other times.

Bristol Brewing, 1647 South Tejon Street, Colorado Springs; (719) 633–2555; www.bristolbrewing.com. Bristol has been brewing its all-natural beers for more than ten years, with much success. The most popular offering is the Laughing Lab, a traditionally brewed Scottish ale, with a nutty, roasted flavor and smooth taste. Another big seller, the Mass Transit Ale, has an auburn color and mellow taste, while the Beehive Honey Wheat, made from Colorado Springs honey, is a refreshing, honey-colored ale with just a touch of sweetness in the finish. Bristol Brewing's beers are available on tap throughout Colorado and are sold in most major area liquor stores. The brewery often makes specialty beers that are served only in the tasting room, which is open from 10:00 A.M. to 9:00 P.M., Monday through Saturday. Tours are available on request.

Irish Brewpub, 108 West Third Street, Pueblo; (719) 542–9974; www.irishbrewpub.com. This family-owned Pueblo pub has been going strong for over sixty years; in 1996 the company began brewing its own trademark beers. The Steel City Light Ale, Irish Red, and dark Pogmahon Porter are among the most popular of the seven beers the pub brews regularly. The brewery offers specialty beers from time to time, and these plus several premium beers from other breweries are on tap at the bar.

The restaurant menu has some surprises; appetizers include alligator, duck sausage, mussels, and oysters. Craving a hamburger? How about a lamb, ostrich, or buffalo burger? The restaurant serves all three, and owner Ted Calantino says lots of people are pleasantly surprised by how good the ostrich is. There are beef burgers too, plus a delicious Philly cheese steak, a mouth-watering Reuben, and a New Orleans-style muffuletta sandwich. At dinner, the pub always prepares two soups, one of which is a delicious clam chowder. Entree choices include pasta, steaks, prime rib, fish, and wild game. The Irish Brewpub is open Monday through Saturday, and restaurant reservations are appreciated.

Judge Baldwin's Brewing Company, 4 South Cascade Avenue, Colorado Springs; (719) 473-5600. This lively pub in the Antlers Adams Mark Hotel consistently serves at least eight of its own handcrafted draft beers. The Blind Dog Bitter is an often-requested light ale with a malty body and crisp hop finish. If you prefer a darker beer, the Dark Munich Lager has a dark ruby color with full body and light hop flavors. Another popular pour is the brewery's ZZ Lager, a northern European–style golden lager. The brewmeisters are constantly introducing new styles and special beers to the lineup. The restaurant offers a full lunch and dinner menu. The menu changes frequently, but recent favorites included barbecued shrimp skewers, fish and chips, potato skins, Surf and Turf, steaks, and an overstuffed Rocky Mountain Club Sandwich. You'll always find salads, sandwiches, and burgers at lunchtime, and a kids' menu is available.

Palmer Lake Brewing Company/ The Warehouse Restaurant, 25 West Cimarron Street, Colorado Springs; (719) 475-8880; www.the warehouserestaurant.com. Palmer Lake has been crafting traditional unfiltered, unpasteurized ales and lagers since 1995, using the highest-quality American and imported malts and hops. Some of the brewery's favorite beers include Sundance Hefeweizen, Peak Pale Ale, General Palmer's Amber Lager, and Locomotive Stout. Teetotalers will enjoy the homemade Front Range Root Beer. Beers are available in pints at the restaurant and to-go in growlers and kegs. In contrast to a typical brewpub, The Warehouse offers a decidedly upscale menu of delicious offerings that pair well with the beers: appetizers like White Cheddar and Caramelized Onion Quesadilla, entrees like Apple Wood–Smoked Pork Medallions and a Locomotive Sundae made with maple-stout ice cream topped with stout-infused chocolate sauce and toasted cashew nuts.

Phantom Canyon Brewing Company, 2 East Pikes Peak, Colorado Springs, CO 80903; (719) 635–2800; www.phantomcanyon.com. Saved from the wrecking ball just in time, the historic old building that houses Phantom Canyon Brewing Company was purchased by John Hickenlooper (owner of the Wynkoop Brewing Company; see page 58) who restored the property and opened the brewery in 1994. Since then Phantom Canyon has been one of the busiest establishments in downtown Colorado Springs. Beer drinkers rave about the microbrewery's Phantom Canyon Indian Pale Ale, reddish copper in color, a bitter, traditionally brewed pale ale. Zebulon's Peated Porter is a smoked porter, dark and rich, with a smoky flavor from the peated malt used in brewing. The Queen's Blonde Ale is crisp, light, and malty with just a touch of German hops. The wide-ranging restaurant menu has something for everyone; two or three specials are prepared every night in addition to regular offerings like shepherd's pie, beer-braised pot roast, fish and chips, burgers, fish, steaks, and much more. The brewery makes its own root beer and has a kids' menu. Lunch and dinner are served daily and a Sunday brunch is served from 9:00 A.M. to 2:00 P.M.

Pikes Peak Vineyards, 3901 Janitell Road, Colorado Springs; (719) 576–0075. Pikes Peak Winery and Restaurant does everything by hand, producing fine wines that include Chardonnay, Cabernet Franc, Merlot, Rieslings, Sauvignon Blanc, and special blends. The winery, located on a historic hundred-acre estate, has its own nine-hole golf course and recreation area. The tasting room is open from 1:00 to 4:00 P.M. daily, offering free samplings and a tour of the vineyard. A restaurant above the winery serves dinner from 5:00 to 9:00 P.M., Tuesday through Sunday.

The Winery at Holy Cross Abbey, 3011 East U.S. Highway 50, P.O. Box 1510, Canon City 81215; (877) 422–9463, www.abbeywinery.com. One of the prettier wineries in our state, this one is located on the grounds of the historic Holy Cross Abbey in Canon City, Colorado. The winery produces Chardonnay, Merlot, and Riesling, plus new offerings which include a Merlot Port, Cabernet Sauvignon, Sauvignon Blanc, and the intriguing "Colorado Nouveau," a sweeter wine made with Colorado Merlot grapes. The winery has won numerous awards, and not only for its excellent wines; it recently won the Silver Medal for label design at the San Francisco International Wine Label Competition. The gift section of the tasting room is filled with temptations: colorful textiles from Provence, exquisite Italian crystal and wine accessories. The tasting room is open year-round Monday through Saturday from 10:00 A.M. to 5:00 P.M. (6:00 P.M. in the summertime), and on Sunday from noon to 5:00 P.M.

Wines of Colorado 8045 West Highway 24, P.O. Box 146, Cascade 80809; (719) 684–0900; www.winesofcolorado.com. As its name suggests, Wines of Colorado stocks exclusively Colorado wines, all available for tasting. You'll generally find fifteen to twenty bottles open in the tasting room at any given time, and free samples are available all day. The store can sell wines seven days a week, even on Sunday. Located in the foothills at the base of Pikes Peak, a full restaurant attached to the store serves lunch and dinner from a casual, but tasty menu; ask for a creekside table during the summer.

Appendix A: Food Happenings

Appendix B: Specialty Foods and Produce

The following businesses, farms, and shops are especially known for these items that they produce or grow.

Bakery Goods
Baked In Telluride, 140

Danish Scandinavian Bakery, 12

Gateaux Bakery, 49

Ingrid's Cup & Saucer, 72

Johnson's Corner, 48, 212

Le Bakery Sensual, 15

Mrs. Mauro's Potica, 5

Baking Mixes
Bear Meadow Gourmet Foods, 160

Barbecue Sauce
Big Mike's Original Barbecue Sauce, 2

Beans
Adobe Milling Co., 118

Mary Ann's Beans, 166

Bratwurst
Bender's Brat Haus, 58

Bubble Tea
Boba Tea Direct, 3

Buffalo Meat/Wild Game Meats
Dale's Exotic Game Meats, 191

High Wire Ranch, 126

Burritos
Chez Jose, 20

Candies and Chocolates
Belvedere Belgian Chocolate Shop, 170

Chocolate Foundry, The, 8

Confre Cellars & Fudge Factory, 69

Enstrom's Candies, 64

Hammond's Candy Company, 4

Michelle Chocolatiers & Ice Cream, 224

Mountain Man Nut and Fruit Company, 226

Nettie's Colorado Candies, 226

Patsy's Candies, 226

Appendix C:
Resources for
Food Lovers

Associations and Organizations

Colorado Brewers Guild
P.O. Box 19736
Boulder, CO 80308
(303) 507–7664
www.coloradobeer.org

Colorado Organic Producers Association
2727 CR 134
Hesperus, CO 81326
(970) 588–2292
www.organiccolorado.org

Colorado Restaurant Association
430 East 7th Avenue
Denver, CO 80203
(303) 830–2972
www.coloradorestaurant.com

Colorado Wine Industry Development Board
4550 Sioux Drive
Boulder, CO 80303
(720) 304–3406
www.coloradowine.com

Community Supported Agriculture (CSA) Farms
To find a CSA farm near you, visit www.nal.usda.gov/afsic/csa/csastate.htm.

International Chili Society
(877) 777–4427
www.chilicookoff.com

International Wine Guild

Metropolitan State College of Denver
P.O. Box 173362
Campus Box 60
Denver, CO 80217
(303) 296–3966
www.internationalwineguild.com

Slow Food

To join, visit www.slowfoodusa.org. *Here are the contacts for the local chapters:*

Aspen/Roaring Fork Valley—Joyce Falcone, joyce@slowfoodaspen.org; www.slowfoodaspen.org

Boulder—Elizabeth Perrault; www.slowfoodboulder.com

Colorado Springs—Jan Webster, webstersdj@aol.com

Denver—Matt Jones and Sally Kennedy, matt4food@mac.com and sallykennedy@aol.com; www.slow fooddenver.com

Durango—Sean Devereaux, devro@frontier.net

Fort Collins—Todd and Stefania Arndorfer, toddandstefania@hotmail .com

Vail Vally—Ebby Pinson, ebbypinson@vailsymposium.org

Western Slope—Eugenia Bone, egbone@aol.com

State of Colorado Department of Agriculture

700 Kipling Street, Suite 4000
Lakewood, CO 80215–8000
(303) 239–4100

To access the Colorado Farm Fresh Directory and the latest information about farmers' markets and Colorado farmers and food producers, visit www.ag.state.co.us

Books about Colorado Food and Spirits

At Mesa's Edge: Cooking and Ranching in Colorado's North Fork Valley, (Houghton Mifflin) by Eugenia Bone

Colorado: A Liquid History and Tavern Guide to the Highest State (Fulcrum) by Thomas Noel

Colorado Bed and Breakfast Cookbook (3D Press) by Carol Faino and Doreen Hazledine

Colorado Cache Cookbook, Crème de Colorado, Colorado Collage, and *Colorado Colore,* published by the Junior League of Denver

Culinary Colorado (Fulcrum) by Claire Walter

The Guide to Colorado Wineries (Fulcrum) by Alta and Brad Smith

Recipe Please (Johnson Books) by Marty Meitus

Books about Colorado Restaurants

Colorado's Finest Small-Town Restaurants and Their Recipes (Fulcrum) by David Gruber

Denver Dines—a Restaurant Guide and More (Johnson Books) by John Lehndorff

The Gabby Gourmet Restaurant Guide (TDF) by Pat Miller

Rise & Dine: Breakfast in Denver and Boulder (Fulcrum) by Joey Porcelli

Radio Shows

The Gabby Gourmet Restaurant Show, hosted by Pat Miller, is on KHOW–630 AM every Saturday from 1:00 to 4:00 P.M.

The Restaurant Show, an always–lively program hosted by Warren Byrne, is broadcast every Wednesday evening from 4:00 to 7:00 P.M., and every Saturday from 9:00 A.M. to 1:00 P.M. on KEZW–1430 AM. To voice your opinion, call in at (303) 631–1430.

Colorado
Eateries Index

Recipe Index

General Index

B

Backcountry Brewery, 104

Baked In Telluride, 140

Basalt, 73

Beano's Cabin, 98

Bear Meadow Gourmet Foods, 160

Beau Jo's, 102

Beaver Creek, 63, 84, 87, 93

Beer at Home, 57

BellFlower Farms, 27

Belvedere Belgian Chocolate Shop, 170

Bender's Brat Haus, 58

Berry Patch Farms, 182

Berthoud, 178, 199

Berthoud Farmers' Market, 178

Big Mike's Original Barbecue Sauce, 2

Big Wheel 'n' Chili Festival, 88

Bingham Hill Cheese Company, 160

Black Bear Restaurant, The, 254

Blacksmith Ridge Farms, 183

Blick's Brewing, 264

Blue Parrot, The, 196

Blues, Brews, & BBQ Festival, 84

Boba Tea Direct, 3

Bonnie Brae Ice Cream, 12

Bonnie Brae Tavern, 12

Book Cliff Vineyards, 217

Boulder, 159, 161, 171, 175, 178, 184, 192–97, 200, 201, 202, 206, 207, 213, 214, 215, 217, 218, 219

Boulder Cheese Company, 171

Boulder County Farmers' Market Farm Tour, 192

Boulder Creek Winery, 218

Boulder Dushanbe Teahouse, 215

Boulder Farmers' Market, 178

Breckenridge, 69, 74, 76, 88, 93, 105

Breckenridge Brewery & Pub, 105

Breckenridge Farmers' Market, 76

Brewery Bar II, 33

Brighton, 182, 191

Bristol Brewing, 264

Broadmoor's Penrose Room, The, 254, 257

Broomfield, 193, 211

Brown Palace Hotel, The, 46, 53

Buckhorn Exchange, The, 19

Buckingham Square Farmers' Market, 24

Burrits Produce, 129

Butcher's Block, The, 68

C

Cake Crafts, 37

Capfire cookout, 101

Canon City, 224, 231, 234, 243, 247, 268

Canon City Farmers' Market, 234

Cano's Collection, 46

Canyon Wind Cellars, 109

Canyon Wind Cellars Tasting Room, 109

Carbondale, 70, 76, 92, 100

Carbondale Farmers' Market, 76

Rogers Mesa Fruit Co., 133
Ron Crist Orchards, 81
R.S.V.P., 231
Runzas, 251

S

Salida, 135, 136, 141, 142, 143, 154
Salsa Fiesta, 141
Salute to Escoffier, A, 241
San Luis Valley, The, 130
SandLot Brewery, 57
Savory Inn and Cooking School, 97
Savory Palette Gourmet Retreats, 194
Savory Spice Shop, 18
Schmidt's Bakery and Delicatessen, 210
School of Natural Cookery, 197
Seabel's, 231
Seasoned Chef Cooking School, The, 44
Seasons Rotisserie & Grill, 147
Sencha, 262
Serranos Coffee Company, 232
Shanaroba Organic Farm, 92
Sheridan, 28
Ship Tavern, 53
Silverton, 136
Six89 Kitchen/Winebar, 100
Ska Brewing, 103, 151
Ski Tip Lodge, 103
Slow Food event, 6
Smith's Corner, 239

Smuggler's Brewpub and Grille, 152
Snowmass Village, 86, 87
Soupçon Restaurant, 149
Southwest Plaza Farmers' Market, 26
Sparrow Hawk, 232
Specialty Food of Aspen & the Cheese Shop, 74
Spero Winery, 61
Spice of Life—An Ingredients Emporium, 233
Spinelli's Market, 20
Spruce Mountain Meadery, 219
Stapleton Farmers' Market, 26
Steamboat Springs, 72, 115
Steamboat Springs Cellars, 115
Steamworks Brewing Company, 153
Steel City Diner and Bakeshop, 263
Stephany's Chocolates, 6
Sterling Farmers' Market, 181
St. Kathryn Cellars, 114
St. Kilian's Cheese Shop, 21
Stir It Up Cooking School, 197
Stoney Mesa Winery, 156
Strasburg, 181
Strasburg Community Council, 181
Suddenly Sonoma, Definitely Denver, 31
Surface Creek Winery, 156
Sushi Den, 54
Sushi, Sake, & Sumo, 32
Sweet Basil, 83, 103

Eliza Cross Castaneda is a food and lifestyle writer whose many articles have appeared in publications like *Mountain Living, The Denver Post, Colorado Homes and Lifestyles,* and *Log & Timber Style.* A Certified Chef of Wine Arts through the International Wine Guild, Eliza has taught cooking classes in a variety of subjects, judged culinary competitions and presented workshops about food writing. She serves on the board of the Colorado Authors' League and is an active member of the International Food, Wine & Travel Writers Association and Slow Food. She lives in Centennial with her family.